THE MASTER'S PLAN FOR THE CHURCH

JOHN F. MACARTHUR, JR.

MOODY PRESS

CHICAGO

© 1991 by
THE MOODY BIBLE INSTITUTE
OF CHICAGO

The Master's Plan for the Church is a revised and expanded edition of *Shepherdology* by John F. MacArthur, Jr.

All Scripture quotations in this book, except those noted otherwise, are from the *New Scofield Reference Bible,* King James Version, Copyright 1967 by Oxford University Press, Inc. Reprinted by permission.

Scripture quotations marked "NASB" are taken from the *New American Standard Bible,* © 1960, 1962, 1963, 1968, 1971, 1972, 1973, 1975, and 1977 by The Lockman Foundation, and are used by permission.

Library of Congress Cataloging in Publication Data

MacArthur, John, 1939-
    The Master's plan for the church / by John F. MacArthur, Jr.
      p.   cm.
    Includes indexes.
    ISBN 0-8024-7841-7
    1. Christian life—1960- 2. Pastoral theology. I. Title.
BV4501.2.M162   1991
262—dc20   91-2224
                                        CIP

3 5 7 9 10 8 6 4

Printed in the United States of America

About the Author

JOHN F. MACARTHUR, JR. (B.A., Pacific College; M. Div., D.D., Talbot Theological Seminary) pastors Grace Community Church in Sun Valley, California. He is a well-known Bible expositor and conference speaker and serves as president of The Master's College and Seminary. His tape ministry and daily radio program, "Grace to You," reaches millions internationally.

Other Books by John MacArthur

The MacArthur Commentary Series
    Matthew 1-7
    Matthew 8-15
    Matthew 16-23
    Matthew 24-28
    First Corinthians
    Galatians
    Ephesians
    Hebrews
The Ultimate Priority
Kingdom Living Here and Now
Jesus' Pattern for Prayer
The Family
You Can Trust the Bible
The Gospel According to Jesus
Our Sufficiency in Christ

To Phillip Johnson,
my true yokefellow,
a man who has faithfully
stood with me
in heart and ministry

Contents

The Dynamic Church

Appendixes

INTRODUCTION

Be on guard for yourselves and for all the flock, among which the Holy Spirit has made you overseers, to shepherd the church of God which He purchased with His own blood.

Acts 20:28; NASB

We are God's fellow workers; you are . . . God's building. According to the grace of God which was given to me as a wise master builder I laid a foundation, and another is building upon it. But let each man be careful how he builds upon it. For no man can lay a foundation other than the one which is laid, which is Jesus Christ.

1 Corinthians 3:9-11; NASB

Shepherds and Construction Workers

Some contemporary church leaders fancy themselves businessmen, media figures, entertainers, psychologists, philosophers, or lawyers. Yet those notions contrast sharply with the symbolism Scripture employs to depict spiritual leaders.

In 2 Timothy 2, for example, Paul uses seven different metaphors to describe the rigors of leadership. He pictures the minister as a teacher (v. 2), a soldier (v. 3), an athlete (v. 5), a farmer (v. 6), a workman (v. 15), a vessel (vv. 20-21), and a slave (v. 24). Each of those images evokes ideas of sacrifice, labor, service, and hardship. They speak eloquently of the complex and varied responsibilities of spiritual leadership. Not one of them makes out leadership to be glamorous.

That's because it is not supposed to be glamorous. Leadership in the church—and I'm speaking of every facet of spiritual leadership, not just the pastor's role—is not a mantle of status to be conferred on the church's aristocracy. It isn't earned by seniority, purchased with money, or inherited through family ties. It doesn't necessarily fall to those who are successful in business or finance. It isn't doled out on the basis of intelligence or talent. Its requirements are faultless character, spiritual maturity, and a willingness to serve humbly.

Our Lord's favorite metaphor for spiritual leadership, one He often used to describe Himself, was that of a shepherd—one who tends

God's flock. Every church leader is a shepherd. The word *pastor* even means "shepherd." It is appropriate imagery. A shepherd leads, feeds, nurtures, comforts, corrects, and protects. Those are responsibilities of every churchman.

Shepherds are without status. In most cultures, shepherds occupy the lower rungs of society's ladders. That is fitting, for our Lord said, "Let him who is the greatest among you become as the youngest, and the leader as the servant" (Luke 22:26; NASB).

Under the plan God has ordained for the church, leadership is a position of humble, loving service. Church leadership is ministry, not management. Those whom God designates as leaders are called not to be governing monarchs but humble slaves, not slick celebrities but laboring servants. The man who leads God's people must above all exemplify sacrifice, devotion, submission, and lowliness.

Jesus Himself gave us the pattern when He stooped to wash His disciples' feet, a task that was customarily done only by the lowest of slaves (John 13). If the Lord of the universe would do that, no church leader has the right to think of himself as a bigwig.

One great difference exists between herding sheep and leading a church. Shepherding animals is only semiskilled labor. No colleges offer graduate degrees in shepherding. It isn't an extremely difficult job. Even a dog can be trained to guard a flock of sheep. In biblical times, young boys—David, for example—herded sheep while the older men did tasks that required more skill and maturity.

Shepherding a spiritual flock, however, is not so simple. The standards are high and the requirements hard to satisfy. Not everyone can meet the qualifications, and of those who do, few seem to excel at the task. Spiritual shepherdology demands a godly, gifted, multiskilled man of integrity. Remember, he is also described as teacher, soldier, athlete, farmer, and slave. Yet he must maintain the perspective and demeanor of a boy shepherd.

That's not all. Church leaders are spiritual construction workers. In 1 Corinthians 3 Paul likens ministers to master builders who follow a set of biblical blueprints, laboring in partnership with God to construct a building—the church: "We are God's fellow workers; you are . . . God's building. According to the grace of God which was given to me, as a wise master builder I laid a foundation, and another is building upon it. But let each man be careful how he builds upon it" (vv. 9-10; NASB).

Wise builders follow the blueprints precisely; the slightest deviation from the architect's plans in the early stages can result in a tottering monstrosity by the time construction is completed. God's Word is the blueprint for spiritual construction, and only those who follow it exactly are building anything that will stand firm.

As builders, then, we must build by the right plan. And as shepherds, we must lead in the right paths. Either way, we determine the direction of our people. Hosea 4:9 says, "Like people, like priests" (NASB). In other words, people emulate their spiritual leaders.

Perhaps that explains the pathetic state of the contemporary church. Many of the best-known and most visible religious leaders utterly fail to measure up to biblical standards for shepherds. Every leader who follows their pattern is destined to fail. They are building with the wrong set of plans, and they are misleading their sheep.

Churches can survive nearly every kind of problem except a failure of leadership. We need a scriptural refresher course for spiritual shepherds, a new look at the Architect's master plan. That's what this book is about.

People often ask me what I think is the secret to Grace Community Church's development during the past two decades. I always point out first of all that God sovereignly determines the membership of a church, and numbers alone are no gauge of spiritual success. In the midst of tremendous numerical growth, however, the spiritual vitality of our church has been remarkable. I'm convinced God's blessing has been on us primarily because our people have shown a strong commitment to biblical leadership. By affirming and emulating the godly example of our elders, the church has opened the door to extraordinary blessings from the hand of God.

Several years ago, we began having regular Shepherds' Conferences at the church. Elders and staff from other churches spend a week on our church campus, studying biblical principles of spiritual shepherding and watching those principles applied in the context of a working church model.

More recently, The Master's Fellowship sponsored Shepherds' Seminars in key cities across the country. The one-day seminars offered in a condensed format the same biblical leadership principles we have taught in the Shepherds' Conferences at the church. The response to those seminars was far greater than any of us anticipated. Many participants asked for a textbook that would consolidate the material into a single resource. *The Master's Plan for the Church* is the outgrowth of those appeals.

Most of the material in this book has appeared in print before. Parts 1, 2, and 3 are revised editions of study guides from series broadcast on the "Grace to You" radio network. The three series —*The Anatomy of a Church, The Dynamic Church*, and *Qualities of an Excellent Servant*—represent some of the most well-received material on church leadership we have ever offered. "Answering the Key Questions About Elders" and "Answering the Key Questions About Deacons" have been published separately as booklets. The remaining appendixes are excerpted from other tape series. Cassette tapes containing all the material in audio format are available individually or in complete series from Grace to You, P.O. Box 4000, Panorama City, CA 91412. Corresponding tape numbers where applicable are given in footnotes at the beginning of each chapter.

You'll note that many of the chapters in this book read like sermons. They are. We've edited them somewhat to literary style, but, desiring to keep their original flavor intact, we have retained many references to the Grace Church family, which was the original audience for most of the messages.

Nothing is more sorely needed today than a return to biblical leadership principles. Solid leaders are appallingly rare in the contemporary church, on the mission field, and in Christian schools and organizations. A church cannot be more successful than its leaders. If the pastor or other leaders fail to meet God's high standards of godliness, authenticity, and spiritual maturity, the church will fail too.

PART ONE

The Anatomy of a Church

[Hold] fast to the head, from whom the entire body, being supplied and held together by the joints and ligaments, grows with a growth which is from God.

Colossians 2:19; NASB

He is also head of the body, the church; and He is the beginning, the first-born from the dead; so that He Himself might come to have first place in everything.

Colossians 1:18; NASB

Chapter 1

The Skeletal Structure*

When Grace Community Church began experiencing tremendous growth, there were so many things happening that I couldn't keep up with all of them. It was an exciting, euphoric time for the church. I like to call that time the years of discovery. When I came to Grace Church, I didn't know much. Every week I'd study and prepare my sermons, and on Sundays the congregation would learn together with me. I'd share what the Bible said, and people would say, "Wow! So that's what the Bible is saying!" We were taking big steps in our spiritual growth and understanding, and the Lord added many people to the church. Those years were like a prolonged honeymoon. Enthusiasm and energy were everywhere.

When I first arrived at Grace Church, my goal was to keep the people already there from leaving. I never envisioned that the church would grow to the size it is now. That's why I often say that the verse I have come to understand the most in the years of my ministry is Ephesians 3:20, which speaks of God as "him who is able to do exceedingly abundantly above all that we ask or think." Throughout my ministry I have seen God do far beyond anything I could ever have imagined!

Churches all seem to follow the same pattern of growth and decline. The first generation fights to discover and establish the truth.

*From tape GC 2024.

Grace Church went through that; the early years were a time of discovery and establishing the truth. The second generation fights to maintain the truth and proclaim it. We have also seen that at Grace Church. The things we have learned, we have put in books and on tapes. We have trained men to become pastors, go out, and start teaching other people. We have shared what we know with other pastors. Yet often the third generation of a church couldn't care less about that. Why? Since they weren't a part of the fight the first two generations faced, they don't have anything at stake. They tend to take for granted the things that have already been established.

That scares me. The toughest thing to deal with in the ministry is indifference. It's heartbreaking to know that those who weren't a part of building the church tend to take everything for granted. Because they weren't a part of the battle, they didn't pay the price or appreciate the sweet taste of victory. They don't know what the battle was like. Those who weren't a part of the process of fighting, discovering, and establishing the truth are often unable to appreciate what God has done.

There are many new people at our church who don't understand the sacrifices of time, talent, effort, and money that people made while the church was growing. Early in our church's history, a young couple forfeited their honeymoon because they wanted to give to the church. That is one of many illustrations of sacrifice. People who haven't been a part of the fight involved in building a church become picky about little things that go wrong. Some people spend too much of their time fooling around with trivial things when they should be more concerned about God's kingdom.

The child of apathy is criticism. It is easy for a person to come to the point where he takes everything for granted and begins to criticize any imperfections he finds. Author Thomas Hardy said he had a friend who could go into any beautiful meadow and immediately find a manure pile. We shouldn't have that kind of perspective.

God has given Grace Church many wonderful people, and we thank Him for that. But I know there are also people who come to church only when it's convenient. For them, going to church is low on the priority list. If they can't afford to go anywhere for a weekend, they come to church. They don't see any need for commitment. Some people don't come on Sunday nights. They think one sermon a week is enough. Those people should be given two hundred sermons in one week to shake them out of their complacency! Kierkegaard observed that people think the preacher is an actor and they are to be his critics. What they don't know is that they're the actors and he's the prompter offstage reminding them of their lost lines (*Parables of*

Kierkegaard, Thomas C. Oden, ed. [Princeton: Princeton University 1978], pp. 89-90).

It is easy for Christians to get to the point where they expect things to be done for them. They show up for church only if they think they will get something out of it.

Building a church is easy. The hard work begins after the church has grown, when you're faced with people who have become complacent.

I received a letter from a young pastor thinking about leaving the ministry, and it broke my heart. This is what he wrote:

> Let me explain to you something I'm concerned about that I have not been able to correct and is causing me to consider leaving the ministry. Perhaps the Lord will use your insights to give me some light.
>
> I firmly believe that the leadership of a church should be the very best, not only in their personal spiritual lives, but also in being an example for people they lead. I am not saying that a leader has to be perfect or superhuman, but he should have a living, growing personal relationship with our Lord. I firmly believe that if the leaders of a church don't present a lifestyle of commitment and dedication to their Lord and church, their followers won't either.
>
> The problem, Pastor MacArthur, is that two-thirds of our elected officers attend only one service a week. I'm not saying they all have to be present every time the doors are open, but I do believe that excepting unforeseen situations, illnesses, and vacations, the leadership of a church should make a double effort to be present at the services, if for no other reason than for the encouragement of the saints and the pastor. I find it extremely difficult to believe that proper leadership can be provided when the leaders do not spend enough time with their people to find out what their hurts and fears are. At our board meetings, I find that by far the majority of the time is spent on items that have no direct relationship to the needs and hurts of people. I believe that because of that, our church has come to a stalemate, which is equal to going backwards instead of moving ahead. I have brought those things to the attention of our board on several occasions (even some of the people on our board are not faithful in their attendance), with absolutely no results.
>
> I am not talking about men and women who simply are not able to make it to church, but people who just will not come. Some of the leaders say they are too busy, too tired at the end of the day, or don't even offer an excuse. But those leaders are not afraid to remind me that they are the power of the church. That happens often. I have come to the place where if this continues on into next year, I am ready to resign the pastorate. How is it possible for a pastor to direct his flock, establish the needed programs, and develop

spiritual leadership if he can't get other leaders to back him? I'm open to your advice. I believe our church has great possibilities. But as long as we are lukewarm, the Lord will not bless us or use us.

That letter could have been written by thousands of different pastors because it is common for people to take for granted the good things God has given them. I don't want that to happen at Grace Church. I don't want people to forget the Lord. I want them to continue to fear His name.

Writing to his congregation, the apostle Peter said, "I will not be negligent to put you always in remembrance of these thing, though ye know them, and are established in the present truth" (2 Pet. 1:12). Peter had a high calling from God, and he didn't want to be irresponsible about how he handled it. He didn't want to be negligent to those he was called to teach, so he continually reminded the people of what they had already learned. He was saying, "I know that you already know these things, but you need to be reminded about them." Continuing in verse 13 he says, "I think it fitting, as long as I am in this tabernacle, to stir you up by putting you in remembrance, knowing that shortly I must put off this my tabernacle . . . I will endeavor that ye may be able, after my decease, to have these things always in remembrance" (vv. 13-15). There is virtue in repeating basics that shouldn't be forgotten. That is what I would like to do now.

Many pastors come to Grace Church to find out why it grows and what we are doing. They usually come to find out how things are done. They desire to know what God is doing, and some of them think they can pick up methods, tools, programs, and ideas and apply them to their own churches. However, that is like going to buy a steer and coming home with just the hide. They're seeing only the flesh of our ministries, not the internal aspects that make those ministries work properly. Beneath the surface of things is a foundation that people don't know about. We try to tell pastors that they may see a ministry functioning, but it is what is behind the scenes that needs to be understood.

For this first part of our study about church leadership, I am going to use the analogy the apostle Paul uses in 1 Corinthians 12:12-31. The church is a body, and we should look closely at its anatomy. Every body has certain features: a skeleton, internal systems, muscles, and flesh. A church needs to have the proper framework (a skeleton), internal systems (certain attitudes), muscles (different functions), and flesh (the form of the programs). Remove any one of those key features, and the body cannot survive. Anatomy is the study of how they fit and function together. Let's look at the anatomy of a church.

We start with the skeleton. For a body to function, it has to have structure. The skeleton gives vertebrate animals their structure. Likewise, there are certain skeletal truths that a church must be committed to if it is to have a sound structure. These doctrines are unalterable and nonnegotiable; they cannot be compromised in any way. Yield on any of these points, and you destroy the skeleton—the church ceases to be a church and becomes an amorphous blob instead.

A HIGH VIEW OF GOD

It is absolutely essential that a church perceive itself as an institution established for the glory of God. I fear that the church in America has descended from that lofty purpose and focused instead on humanity. Today the church seems to think its goal is to help people feel better about themselves. It offers people nothing more than spiritual placebos. It focuses on psychology, self-esteem, entertainment, and a myriad of other diversions to try to meet felt needs.

The church has been reduced from an organism that emphasizes knowing and glorifying God to an organization that focuses on man's needs. Yet if you know and glorify God, the needs of your life are answered. "The fear of the Lord is the beginning of wisdom" (Prov. 9:10). When you have a right relationship with God, everything else will fall into its proper place. I am not saying that we should ignore people's needs. We are to be concerned about people the same way God is. But a balance must be found, and that begins with a high view of God. We must take God seriously.

I feel righteous indignation toward preachers and others who want to take God off His throne and turn Him into a servant who has to do whatever they demand of Him. People tend to be irreverent; they do not know how to worship God. Some people think that worship is anything that induces a warm feeling. They know little about God. There are too many Marthas and not enough Marys in the church (Luke 10:38-42). We are so busy serving that we don't take the time to sit at Jesus' feet. We don't tremble at God's Word. We don't allow ourselves to be confronted by God's holiness and our sinfulness so that He can use us for His glory.

When a person dies, we have a tendency to say, "How could God let that happen?" We have no right to ask that. We should ask, "Why are we still alive?" God, being holy, could have destroyed man when he first fell into sin. Just because God is gracious toward us is no cause for us to be indifferent. God must be taken seriously.

Look in your Christian bookstore. The vast majority of books written today attack only trivial problems. During the eras when the church was most holy, Christians had very few books to read, but the books they did have told them how to have a relationship with God. Most books today don't do that.

A survey taken at a nationwide pastors' conference revealed that most pastors feel they need more help in dealing with families. In spite of all the books available on family-related issues, that's still an area where Christian leaders need more help. So the answer isn't to write more materials about the family. The problem is that people aren't taking God seriously enough to walk according to His laws. If families were taught a high view of God, there would not be as many family problems in the church.

James 4:8 says, "Draw near to God, and he will draw near to you." Would you like to live your life with God near you? If you draw close to God, He will come close to you. But you say, "When I get near God, it is easy to become nervous." That's why James 4:8 also says, "Cleanse your hands, ye sinners." The closer you get to God, the more you see your own sin. Consequently, you will humble yourself and mourn over your sin. James 4:10 says that when you've humbled yourself before the Lord, "He shall lift you up."

We must take God seriously and exalt Him; we don't want to have a man-centered church. We are to reach out to people in the love of Christ, but God is still to be the focus of our worship and our life.

THE ABSOLUTE AUTHORITY OF SCRIPTURE

A second nonnegotiable truth that makes up the skeleton of the church is the absolute authority of Scripture. The Bible is constantly under attack, even from within the professing church. I recently read an article by a seminary professor who argued that Christians should not view homosexual behavior as sinful. If a person advocates that view, he must be disregarding the Bible. How inconsistent for a seminary professor to deny the Bible when he is training men to minister the Word of God! But that is happening today. The Bible is being attacked head-on.

I believe charismatics attack the Bible when they add their visions and revelations to it. It is a subtle and often unintentional attack, but it is an attack just the same. They say that Jesus told them this and that God told them that. They are undermining the Bible when they do not regard it as the single authority. Those who believe God speaks regularly with special messages for individual Christians trivialize His Word. God reveals Himself primarily through the pages of Scripture, and that written revelation must be held up as the absolute authority.

One of the worst assaults on God's Word comes from people who say they believe the Bible but don't know what it teaches. That is the subtlest kind of attack. People all across America say they believe the Bible from cover to cover but don't know one paragraph of it. How can they believe what they don't know?

Jesus said, "Man shall not live by bread alone, but by every word that proceedeth out of the mouth of God" (Matt. 4:4). If we are fed by every word that comes out of the mouth of God, we ought to study every word. Today, preachers have lost sight of that.

A pastor once told me, "I pastor a church for only two years, and then I leave."

I said, "Have you been doing that for a long time?"

"Yes, I spend two years here, two years there, and two years in another place."

"Why?" I asked.

"I have fifty-two sermons. I preach each one twice, and then I leave."

I said, "Why don't you teach the whole counsel of God (Acts 20:27)?"

He answered, "I don't teach all of it, just the parts I think are important." But every word that proceeds out of the mouth of God is important!

SOUND DOCTRINE

The third thing that a church must have as a part of its skeleton is sound doctrine. If you have a high view of God and are committed to Him, you must adhere to what His Word teaches. The teachings of God's Word make up sound doctrine.

Many Christians today are vague about doctrine. Many pastors offer "sermonettes for Christianettes"—little sermons that are nice and interesting. Sometimes they make you feel warm, fuzzy, sad, or excited. But seldom do we hear doctrine taught or discussed. Very few preachers explain the truths about God, life, death, heaven, hell, man, sin, Christ, angels, the Holy Spirit, the position of the believer, the flesh, or the world. We need truths that we can hold onto. You need to read a text, find out what it says and means, draw out a divine truth, and plant that truth in the minds of people by repeating it.

I picked up that style of preaching when I graduated from high school. My father gave me a Bible and wrote a note in it encouraging me to read 1 and 2 Timothy. I did that, and Paul's message to Timothy kept running through my mind: "If thou put the brethren in remembrance of these things, thou shalt be a good minister of Jesus

Christ, nourished up in the words of faith and of good doctrine, unto which thou hast attained" (1 Tim. 4:6; cf. 1 Tim. 1:3, 10; 4:13, 16).

Early in my ministry at Grace Church, I taught from the book of Ephesians, explaining a believer's position in Christ. That study was foundational to the church. Recently I visited my high school football coach, whom I hadn't seen for a long time. He is a Christian and also teaches the Word of God. We were reminiscing about some of the silly things that happened when I played football in high school. Then he said to me, "John, you have made concrete for me the position of the believer in Christ. I have listened to your tapes on Ephesians chapter one many times, and I've taught from that passage repeatedly over the years to young people. Understanding the doctrine of the believer's position in Jesus Christ has given me a foundation for my entire life."

I didn't give my coach that foundation; the book of Ephesians and the Holy Spirit did. The point is that people need solid doctrine to build their lives on.

Personal Holiness

We have to draw lines when it comes to personal holiness. We need to be careful about what we expose ourselves and our children to. It is impossible to watch some of the films in movie theaters and read some of the books being published today without paying a price. I sometimes wonder what is going through the minds of Christians who expose themselves to movies, television programs, and publications that propagate immorality and an unbiblical value system.

We dare not lower our standards along with the world. What our society tolerates is shocking. Things that were not spoken of except in hushed whispers a decade ago are now openly flaunted. I wonder that our culture could degenerate so far in such a short time. Christians are called to live a pure life, and we can't compromise that. We should enforce a standard of purity among ourselves.

Second Corinthians 7:1 says, "Having, therefore, these promises, dearly beloved, let us cleanse ourselves from all filthiness of the flesh and spirit, perfecting holiness in the fear of God." A church should enforce that standard (see Matt. 18:15-17). That's why we implement church discipline at Grace Church. If someone sins, we confront him.

Many Christians aren't as concerned about personal holiness as they should be. Where are you in terms of holiness and communion with the living God? We can't live semicommitted Christian lives and still expect God's work to be done.

Spiritual Authority

One final component of the skeletal structure of a church is spiritual authority. A church must understand that Christ is the Head of the church (Eph. 1:22; 4:15) and that He mediates His rule in the church through godly elders (1 Thess. 5:13-14; Heb. 13:7, 17).

Hebrews 13 says to submit to those over you in the Lord, for they watch over your souls. Follow their example. First Thessalonians 5 says to "know them who labor among you, and are over you in the Lord, and admonish you, and to esteem them very highly in love for their work's sake" (vv. 12-13).

We have many leaders at Grace Church; I'm just one of them. I happen to be the one whom God has chosen to preach. Jesus had twelve apostles. Every time the biblical writers list them, Peter's name is first (Matt. 10:2-4; Mark 3:16-19; Luke 6:14-16; Acts 1:13). He was always the spokesman. That doesn't mean he was better than the others. He simply had the gift of speaking, whereas the others were gifted in other ways.

Peter and John always traveled together. Because of that, you would think that John didn't say much. But he wrote the gospel of John; 1, 2, and 3 John; and Revelation. There is no doubt that with the intimate friendship he had with Christ, he could have related even more great things to us. But every time he was with Peter in the first twelve chapters of Acts, he was silent. Why? Because Peter had the gift of speaking.

Barnabas was a great teacher—probably the leading one in the early church. But when Barnabas and Paul traveled together, even unbelievers realized that Paul was the chief speaker.

So there are variations in the giftedness of spiritual leaders. But in totality, there is still an equality of spiritual authority given to those the Bible calls elders or overseers.

Let's sum up what we've learned. For the church to be effective as the Body of Christ, it has to have the right framework. It has to have a high view of God. The pursuit of a church should be to know God. In seeking to know God, the authority of Scripture must be recognized, for it is through the Bible that we can know God. A church should have a high view of Scripture and a commitment to teaching sound doctrine. The people of a church should also seek personal holiness and submit their souls to the care of those the Lord has placed over them as spiritual authorities.

Chapter 2

The Internal Systems*

As we have noted, the skeleton of a church consists of nonnegotiable truths on which we cannot afford to yield. Like a skeleton, they are rigid and unbending, the backbone of a biblical ministry.

But like any living body, the church cannot exist as a skeleton alone. A skeleton provides a framework, but it isn't alive. A physical body has organs and fluids that keep it alive and functioning. So a church must have internal systems—certain spiritual attitudes. The life of a church comes from those systems.

The goal of a pastor and the leaders of a church should be to generate proper spiritual attitudes in the hearts of the people. They can't just say, "You need to do this, and you need to do that." They must generate the spiritual attitudes that will motivate people to proper behavior. A person can do something good outwardly, yet have a bad attitude. However, good outward behavior should come from good attitudes. That's why it's important to emphasize the fruit of the Spirit (Gal. 5:22-23)—the internal attitudes.

Sometimes young men go into a pastorate and see certain things missing in their church. They see a lack of organization and become tempted to reorganize the church. They'll say, "Let's appoint some elders and reorganize this church!" But do you know what will happen after the reorganizing is finished? They're going to have the same

*From tapes GC 2025-2028.

31

people with the same attitudes in a different structure, and the people are not going to understand the purpose behind the change.

When I first came to Grace Church, I had a new idea about how to run the Sunday school. I wrote out my idea and presented it to the Education Committee. They unanimously turned it down. They said, "Who are you, kid? We've been here longer than you." In effect, they were saying, "Prove yourself first." Several years later, the Education Committee came up with the same system I had proposed. I learned that it's important to develop in people the spiritual attitudes that will bring about the right kind of responses. If the right kind of spiritual attitudes are present in a church, the structure will take care of itself, because Spirit-controlled people are going to do Spirit-led things. They will naturally conform to the biblical pattern of the church.

A church should work on the attitudes of its people. I'm not interested in trying to make sure the people of Grace Church behave a certain way by giving their money; coming to church Sunday mornings, Sunday evenings, and Wednesday nights; praying five hours a week; and reading the Bible every day. Those things are not to be approached on a legalistic or superficial basis. The emphasis of a ministry should be on generating proper spiritual attitudes. Sometimes that's difficult to do because some people don't want to have right attitudes, and it becomes easy to let them do "good" things with a bad attitude. But doing that will allow the people with bad attitudes to derive satisfaction from legalistic behavior.

OBEDIENCE

Obedience stands above all other attitudes. An obedient person does whatever God says to do. He does not compromise. If God says something, that's it—there is nothing to argue about. It's important for us to have God's Word in our hearts and minds so that we know how to be obedient. Obedience is the *sine qua non* of all right attitudes. It is the all-pervasive attitude that makes other spiritual virtues possible. Behavior without an attitude of obedience is meaningless; internal obedience is better than any external act of worship (1 Sam. 15:22). Furthermore, obedience leads to other right spiritual attitudes.

There are several other important reasons to live an obedient life: to glorify God, to receive blessings, to be a witness to unbelievers, and to be an example for other Christians. Being obedient also allows us to be filled with the Spirit. When we're filled with the Spirit, we're able to reach out to unbelievers and set an example for those who watch how we live.

Jesus says in Luke 6:46, "Why call ye me Lord, Lord, and do not the things which I say?" If Jesus is Lord of your life, you should do what He asks you to do. Matthew 7:13-14 says that the path to salvation is narrow. That's because it is confined by God's will, law, and Word. We are to affirm Christ as Lord (Rom. 10:9-10) and submit to His lordship. That means living a life of obedience.

A man who listened to our radio program sent a letter and a tape to me, telling me about a matter that was on his heart. During the first ten minutes of the tape, he talked about how he appreciated our study of the Bible on our radio program. Then he said he had many sins in his life that God was working on, one of which he wanted to ask me about. He said that he had never had normal feelings toward women; instead, he had a strong sexual attraction to large farm animals.

He went on to add, however, that he didn't think his desire for animals constituted a problem because he didn't feel guilty about it. He said that the Lord was refining him in other areas, not that one. A four-page letter was sent back to him explaining that his problem is a serious sin in the eyes of God. In fact, if he had lived in the Old Testament era, he would have been killed, for Leviticus 20:15 says, "If a man lie with a beast, he shall surely be put to death." The letter kindly expressed that God doesn't select certain sins to work on and leave others alone. Every sin is an affront to His holy name. Several Scripture references were given in the letter to support what was said.

A while later, that man sent another tape to me. He said, "I don't think anybody understands. Christians are so tangled up in the Bible that they don't understand how God works and feels."

That's a revealing statement. Unfortunately, it reflects a widespread attitude. But it is disastrous theology. How are we going to know how God feels about something except by reading the Bible? That man didn't want to listen to what God had to say about his problem because he didn't want to be confronted with his own guilt. First John 2:5 says, "Whosoever *keepeth his word*, in him verily is the love of God perfected; by this know we that we are in him" (emphasis added). A person who can tolerate that kind of abomination in his life and says he knows how God feels without reading the Bible has a problem. Sin causes a person to become self-justifying.

That's an extreme illustration, but it points out the fact that God has called us to be obedient to His Word. We should know how He feels about things because He tells us in His Word. The goal of ministry should be to build an obedient people. That is what God intended to do in both the Old and New Testaments. When God speaks, we are to obey.

It is sad that when some people are confronted with divine truth that convicts them of something in their lives that isn't right, they continue in their pattern of disobedience. For example: suppose you hear a sermon about forgiveness, and there is someone you know that you need to forgive. But you push that sermon out of your mind and continue to have a bitter, unforgiving spirit. That is disobedience. It is diametrically opposed to all that God wants to accomplish in your life.

Someone will say, "I go to church. Isn't that enough?" First Samuel 15:22 says, "To obey is better than sacrifice." Ritual will never replace obedience. In 1 Peter 1 the apostle says to "gird up the loins of your mind" (v. 13). In other words, make sure your priorities are right. Be "obedient children, not fashioning yourselves according to the former lusts in your ignorance" (v. 14). Don't live the way you did before you became a Christian. You are to be an obedient child.

Jesus said, "Blessed are they that hear the word of God, and keep it" (Luke 11:28). Paul, commending the Roman Christians, said, "Your obedience is come abroad unto all men. I am glad" (Rom. 16:19). A pastor's heart is made happy when the obedience of his people is manifest.

I once heard Howard Hendricks say that people who have been Christians for a long time and are more than fifty years old should be the most excited, committed, pure, servant-like people in a church. The very energy of a church ought to come from them. They should be on the forefront in evangelism and prayer. Why? Because they've lived with God the longest. They've applied the Word to their lives for so long that they've become more obedient and mature than those who have been Christians for only a few years.

It is wonderful that Grace Church has many young people. I like young people because they are energetic. But it's sad if the energy of a church only comes from its young people. Often I hear young pastors say, "My church is good and is in a nice area, but it's full of old people."

If you're a Christian but don't apply God's Word to your life, you'll just become one of those inert older people. You'll pass fifty years old, and you'll want to retire spiritually. You'll say, "I've been going to church for many years. I don't want to get involved in evangelism; I'd rather leave that kind of thing for younger people." Look at the Old Testament leaders of Israel: Many of them were older people! The early church found its energy in its mature saints. Today the church is deriving its energy from young people. We need the energy that young people have, but we also need the power that older believers have developed from long, obedient lives. An older believer should be ready to blast off into heaven from the energy he has built up! But because many believers don't apply what they hear as they get older, their lives don't change. They may know a lot of spiritual facts, but they have no power. I don't want that to happen in my life. Perhaps the reason many people eventually stop serving Christ is that they allow themselves to hear the Bible without applying it.

We must be committed to obeying God's Word. If the Spirit teaches you a truth, apply it. When you're confronted with conviction, don't say, "I wish So-and-so could have heard that sermon." Apply the sermon to yourself. When you obey Christ, you grow in spiritual maturity and become more useful to God.

HUMILITY

The second attitude a Christian should have is humility. I've struggled with pride. I'm sure that you've had problems with it, too. Humility is very elusive because when you say to yourself, "I'm humble," you're being proud.

At Grace Church, when we built the auditorium that we now use as a gymnasium, someone ordered five big chairs with crowns at the top of their backs. Before the services started, I was supposed to sit in the chair in the middle. I tried that for a couple of weeks but didn't like it. I preferred to sit in the front row of the pews with the congregation. I didn't want people thinking I was proud of myself or better than they. Sitting in the front row of the pews gives me the same perspective as everyone else: I am in church to worship God. The only difference between my congregation and me is that God has called me to be a preacher and given me the gift of preaching.

I hope that when you became a Christian you weren't under the illusion that God needed you. Some people say, "If the Lord could only save that person! He has such great talent and is a good leader." That's ridiculous. The Lord can save anybody He wants. And we have nothing to offer God. We're like the man in Matthew 18:23-34 who couldn't pay his ten-thousand-talent debt. He had nothing to offer. Matthew 5:3 says, "Blessed are the poor in spirit; for theirs is the kingdom of heaven." In other words, when we came into God's kingdom, we came as destitute beggars who had nothing to offer. We were spiritually bankrupt. If we have anything now, it isn't because we earned it; God gave it to us. The only thing I have to offer back to God is what He gave me through His gift of salvation and His Spirit. I can't take any credit for what I am; I must give God the glory. I have no reason to be proud.

The leaders of Grace Church have endeavored to withstand the preoccupation with self-esteem and the selfishness of our contemporary society. We point out that God has called Christians to be sacrificial and humble. The Bible talks repeatedly about humility. In essence Jesus says in Matthew 10:38-39, "Let a man deny himself, take up his cross, and gain his life by following Me." He says the same thing in Matthew 16:24-25: Deny yourself and follow Me. Pay the price of self-effacement and set yourself below others. In Philippians 2:3-4 we read, "In lowliness of mind let each esteem others better than themselves. Look not every man on his own things, but every man also on the things of others." Seek to honor others and meet their needs. If the people of a church are fighting for positions of authority, they are going to experience the same chaos as when all the disciples were seeking to be the greatest (Matt. 20:20-21; Mark 9:33-35; Luke 22:24).

We should earnestly desire to be humble. That doesn't mean we are to undervalue ourselves, because in Christ we are eternally priceless. We aren't to walk around saying, "I'm a worm; I'm a rat; I'm a bum; I'm nothing." (However, remember that Christ is the One who made us priceless—we didn't do that ourselves.) We're of value to God because we're redeemed and sanctified. That enables us to serve Him.

LOVE

Only those who are humble can show love. I'm not talking about the worldly kind of love that is counterfeit and object-oriented. That's the reason many marriages don't last. Worldly love is only an emotion, and when the emotion is gone the relationship is over. That kind of love seeks only to get and not to give.

Biblical love is not like that. It's not an emotion; it is an act of sacrificial service. It's not an attitude; it's an action. Love always *does* something. The words used to describe love in 1 Corinthians 13:4-7 are all verbs. Love is an act of service that flows from a heart of humility.

Biblical love meets people's needs. Jesus says in Luke 10:27, "Thou shalt love . . . thy neighbor as thyself." A lawyer replied, "And who is my neighbor?" (v. 29). Jesus answered with the story about the Good Samaritan (vv. 30-35). The Samaritan was walking along a road and came upon a man who had been badly beaten. He helped the man and met his needs. Who is your neighbor? Anyone who has a need that you are able to meet. Who are you to love? Anyone who has a need. How do you love him? Meet his need, even if you don't feel an emotional attachment or an attraction for him.

A classic illustration of the humility of love is in John 13. Jesus and the disciples were to have supper together. The disciples were arguing among themselves about who was the greatest (Luke 22:24). In those days, people ate meals in a reclining position, which meant that a person's head would be about eight inches from someone else's feet. It was common courtesy for everyone's feet to be washed before they reclined for eating. But no servant was available to wash the disciples' feet. None of the disciples was willing to assume that chore because they were all arguing about who was the greatest. So Jesus took off His outer garment, put a towel around His waist, and washed their feet Himself (John 13:4-5). He taught them an unforgettable lesson. When finished He said, in effect, "You're to love one another as I have loved you" (v. 15). How did He show His love For them? Not with an emotional attachment. Probably the only emotion He had was disgust because the disciples were full of selfishness and pride. He showed them His love by meeting their need. Likewise, we should meet the needs of others.

We should meet other people's needs spontaneously and voluntarily. Our love should be like a reflex from a humble heart. That kind of heart will always manifest itself. The following is a letter I received that illustrates spontaneous sacrificial love:

> Some time ago my husband and I had the opportunity to visit Grace Community Church and I want to tell you what your church is like from a visitor's point of view. Our church is large, too, and our motto is, "The church is where love is." I have never felt more welcome anywhere than I did at Grace Church. The people were terrific. They treated us like royalty. One gentleman gave me an early morning tour. During the break between the first and second services, I talked with another man for a while. He asked me if I would like a tape from that morning's service. I said yes! A few weeks later, I received not just one tape, but the whole series on Jesus' teaching on divorce. Many of my friends have listened to that series and had many questions answered for them. I just wanted to let you know how wonderful your congregation is.

That is wonderful, isn't it? I know the people she was talking about. The person who gave her the tour didn't really have the time to do that because of his many responsibilities. The person who sent her the tapes didn't really have the money to do it, but that's how love acts. Love flows from a humble heart. Love seeks the comfort and joy of others.

UNITY

Jesus prayed that all Christians would be one, just as He and the Father are one, so that the world would know He was sent by the Father. He prayed that we would be unified (John 17:21). That basically refers to the unity of believers as a result of salvation, but Jesus also wants us to have unity in the life and purpose of the church. The apostle Paul told the Ephesians to endeavor "to keep the unity of the Spirit in the bond of peace" (Eph. 4:3). He didn't tell them to generate unity; they already had it. They were to maintain the unity God had already given them.

Unity is an important part of church life. That's why Satan constantly attacks it. Some time ago, my wife and I went to a Bible conference and had the opportunity to talk with the daughter of Dr. Criswell, who pastors the First Baptist Church of Dallas. She told us, "Dad once had a man on his church staff who tried to split our church. He was very torn about that. One Sunday he became so concerned about it that he called a construction company and said, 'Before next Sunday, I want kneeling benches installed in every pew in this church.' By the next Sunday, every pew had kneeling benches. (They're still there today.) When everyone came into the church, he said, 'By the grace of God there has never been a split in this church, and there never will be.' Then he told the entire congregation to kneel on the benches in prayer. God healed the rifts that had been developing in the congregation."

Unity brings God glory. It honors His name. Satan is incessantly trying to divide churches. I praise God that Grace Church has never experienced a split. There have been people who wanted to leave because some little thing didn't happen the way they wanted it to. Even if they were right, humility and love don't act to bring about division.

No one is perfect, so there will always be little things that people disagree about. Nevertheless, we should always get on our knees together and seek to maintain the unity of the Spirit and the bond of peace (Eph. 4:3). That was the desire of the New Testament writers. Paul poured his heart out to the Corinthians, saying, "I beseech you, brethren, by the name of our Lord Jesus Christ, that ye all speak the same thing, and that there be no divisions among you, but that ye be perfectly joined together in the same mind and in the same judgment. For it hath been declared unto me of you, my brethren, by them who are of the house of Chloe, that there are contentions among you" (1 Cor. 1:10-11). He couldn't stand to see divisions in the church. He told the Philippian church to be "striving together for the faith of the gospel" (Phil. 1:27). His words are just as applicable today. Do you see the attitudes mentioned above in your life? Is your life characterized by obedience? Are you progressing in maturity and becoming more sanctified as you hear the Word and apply it? Do you see yourself growing in such a way that as you get older, you will reach the peak of dedication in your spiritual life? Do you have an attitude of humility? Are you meeting other people's needs with loving acts that come from a humble heart? Do you truly seek to make peace and maintain the unity of the Spirit? We should seek all those things in our lives. That is God's will for us.

WILLINGNESS TO SERVE

Large churches have large needs. Because of our church's size, there are multiple opportunities for service. Ironically, people tend to think they are not needed in such a large church. They find it pleasant to sit on the sidelines, get comfortable, and watch while others minister. That can be deadly!

In 1 Corinthians 4:1 Paul says, "Let a man so account of us, as of the ministers of Christ." In other words, "When the time comes to render a judgment about my co-workers and me, let it be said that we were servants of Christ."

There are several words in the Greek language for servant, and Paul used the one that best conveyed the idea of a lowly servant (Gk., *hupēretēs*, "an under rower"). In those days, large wooden three-tiered ships called *triremes* were propelled by slaves chained to their oars in the hull. The slaves on the lowest tier were called "under rowers." Paul and his co-workers didn't want to be exalted; they wanted to be known as third-level galley slaves who pulled their oars.

Many people want to be hotshots, but God wants obedient servants. In 1 Corinthians 4:2 Paul says, "It is required in stewards, that a man be found faithful." God doesn't want a person to come up with a clever new way to pull his oar and shear off everyone else's in the process! He wants faithful rowers who see themselves as willing servants.

Service to others doesn't necessarily have to be related to church-designed programs. In Romans 12 Paul talks about the function of servants, using the human body as an analogy: "As we have many members in one body, and all members have not the same office [function], so we, being many, are one body in Christ, and every one members one of another. Having then gifts differing according to the grace that is given to us, whether prophecy, let us prophesy . . . or ministry, let us wait on our ministering; or he that teacheth, on teaching; or he that exhorteth, on exhortation; he that giveth, let him do it with liberality; he that ruleth, with diligence; he that showeth mercy, with cheerfulness" (vv. 4-8). Paul is saying, "Use the God-given ability you have to minister to others!" You don't need to have a program to be able to minister to others. Let the abilities God has given you flow from your life, whether it be in a structured program or personal interaction. A believer is indwelt and empowered by the Holy Spirit for the purpose of serving others. If you don't serve you'll be creating a bottleneck. Don't go to your church and say, "There are too many people! I don't know where I can serve." If you're filled with the Holy Spirit, God wants to cultivate a ministry through you that is essential for that church.

Paul mentions various categories of ministry in Romans 12:6-8: prophecy (preaching), ministry, teaching, exhorting, giving, ruling, and mercy (see also 1 Cor. 12:4-11). Each of those categories is very broad. Within the category of giving, there are many ways to give. Within the category of showing mercy, there are many ways to show mercy. There are many different styles of preaching and teaching. The Lord has given each of us a blend of gifts enabling us to minister the way He wants us to. In my own life I can see that God has called me to preach, teach, lead, exhort, and perhaps demonstrate the gift of knowledge. He blends certain gifts in such unique ways that we are like spiritual snowflakes—no two of us are alike. That's why the church misses out when we don't serve in the way we are gifted. God doesn't want us to be spectators.

Several years ago *Moody Monthly* published an article about Grace Church. At the time we were in a smaller building and bursting at the seams with people. After surveying the church and interviewing different people, the writer decided to title his article "The Church with Nine Hundred Ministers." He did that because we had nine hundred people and everyone was actively serving. We didn't have many formal programs, but everyone was ministering his gifts. People were always calling the church and asking if they could visit someone in the hospital, if the nursery needed more helpers, if someone was needed to clean the restrooms and windows, if help was needed to evangelize, or if someone was needed to teach a class. Everyone made himself available. People would also tell each other how God was blessing their ministry, and they gave God the glory for what was happening. That's the way a church should be.

There are many other areas of ministry a person can get involved in. Cultivate the giftedness that God has given you and become active in whatever ministry God leads you to.

In Colossians 4:12 Paul writes, "Epaphras . . . is one of you, a servant of Christ." Notice that Paul didn't say anything like, "Epaphras, the seminary graduate," or, "Epaphras, the Phi Beta Kappa member with a Ph.D." He just said, "Epaphras is one of you, a servant of Christ." Being a servant of Christ is a very high calling!

Paul writes about another man with a true servant's heart in Philippians 2:25: "Epaphroditus, my brother and companion in labor, and fellow soldier, but your messenger . . . ministered to my need." Epaphroditus was a companion to Paul. Do you know how valuable a companion is when you're in a battle defending the gospel? Many people need that kind of support.

People like Epaphroditus are going to be noticed in heaven. It's hard to find people like him. Paul says to the Philippians in verse 29, "Receive him . . . and hold such in reputation." Why? Because he was a helper and companion.

A willing servant is spontaneous in what he does. You can either sit back and say, "I don't know if I want to get involved in that; I don't know if I want to work with those people," or you can just get involved and serve.

JOY

What is joy? It's an outward exuberance. It's also the response of the heart, soul, and mind to one's relationship with Jesus Christ. One of the things the leaders of Grace Church have endeavored to cultivate in the congregation is joy.

There is a seriousness in the Word of God and in being before the infinitely holy, all-wise, sovereign God. There is a great seriousness in struggling with the terrible anxieties of life and death and all that our humanity brings upon us. Many things fill us with pain. But at the same time, we are to be filled with joy. We have a knowledge deep in our souls that all is well and that ultimately everything will be glorious.

When we study the Word of God and obey Him, we will experience joy. First John 1:4 says, "These things write we unto you, that your joy may be full." Romans 14:17 says that the kingdom of God is "righteousness, and peace, and joy in the Holy Spirit." Jesus says in John 17:13 that He came to give us joy. Paul said, "Rejoice in the Lord always; and again I say, Rejoice" (Phil. 4:4).

I'm convinced that joy is linked to a willingness to serve. When people get involved in serving and using the gifts God gave them, they experience joy. People who are overly introspective are always trying to meet their own needs and solve their own problems. Therefore they become ingrown, self-contemplating, miserable human beings.

A person can choose to lose his joy. He can look for the manure pile in every meadow if he wants to. It's a choice everyone makes. I choose to be joyful and excited about what God does. With the strength the Holy Spirit has given me, I won't let anyone take away my joy because the Bible commands that I rejoice always (Phil. 4:4). I tell myself, "Rejoice in the God who redeemed you and loved you in spite of your sin. Rejoice that you are going to heaven someday." We will have problems, but there is coming a day when all true believers will be in heaven and all of us will be perfect.

PEACE

Peace is a beautiful word, isn't it? Jesus said, "Peace I leave with you, my peace I give unto you; not as the world giveth, give I unto you. Let not your heart be troubled, neither let it be afraid" (John 14:27). Jesus gave us His peace. First Corinthians 7:15 says that "God hath called us to peace." Philippians 4:7 says to let the peace of God rule your heart. Second Corinthians 13:11 says to "live in peace." First Thessalonians 5:13 says to "be at peace among yourselves."

Whereas joy is an outward exuberance, peace is an inward contentment that senses everything is under control. If there is sin in your life, you won't experience peace. But when your life is cleansed of sin and you're walking in the Spirit, you'll have peace. Never allow anyone or anything to take away your peace.

At Grace Church we try to cultivate an attitude of peace, rest, and confidence in God. There is no reason to be troubled. Paul said to "be anxious for nothing" and let the peace of God rule your souls (Phil. 4:6-7). All of us experience trials that make us anxious. We don't live in perfect peace, yet we are to have an attitude of peace.

In Matthew 5:9 our Lord says, "Blessed are the peacemakers; for they shall be called the sons of God." Christians should be peacemakers. You couldn't do anything more wonderful for the kingdom of God and the church of Jesus Christ than to be a peacemaker. Human nature tends toward conflict. Job said, "Man is born unto trouble, as the sparks fly upward" (5:7). People continually experience personality conflicts. Yet we are called to be peacemakers. We're to help soothe conflict, not foment it. Sometimes an insignificant problem can be blown out of proportion and become a tidal wave. People are more inclined to increase trouble than to make peace.

Say to yourself, "I am at peace, God is in control, and I'll be a peacemaker." Every time you get into a conflict, be a peacemaker. When you see two people in a conflict, help them embrace one another in peace. Don't take sides. Try to find the good in a person instead of focusing on the bad. Cultivate proper relationships, starting in your own family. If you know that saying a certain thing will irritate someone, don't say it. Sometimes when I'm right about something and someone else thinks I'm wrong, I won't assert that I'm right because I don't want to disrupt the peace between us. I won't compromise my convictions, but I'm also not going to unnecessarily defend my rights. Peace is more important to me than having my own way. However, if someone denies the truth of God, I will battle for what is right. With the people in the family of God, though, we are to be peacemakers. How simple life would be if we were all peacemakers!

THANKFULNESS

First Thessalonians 5:18 says, "In everything give thanks; for this is the will of God in Christ Jesus concerning you."

People say, "If only I had a better job," or, "If only I had a better spouse," or, "If only I didn't have so many problems." But we're to be thankful.

Giving thanks can be a powerful thing. If you can cultivate a thankful heart, you will solve many of your problems. Offering thanks and praises to God helps you to stop focusing on your problems. That was certainly true for the psalm writers. Whenever a problem developed, they would cry out to the Lord in despair. One said, "Why are the wicked allowed to prosper?" King David had that attitude when he fled from his son Absalom, who wanted to take over his throne. But eventually he started thinking about all the good things God had done for him. When he cultivated an attitude of thankfulness—even in the midst of fleeing from Absalom—he was no longer in despair.

We have many things to be thankful for:

Psalm 30:4—"Give thanks at the remembrance of his holiness."

Psalm 106:1—"Give thanks unto the Lord, for he is good; for his mercy endureth forever."

Daniel 2:23—Daniel expressed thankfulness to God for the wisdom and strength given him.

Romans 1:8—Give thanks to God for people who exhibit their faith.

Romans 6:17—Be thankful for the conversion of people.

Romans 7:23-25—Be thankful that Christ has delivered you from the power of indwelling sin.

1 Corinthians 1:4—Thank God for the grace He bestows on believers.

1 Corinthians 15:57—Give thanks to God that He has given us victory over death.

2 Corinthians 2:14—We should be thankful for the triumph of the gospel.

2 Corinthians 8:16—Be thankful for those who have a zeal for Christ.

2 Corinthians 9:15—We are to be thankful for the gift of Christ.

1 Thessalonians 2:13—Be thankful for those who receive and apply the Word of God.

2 Thessalonians 1:3—We should be thankful when we see believers working hard for the sake of the kingdom and showing love to one another.

Revelation 11:17—We should be thankful for Christ's power and His coming kingdom.

Don't complain when you're in bad circumstances; cultivate a heart of thankfulness instead. If you're not a thankful person, it's because you think you deserve better circumstances than those you currently have. But if you got what you deserved, you'd be in hell. That goes for all of us. So be thankful for whatever God gives you. That will t⸰ke all the sourness out of your life.

SELF-DISCIPLINE

Christians need to realize how important it is for us to conform to God's divine standard. Self-discipline means staying away from sin and doing only what is right. The disciplined person understands the law of God and doesn't do anything outside the bounds of that standard.

Paul talks about self-discipline in 1 Corinthians 9:24-27, where he uses a familiar metaphor to illustrate his point: "Know ye not that they who run in a race run all, but one receiveth the prize? So run, that ye may obtain." Everyone in a race runs to win the prize; that's why they're in the race. Believers have been called to race (Gal. 5:7; Phil. 2:16; Heb. 12:1-2) and to run to win. What is necessary to accomplish that goal? Paul tells us in verse 25: "Every man that striveth for the mastery [competes in athletics] is temperate in all things." In other words, if a person wants to experience victory, he has to be self-disciplined. A man can't win a race if he is thirty pounds overweight. Tremendous discipline is required to keep in shape.

The number of hours an athlete must train so he can win in competition is staggering. An athlete who competes internationally frequently trains several hours a day for as long as five to ten years of his life. He must push himself to the point where he will no longer experience pain, to a point beyond a second wind. There is a euphoria beyond pain that only athletes can experience. That euphoria is like an incredible sense of freedom and energy, and it comes only beyond pain.

In verse 26 Paul continues, "I, therefore, so run, not as uncertainly." He made sure he stayed on course. In 2 Timothy 2:5, Paul tells Timothy that for an athlete to win the crown in a race, he must "strive lawfully (Gk., *nominos*)." He must obey the rules of the game. He can't go out of bounds. If he wants to win, he must conform to the rules.

In verse 27 Paul adds, "I keep under my body, and bring it into subjection, lest that by any means, when I have preached to others, I myself should be a castaway [be disqualified because of sin]." He didn't want to sin and lose the chance for a spiritual victory any more than an athlete would want to do anything that would disqualify him.

I once had the opportunity to teach a Bible study for the Miami Dolphins football team before they played a game against the Los Angeles Raiders. I taught them from Ephesians 6. Some of the players already had their legs and ankles taped, ready for battle. I told them that they had spent a tremendous number of hours and much energy to reach the peak of athletic performance they were at. Soon they were going to put on their armor, so to speak, to do battle for a corruptible crown (1 Cor. 9:25). I told them that there was another warfare more important than that: spiritual warfare for an incorruptible crown—an eternal inheritance that "fadeth not away" (1 Pet. 1:4). The armor for that kind of warfare is more important than shoulder pads, chest pads, hip pads, helmet, and all the other things football players wear. It is vital to wear that armor if one is going to know victory in spiritual warfare. I read Ephesians 6:11: "Put on the whole armor of God, that ye may be able to stand against the wiles of the devil." Then I said, "Fighting unprepared against the enemies of your soul would be like fighting the Raiders in your gym shorts, 'for we wrestle not against flesh and blood, but against principalities, against powers, against the rulers of the darkness of this world, against spiritual wickedness in high places'" (Eph. 6:12). We are caught in a spiritual battle, and the battle isn't against men but against demons.

I will never forget a battle with a demon-possessed girl one night at church. She was in a room kicking, screaming, and throwing furniture around. When I walked into the room, she said, "Don't let him in!" But the voice that spoke wasn't her own. My first response was, "Fine, I'm leaving!" But I began to realize that if the demons didn't like me, it was because I was on God's team. In the power of God, several of us spent hours there until she confessed her sin. God, in His grace, purified her. Since that encounter I've never doubted that man's battle is against demons.

It's important for us to understand the seriousness of the spiritual warfare wrought against Christ and all who belong to Him. We need to put on "the whole armor of God, that [we] may be able . . . to withstand" (Eph. 6:13). We have to be prepared for battle.

There are two elements of that armor I'd like to emphasize. They are mentioned in Ephesians 6:14.

THE BELT OF TRUTH

Paul said to "stand, therefore, having your loins girded about with truth." He was envisioning a Roman soldier preparing for battle. If a Roman soldier were to go into battle without a belt, his tunic would fly loosely around him. In hand-to-hand combat, a loose tunic could interfere with a soldier's moves and cause his death. It would also make him vulnerable to being grabbed by an enemy soldier. To prevent that from happening, a Roman soldier put on a belt to gather his tunic tightly around him. Paul called it the belt of truthfulness. He associated it with a sincere commitment to self-discipline. We must be serious about being prepared for spiritual battle. The battle we are in is not trivial. We need to be committed to walking the narrow path that God has called us to walk. That isn't easy; there are little voices all along that path calling us to divert from it. If we love pleasure more than we love God, we'll divert from the path of self-discipline that God has called us to and enter into sin.

THE BREASTPLATE OF RIGHTEOUSNESS

A Roman soldier wore a breastplate over his chest to keep his vital organs from being vulnerable to arrows and knives. Paul called it the breastplate of righteousness (or holiness). We need to live righteously—to obey God's laws—or we'll be vulnerable in battle. In 2 Corinthians 7:1 Paul says, "Having, therefore, these promises, dearly beloved, let us cleanse ourselves from all filthiness of the flesh and spirit, perfecting holiness in the fear of God."

I grieve when I see undisciplined Christians. They know that they're to be obedient, but they're not committed to that command. In Philippians 4:8 Paul says, "Whatever things are true, whatever things are honest, whatever things are just, whatever things are pure, whatever things are lovely, whatever things are of good report; if there be any virtue, and if there be any praise, think on these things." Self-discipline is related to the mind. Proverbs 23:7 says, "As [a man] thinketh in his heart, so is he." A pure, self-disciplined life comes from being saturated with the Word of God. The psalmist said, "Thy word have I hidden in mine heart, that I might not sin against thee"

(Ps. 119:11). Colossians 3:16 says to "let the word of Christ dwell in you richly." God's Word is the source of discipline, and you must be committed to knowing it.

Don't give in to the cries of the world that say, "Come over here; we'll give you a good time." If you preoccupy yourself with ungodly movies or other sinful activities, you are not giving your life fully to the commitment that God calls for. I have heard all the arguments Christians put forth to try to justify questionable activities, but I'm not impressed by any of them. We're not to be wallowing in the gray areas. Paul commands us in Philippians 4:8 to think about things that are *good,* not things that don't seem bad.

ACCOUNTABILITY

It is essential to teach everyone in a church to be accountable to one another. We should be concerned about *each other,* not what color the carpeting and wallpaper is. People are more important than programs. In Matthew 7 Jesus says, "Why beholdest thou the mote that is in thy brother's eye, but considerest not the beam that is in thine own eye?" (v. 3). In other words, "Why are you more concerned about the little problem in your brother's life than the bigger problem in your own life?"

The principle is this: We have a responsibility to point out one another's sin, but before we can do that, we must deal with our own sin (v. 5). Accountability among the people of a church is an important thing. In a relationship of accountability, a person is not just responsible for taking care of others; he is also responsible for making sure his own life is right before he tries to take care of others.

Let's look at a practical application of accountability. Suppose someone you know at your church stops attending. It is your responsibility to go to that person and say, "You're forsaking the assembly (Heb. 10:25). You need to be more committed to worshiping with God's people." You might think, *Who am I to say that? I've got problems in my own life.* Then clean up your life—get the beam out of your eye—so that you can confront that other person's sin. Accountability requires us to be pure.

Galatians 6:1 says, "Brethren, if a man be overtaken in a fault, ye who are spiritual restore such an one." It takes a person walking in obedience to help someone who isn't.

Matthew 18:15 tells what to do after you've dealt with the sin in your life: "If your brother sins, go and reprove him in private" (NASB). If a person in your church sins, approach him about it alone. If, for example, you know a professing Christian who is a dishonest businessman who mistreats his employees, you have an obligation before God to go to that person and—in a loving way—say, "What you are doing is wrong." Some other examples of when you should confront other Christians are if you know someone who is not being faithful to his spouse, parents who aren't bringing up their children as they should, or children who aren't obeying their parents. Galatians 2:11-14 tells us Paul rebuked Peter publicly for doing something wrong. Elders and leaders are not exempt from rebuke. If they need rebuking, it is to be done before the church so that others may fear and avoid sin (1 Tim. 5:20).

When I received a letter from someone who noticed something wrong in my life, I wrote back to him asking for his forgiveness and thanking him for bringing it to my attention. If something is wrong in my life, I want to know it. But if someone doesn't tell me because he or she is afraid to, I'm apt to keep making the same mistake. Everyone in a church should have that kind of accountability with one another so that everyone's life is pure. Husbands and wives especially should hold one another accountable. It isn't right for anyone's sinfulness to be tolerated. Anyone in sin should be lovingly confronted.

But what if the sinning person doesn't listen? Matthew 18:16 says, "If he will not hear thee, then take with thee one or two more, that in the mouth of two or three witnesses every word may be established." If the person you are confronting still doesn't listen, verse 17 says to "tell it unto the church." Have everyone in the church encourage the sinning brother to repent.

When church discipline was first applied at Grace Church, a couple of the pastors said to me, "It won't work. The church will be wrecked. You can't have everyone watching out for other people's sins." I said, "The Bible says we're supposed to be accountable to one another. Let's just do it and see what God does." We are not to worry about building the church; Christ said He would take care of that (Matt. 16:18). All we are supposed to do is be obedient to God, and He will take care of everything else.

I have a wonderful illustration of how church discipline worked for the good of Grace Church. A woman called me one day and said, "My husband just left me. He is going to live with another woman." I asked her for the name of that other woman, and she gave it to me. I looked up the woman's telephone number and called her. The husband of the woman who had called me answered the telephone. I said, "This is John from Grace Church. I'm calling in the name of Christ for you to move out of that woman's place before you sin against God, your wife, and your church." He was shocked and said he would go right back to his wife. The next Sunday he came up to me, embraced me, and said, "Thank you! I didn't want to be there. I was tempted, and I thought no one would care about that." He wasn't alienated by my rebuke. Rather he was brought back to the fellowship and obedience. (For more specifics on the issue of church discipline, see appendix 4.)

Confrontation is necessary to help restore a sinning brother. Sometimes a Christian will do something he doesn't want to do, and it will require the rebuke of another Christian to pull him out of it. Paul said he struggled with the flesh: "That which I do I understand not; for what I would, that do I not; but what I hate, that do I" (Rom. 7:15). Confrontation is not intended for invading people's privacy; it's for the purpose of helping others in their battle with sin. We need to be concerned about accountability. That's one reason Communion is important. It reminds us to make sure our lives are right so that we can restore each other in love and stimulate one another to love and good deeds (Heb. 10:24).

Accountability involves the "one anothers" of Scripture. We are to exhort one another (Heb. 10:24-25), pray for one another (James 5:16), love one another (Gal. 5:13; Eph. 4:2; 1 Pet. 1:22), teach one another (Col. 3:16), edify one another (Rom. 14:19; 1 Thess. 5:11), and admonish one another (Rom. 15:14; Col. 3:16). Those things make up the life of the church.

FORGIVENESS

The church can't survive without forgiveness. It's an important attitude because we're human and we all sin. If you can't forgive someone who sins, particularly someone who sins against you, you have a cancer in you that's infecting the Body of Christ.

Look how Jesus instructs us to pray in Matthew 6:12: "Forgive us our debts, as we forgive our debtors." In other words, "God, forgive us in the same way we forgive others." Verses 14-15 tell us, "If ye forgive men their trespasses, your heavenly Father will also forgive you; but if ye forgive not men their trespasses, neither will your Father forgive your trespasses." If you don't forgive other people, God won't forgive you.

Now that isn't talking about the eternal, redemptive forgiveness we receive when we accept Christ as our Savior. It's talking about a parental, temporal forgiveness. It's a forgiveness related to current sin. We need to have a forgiving attitude if we want to have pure, blessed fellowship with God and fellow brothers and sisters in Christ.

If you want to be forgiven by the Lord on a daily basis and maintain a pure, sweet fellowship with Him, you need to have a forgiving heart toward others. How can you possibly not forgive others? Matthew 18:23-34 is a parable about a man who owed his master ten thousand talents (an incomprehensible debt). The master forgave that man and erased his debt. Later that man found a friend of his who owed him a hundred denarii (a trivial amount compared to the former debt). He had him put in jail. Jesus graphically pointed out how greatly such behavior angers God.

Ephesians 4:32 says, "Be ye kind one to another, tenderhearted, forgiving one another, even as God, for Christ's sake, hath forgiven you." We should forgive one another because God has forgiven us. How can we be forgiven so much and forgive others so little? The church needs to be filled with forgiving people because in this life people are always going to do things that irritate others or cause problems. If you're willing to forgive an offender, you'll be free from the bondage of bitterness. You'll also be free to be forgiven by God and experience blessing from Him.

DEPENDENCE

Put in negative terms, dependence is an attitude of insufficiency. That kind of attitude is hard to develop in capable people. If a church isn't careful, it can arrive at the point of eliminating God in its ministries because it's depending on the strength of its people and programs. That wouldn't happen so easily if we had the same problem believers who lived behind the Iron Curtain had. Many there lived daily in fear of death and had few resources. Those of us who have been abundantly blessed by God can easily forget Him. Remember when the Lord gave Israel the Promised Land? He gave them "great and goodly cities, which [they] buildedst not, and houses full of all good things, which [they] filledst not, and wells digged, which [they] diggedst not" (Deut. 6:10-11). Yet they forgot all about God (cf. Deut. 8:10-18).

It's easy to get absorbed with activities, great ideas, and bright hopes. But we have to make sure that we don't get so involved in them that we do things that aren't in God's will. We must maintain an attitude of dependence on God.

In Psalm 19 David says, "Keep back thy servant also from presumptuous sins" (v. 13). It's so easy to do things without relying on God—without searching for the heart and mind of God. It's important that when you make decisions, you pray to God with patience and commune with Him until you know that whatever you do will be the work of God. I've always feared doing something in my ministry that God isn't part of. I want to walk at the same pace Christ does.

When I went to seminary all the students had to preach at least twice in chapel. As we preached, members of the faculty sat behind us on a platform with critique sheets that they would fill out during the sermons. If a student was only ten minutes into his sermon and he could hear the critique sheets being turned over to fill out the back, he knew he was in trouble! Nevertheless, everyone tried his best.

I was assigned to preach on 2 Samuel 7. I wanted to make sure that I did a good job on it, so I literally memorized my sermon. I even memorized where my pauses were! I started my sermon by talking about David's desire to build a house for the Ark of God. David felt bad because he lived in a beautiful palace while the Ark of God was still in a tent. He told Nathan the prophet, "See, now, I dwell in an house of cedar, but the ark of God dwelleth within curtains" (v. 2). Nathan commended David and told him to go ahead and do what was on his heart (v 3). But God said, "David will not build a house for me, for he is a man of war and has shed blood" (1 Chron. 28:3). Solomon was the one that would build the house of God (2 Sam. 7:12-13). Although God did not allow David to build His house, He did give him a wonderful promise (vv. 8-16).

Using those verses, I preached on the sin of presuming on God. It was a life-changing experience for me because that message has stuck in my mind through the years. When I finished preaching, one of the professors handed me his critique sheet. I opened it up, and he hadn't even used it. Instead, he wrote on it, "You missed the entire point of the passage." That ruined my day, but it was a very good lesson. The professor thought I should have preached on the kingdom promise that God gave David. I know the passage talks about the kingdom promise, but it also talks about presumption, and I believed that was what my own heart needed to hear because I tend to move ahead too fast on things sometimes.

Prayer is a key element in preventing presumptuousness. When the disciples asked Jesus to teach them how to pray, He said, "When ye pray, say, Our Father, who art in heaven, hallowed be thy name" (Luke 11:2). When you say, "Hallowed be thy name," you are saying, "Lord, let Your name be glorified and exalted." The prayer continues, "Thy kingdom come. Thy will be done, as in heaven, so in earth." We should pray that God will do on earth what He is doing in His heavenly kingdom. The Disciples' Prayer doesn't begin by saying, "Give us this and that." Rather it teaches us to pray in a dependent way—to pray for God to do His work His way.

FLEXIBILITY

Someone once said that the seven last words of the church are, "We never did it that way before!" There's truth in that. A church that is not flexible is destined for failure. Sadly, some Christians think it is a virtue to be inflexible. They wear their stubbornness like a merit badge.

Mindless rigidity was a trait of the Pharisees. In Matthew 15 we read that some Pharisees and scribes came up to Jesus and confronted Him, saying, "Why do thy disciples transgress the tradition of the elders? For they wash not their hands when they eat bread" (v. 2). They meant the disciples were not doing the required ceremonial rituals before they ate, not that they weren't washing their hands. Jesus responded, "Why do ye also transgress the commandment of God by your tradition?" (v. 3). Some churches are obsessed with tradition. They see a command in the Bible and say, "We can't do that; we must maintain tradition."

People often ask me to send them an organizational chart of Grace Church so they can learn how we are set up. However, organizational charts are useless in our church because things are always changing. God is always working through different people who at different times are strong, weak, very committed, or less committed. New people are always joining the church, and God works through them. The constant change is wonderful because it keeps us from falling into routines that obscure the pattern set forth in God's Word. We don't want tradition to get in the way if we learn something new about what God wants us to do.

We were visiting with a relative one Christmas who asked, "John, do you have a Christmas Eve service at your church?" I said, "No, we don't. We encourage everyone to be at home with their families and talk about the meaning of Christmas and the birth of the Lord." She said, "That's too bad. At our church, we've *always* had a Christmas Eve service." I said, "Do you go to them?" She said, "No one goes, but we've always had a Christmas Eve service." What creatures of habit we are!

I'm very grateful that at Grace Church we've tended to be flexible. When I first started pastoring and the congregation and I studied the Word of God together, we realized that certain things needed to be changed so that they would be in line with God's will. That attitude continues to prevail. Sometimes we send out young pastors to other churches, and they come back saying, "I've tried to break down the wall of tradition at that church, but I don't know if the people there will ever change."

We need to be flexible in our personal lives, too. When Paul had finished his ministry in Galatia and Phrygia (provinces in the area now known as Turkey), he wanted to go south into Asia (the seven churches of Asia Minor were there). He started going in that direction, but the Holy Spirit stopped him (Acts 16:6). Paul didn't let that keep him from ministering elsewhere. He said to his companions, "We've already been east, and we can't go south, so let's go north to Bithynia." The Holy Spirit didn't allow that either (v. 7). The only direction they could go now was west, and the ocean was in that direction. Not knowing what to do, Paul probably prayed to God about where he should go. When he and his companions were asleep, Paul had a vision. In it was a man from Macedonia who said, "Come over into Macedonia, and help us" (v. 9). So Paul went to Macedonia, and that began the gospel's spread beyond the Middle East to the rest of the world. Paul was flexible about where he went.

Some time ago, one of our elders at Grace Church, a Jewish Christian, had a strong desire to reach Jewish people for Christ. Because he speaks French fluently, his desire was to go to Paris and reach out to the many Jewish people there. He got involved in the Bible Christian Union, a mission group that serves in France. They helped train and prepare him. But when he was ready to be used by God, the Lord placed him in Montreal, Canada. There are many French-speaking Jewish people there, just as there are in Paris. God had a different place in mind, and the missionary was flexible.

The church has to be flexible, too. It has to be able to say, "God, we depend on You to lead us, and we're willing to move wherever You take us."

A DESIRE FOR GROWTH

First Peter 2:2 says, "As newborn babes, desire the pure milk of the word, that ye may grow by it." That analogy isn't talking about the milk of the Word as opposed to the meat (1 Cor. 3:2). Peter is simply saying, "In the same way babies desire milk, you must desire the Word so you can grow." How much do babies desire milk? If you've had one, you know they will kick and scream when they want milk. They have a single-minded devotion to milk. Peter says we're to have that same consuming desire for the Word.

How strong is your desire for the Word? Do you have to exert effort to open the Bible and read it, or is your heart drawn to it? Are you growing? We grow by feeding on the Word of God. We don't all have the same capacity to grow, but whatever capacity we do have, we should use to the fullest. Even though we all have different abilities, the Spirit of God works in all our hearts to help us love His Word and grow at the pace that we can grow. The thing that would give me the greatest fear in my heart would be if Grace Church stopped growing. It would be terrible to hear people say, "I've had enough theology; I've heard so much exposition of Scripture that I know more than I want to. I think I'll just leave." I pray that the people of Grace Church will never lose their desire to grow.

In 2 Peter 3:18 Peter says, "Grow in grace, and in the knowledge of our Lord and Savior, Jesus Christ." When we grow, we're not just learning facts in a book; we're getting to know Christ Himself. First John 2 says that as a new member of the family of God, you are a child and you know the Father (v. 13). As you grow and become a spiritual youth, the Word of God dwells in you and you "overcome the wicked one" (vv. 13-14). First you know God in a simple way, then you become familiar with doctrine. You mature into a spiritual adult when "ye have known him that is from the beginning" (vv. 13-14). In other words, you're not just learning doctrine; you're learning to know God. The more you know God, the more enriching your fellowship with Him will be. Think of the most wonderful person you've ever met, and how great it would be to have a friendship with him or her that continually grew. You should desire to have that kind of growing relationship with the infinite, holy God of the universe.

Do you have a hunger for the Word? Do you meditate on it? Do you feed on it daily? Can you say with Job that you love the Word of God more than your necessary food (Job 23:12)? When I study a passage in the Bible, I always try to learn more about God's character so that I can get to know Him better.

FAITHFULNESS

Many Christians are spiritual sprinters—they get involved, serve for a while with all their energy, but then go into spiritual retirement. God is looking for marathon runners—people who will run a long distance. First Corinthians 4:2 says, "It is required in stewards, that a man be found faithful." Long-term spiritual commitment is wonderful. A person in his eighties in our fellowship said to me, "Could you slow down when you preach? I'm having trouble keeping up as I take notes." I love that! He's more than eighty years old and still taking sermon notes! He's still excited about the Word, the life of God, and the church. He's faithful to the ministry. He hasn't quit in his commitment to God. It's the people who teach, disciple, and serve others for years who are the stalwarts of the faith.

In 2 Timothy 4:6-7 Paul says, "I am now ready to be offered, and the time of my departure is at hand. I have fought a good fight, I have finished my course, I have kept the faith." He was saying, "I can die now; I'm done. I've finished the task God gave me. I've fought the fight and kept the faith."

It's sad when you see an older Christian become indifferent about his commitment to God. Sometimes you see that happen to preachers, teachers, or other Christian workers. They become bitter and self-centered. In contrast, it's beautiful to see a person grow old and continue in a life of faithful service.

Not everyone at Grace Church attends faithfully. Sometimes when my wife and I go to a store, someone will come up to me and say, "I know you. You're John MacArthur. I go to your church." I'll say, "How wonderful! I haven't seen you before. Were you there last Sunday?" I'll often hear, "No, I wasn't there last Sunday. It's been a while since I've gone. But I love Grace Church." It makes me sad when people come to church only when it's convenient. A faithful Christian always makes a priority of worshiping, serving, and praying consistently. It's sad when people are distracted by other things and don't keep their priorities right.

HOPE

Hope is a great word. For the Christian, hope means security for the future. There is no fear of death. We can actually look forward to what's ahead of us in life and death.

I love Paul's expression in Romans 12:12, "Rejoicing in hope." Death holds no fear for us. A funeral service for a Christian should be a cause for rejoicing and praising God because that person has gone from this place of tears, disease, death, and limitations to a place that's free of those things. We look forward to the fulfillment of Romans 8:23, which says we'll have a redeemed body to go with our redeemed soul. We live in hope.

It's important to maintain an attitude of hope. Practically speaking, that means we shouldn't become too obsessed with earthly things. Jesus said, "Lay not up for yourselves treasures upon earth, where moth and rust doth corrupt, and where thieves break through and steal . . . for where your treasure is, there will your heart be also" (Matt. 6:19, 21). If our hearts are focusing on our hope in eternity, then our treasure is going to be in eternity, too. I hope you aren't living for the moment. Don't live for what is temporal. We should be living in hope, and that means being more committed to investing in eternity than investing in what is temporary. Remember, we have a wonderful future before us!

We have to keep on track. We must be reminded of God's truth so we don't wander from it. The virtues we have studied may be present in the hearts of the people and the ministries at your church. But be sure to remind them of their commitment to each one.

Chapter 3

The Muscles*

Having studied the skeleton and the internal systems that give the body life, we turn our attention to the muscular system.

Muscles enable a body to function. The body gets its form from its skeleton and its vitality from its internal systems. But the muscles are necessary if it is to move and operate. What are the muscles of the church? What motion takes place in the Body of Christ? Several spiritual activities constitute the movement of the church.

PREACHING AND TEACHING

I've put preaching and teaching together because they are both related to the proclamation of biblical truth. Proclaiming the Word of God is a primary function of the church. I grieve over the sermonettes people hear in some churches. Some preachers merely counsel from the pulpit or deal with ethical issues. In many Sunday school classes people don't learn much about the Bible, and they guess about what it teaches. But the church's most important function is to proclaim the Word of God in an understandable, direct, authoritative way.

Let's look at excerpts from the two epistles Paul wrote to Timothy. First Timothy tells us how we are to behave and function in the

* From tapes GC 2029-2029A.

church (3:15), and both 1 and 2 Timothy emphasize that we are to make a priority of proclaiming the Word of God.

First Timothy 3:16 talks about the wonder of the incarnation of Jesus Christ: "Without controversy great is the mystery of godliness: God was manifest in the flesh, justified in the Spirit, seen of angels, *preached unto the nations,* believed on in the world, received up into glory" (emphasis added). One of the essential elements of God's manifesting Himself in the flesh is preaching. At the heart of the church is the incarnation, and at the heart of the incarnation is its proclamation. Preaching has a central place in the life of a church.

I believe God has blessed Grace Church because it has made a priority of proclaiming the Word of God. We don't just talk about the Bible; we teach it. Many hundreds of people over the years have said they come to Grace Church because they want to be fed the Word of God. That's our commitment; that's our function. It isn't just my job to proclaim the Word; it's everyone's job! Some people are gifted to preach or teach, but we're all to proclaim the Word.

Paul told Timothy that if he reminded the brethren of the truth he would be "a good minister of Jesus Christ, nourished up in the words of faith and of good doctrine" (1 Tim. 4:6). He adds in verse 11, "These things command and teach." In other words, "Teach with authority."

I was invited to speak at a commencement ceremony at the Los Angeles Police Academy. The man next to me told me about the various graduates. He said, "We had to flunk one man because of his voice. It wasn't authoritative enough. A policeman needs to have authority in his voice." That makes sense: a policeman's authority is the law. If I sound like I speak with authority, it's because my authority is the Word of God.

In 1 Timothy 4:13 Paul continues, "Till I come, give attendance to reading, to exhortation, to doctrine." Timothy was to read the Bible, explain its doctrines, and exhort people to apply it. He was told not to neglect preaching (v. 14) but to meditate on God's truths (v. 15), obey them, and continue following them (v. 16).

We see another dimension of preaching and teaching in 1 Timothy 5:17: "Let the elders that rule well be counted worthy of double honor, especially they who labor in the word and doctrine." That indicates the leadership of a church should focus on preaching and teaching. Indeed, the church's primary function is to proclaim God's Word.

I've heard people criticize Grace Church saying, "There's too much preaching and teaching there and not enough of other things." I don't see how there could ever be too much preaching and teaching!

The reason we put so much emphasis on preaching and teaching is that they help everything else to happen. We have to know what the Bible says about something before we know how to act. We won't know how to worship, pray, evangelize, discipline, shepherd, train, or serve unless we know what the Word of God says.

In 2 Timothy 2:15 Paul says, "Study to show thyself approved unto God, a workman that needeth not to be ashamed, rightly dividing the word of truth." Paul wanted Timothy to handle the Word correctly. In 2 Timothy 1:13 he says, "Hold fast the form of sound words." A person proclaiming God's Word must first commit himself to it and then dispense it.

Scripture makes people "wise unto salvation" (2 Tim. 3:15). It is the Word that "is profitable for doctrine, for reproof, for correction, for instruction in righteousness, that the man of God may be perfect, thoroughly furnished unto all good works" (vv. 16-17). Based on those realities Paul issued this charge: "Preach the word; be diligent in season, out of season" (2 Tim. 4:1-2). In other words, "Work hard at proclaiming God's Word. Keep preaching all the time. Don't worry about whether people are offended by what you say."

Paul then told Timothy to be confrontive in his preaching and to do it "with all long-suffering and doctrine" (v. 2). Preaching should make people face the failures in their lives, but we can't expect people to come to complete understanding immediately. In the process of confrontive preaching, we must be patient and teach doctrine. It is the Word that convicts. One of the functions of the church is to patiently teach the Word of God in a confrontive way so that people are made accountable before God to make sure their lives are right.

Ephesians 4:23 says, "Be renewed in the spirit of your minds." Romans 12:2 says, "Be not conformed to this world, but be ye transformed by the renewing of your mind." You need to have the Word in your mind so that right behavior will follow. Preaching and teaching the Word puts Scripture at the forefront of people's minds; there is no substitute for them.

EVANGELISM AND MISSIONS

A second function of the church is evangelism and missions. I use those terms together to provide a comprehensive perspective. Evangelism is generally carried out on a personal basis, whereas mission work usually covers broad areas. The church exists for the sake of the world. We are to desire to live as God wants us to so we can be a shining light in the midst of a dark and perverse generation (Phil. 2:15). The ultimate goal of all ministry is to reach others for Christ.

There are two ways to evangelize: through our lives and through our words. Our lives make our testimonies believable or unbelievable. If Christ is exalted and people are living in obedience to God in our church, then we're going to establish credibility for our corporate testimony. The way we live in the world is important.

It's wonderful when people come to Grace Church and say, "The people here really live out their message. They obey the Word of God." But how many times have you heard people say, "I went to that church over there, and they have a lot of hypocrites. They don't care about anyone. The pastor embezzled money from the church and ran off"? Satan does everything he can to corrupt churches so that the integrity of the gospel message is undermined and there is no foundation for individual testimonies.

We have been called to live an evangelistic lifestyle in our communities. In Matthew 5:13 our Lord says that we are the salt of the earth: "If the salt have lost its savor, with what shall it [the earth] be salted?" We are a preservative on the earth; we are distinct. That's why we're called to live pure lives. I am concerned that we live godly, virtuous lives not just so we can glorify God but so unbelievers can glorify God. We are to live holy lives because that will draw others to purity. We are to be godly examples.

In Matthew 5:14 Jesus says that we are also the light of the world. Verse 15 notes that a light is not supposed to be hidden under a bushel, which is anything that clouds the testimony of your life.

I sometimes see people I know in circumstances that embarrass them. I can't tell you how many people have tried to swallow a cigarette when they see me! Sometimes I'll go into a restaurant and see someone I know with a drink in his hand. I'll just smile and wave, and he'll go into instant panic. I don't have to say anything. Jesus summed up our responsibility to live a righteous life when He said, "Let your light so shine before men, that they may see your good works, and glorify your Father, who is in heaven" (Matt. 5:16). Unbelievers should be able to look at your life and say, "Only God could do that in a person's life. What a wonderful life!"

We also evangelize through our words. First Peter 3:15 says to "be ready always to give an answer to every man that asketh you a reason of the hope that is in you." Someone once joked that most Christians are like an Arctic river: they are frozen over at the mouth! We ought to be as eager to speak about the Lord as we are to speak about mundane things. One reason some of us have difficulty proclaiming the gospel is that we don't know many non-Christians. Our world is narrow. It's like a pyramid: the longer you've been a Christian, the fewer non-Christians you know. Work hard to keep that from happening to you.

When we proclaim the gospel, we have to make sure we know what to say. That's why at Grace Church we spend a lot of time articulating the gospel. We want to make sure everyone understands how a person becomes saved. We study Christ's words to the rich young ruler in Matthew 19:16-26 and His Sermon on the Mount (Matt. 5-7). Churches all over the world are filled with people who think they are saved but are not because they misunderstand how a person obtains salvation.

Missions is a worldwide view of evangelism—it involves reaching across the globe to whatever areas God will open to us. I received a letter from a pastor in the Philippines, and he said, "I've heard about Grace Church. I want to build my church the way God would want it built. Could you send me some information so that I know what to do?" There are people at our church strategizing for us to reach as far beyond our own walls as God will allow us. Jesus said, "Go ye, therefore, and teach all nations, baptizing them in the name of the Father, and of the Son, and of the Holy Spirit, teaching them to observe all things whatsoever I have commanded" (Matt. 28:19-20). The church is to be committed to preaching, baptizing, and teaching wherever it can.

WORSHIP

Paul said to the Philippians, "We . . . worship God in the spirit, and rejoice in Christ Jesus, and have no confidence in the flesh" (Phil. 3:3). John 4:23 says that those who "worship the Father in spirit and in truth" are true worshipers. We are called to offer our bodies as a living sacrifice to God in a holy act of worship (Rom. 12:1). Peter said that we are "an holy priesthood, to offer up spiritual sacrifices, acceptable to God by Jesus Christ" (1 Pet. 2:5).

When you go to church, do you really think about the songs you are singing or meditate on the things of God that you hear taught and preached? You need to cultivate a worshipful heart. And your worship should not be confined to when you're in church. The church service should be a catalyst to get you to worship at all times. In *The Ultimate Priority* (Chicago: Moody, 1983) I said that we worship best when we are fully obedient. Obedience is the basic definition of worship. Like obedience, worship is to be a way of life rather than just an exercise on Sundays.

Hebrews 10:22 tells us to draw near to God. James 4:8 gets more specific: "Draw near to God, and he will draw near to you." Do you ever draw near to God in an unhurried way? Do you let your heart and mind ascend when you hear the hymns, Scripture readings, or prayer? Do you meditate in deep devotion? Remember, we are to be worshipful people.

PRAYER

Prayer may well be the most difficult spiritual exercise we engage in. It is hard work first of all because it is selfless. True prayer embraces the kingdom of God: "Our Father, who art in heaven, hallowed be thy name. Thy kingdom come. Thy will be done" (Matt. 6.9-10). True prayer also embraces the people of God. "Give us this day our daily bread. And forgive us our debts, as we forgive our debtors. And lead us not into temptation" (Matt. 6:11-13). There is no "I" in the Disciples' Prayer.

It's hard work to pray on behalf of God, His will, and His people. It's easy for us to pray when a problem hits us. When we get injured, get sick, lose a loved one, get caught doing something wrong, or despair over a child who strays from the Lord, we find it rather easy to pray on our own behalf.

A person who prays only in times of personal need has a weak prayer life. The person who is able to abandon himself in unceasing prayer on behalf of God's eternal kingdom and the needs of His redeemed people brings glory to God. Luke 11:5-8 tells about a man banging on his friend's door for bread at night so that he could feed a guest. If I were hungry myself, I would have no problem banging on someone's door all night for bread. But would I be able to bang on that door for bread for someone else?

On a radio interview in Chicago, I said that one of the benefits of growing older is that you have a longer list of answered prayers than younger people. You've had more chances to see God demonstrate His powers. The more you see God answer prayer, the more confident you become in your prayers. Perhaps older people tend to pray better than younger people because they have seen a larger number of God's responses to prayers.

Another reason prayer is difficult is that it is private. When you pray, you usually do it by yourself. No one knows how much you pray. It requires self-discipline. We tend to perform much better when we know people are watching us. I spend a great amount of time preparing my sermons because I know that many people are going to listen to what I say. I confess it's easier for me to neglect prayer because it's private.

Prayer is hard work. It is selfless and is to be done without seeking the attention or approval of others. We have a small group of older people at our church who get together every Monday to pray. They've been praying together for more than ten years. They pray, and God answers their prayers. The church benefits from their faithfulness. I don't know how God's sovereignty and our prayer requests work together, but I do know that God answers prayers. James said, "The effectual, fervent prayer of a righteous man availeth much" (5:16). I want to be a prayerful person because I want to see God do His work and give Him the glory due His name.

We must be committed to prayer. Paul couldn't have said that more clearly when he said, "Pray without ceasing" (1 Thess. 5:17). Offer your whole life as a prayer to God—be aware of Him every time you think, act, or talk. Say in your heart, "I'm thinking about doing this, Lord. Is that all right?" To pray unceasingly is to live life as if you were looking through the mind and heart of God. It doesn't mean walking around mumbling with your eyes closed all the time. Prayer is living life in a God-conscious way.

DISCIPLESHIP

In Matthew 28:19-20 our Lord says, "Go therefore and make disciples of all the nations, baptizing them . . . teaching them to observe all that I commanded you" (NASB). Discipleship involves bringing people to Christ and leading them to maturity.

In Acts 1:1 Luke writes, "The former treatise have I made, O Theophilus, of all that Jesus began both to do and teach." In other words, the book of Luke ("the former treatise") is about what Jesus began to do, and the book of Acts is simply a continuation of that. Christ discipled the twelve, and in the book of Acts we see them discipling others. Two thousand years later, you and I are carrying on the work Jesus began. We are to continue that succession: "The things that thou hast heard from me among many witnesses, the same commit thou to faithful men, who shall be able to teach others also" (2 Tim. 2:2). Every Christian is in a relay race. Each of us is to take the baton and hand it on to others. None of us is in a solo effort. Somebody invested the gospel in us, and we are to invest it in others.

You may feel that you don't know much. Find someone who knows less than you do and tell him what you know. Find someone who knows more than you do and listen to him. Teach and be taught. I pour my heart into the people I disciple, and I learn from others. All of us have to be in that flow. We're not to be isolated; we're a chain all linked together.

In 1 Corinthians 4 are some verses that give us a wonderful, indirect insight into the discipling process. Paul was writing a letter of rebuke to the Corinthian church, which he himself brought into existence by the grace of God and the power of the Spirit. He was rebuking them because they had departed from the basics of the faith and were involved in sinful things. He wanted to correct them.

In verses 14-15 he says, "I write not these things to shame you, but as my beloved sons I warn you. For though ye have ten thousand instructors [Gk., *paidagogos*, "moral guardians who give spiritual advice"] in Christ, yet have ye not many fathers; for in Christ Jesus I have begotten you through the gospel." He said that because the Corinthians were wondering what gave him the right to rebuke them. Paul explained why. He was their spiritual father. He brought their church into existence.

Note that Paul referred to the Corinthians as "my beloved sons." Discipleship is to be done with an attitude of love. You need to be able to say, "I'll give my life and time for you. I'll pray for you and give you my insights." If you don't care about a person and are not willing to make sacrifices for him, you're fooling yourself if you think you can disciple him.

Paul also warned the Corinthians. Discipling is corrective. It is like raising a child. You have to warn your children what to stay away from. You can't give children positive instruction only; they need negative instruction, too. Paul said to the Ephesian elders at Miletus, "Remember, that for the space of three years I ceased not to warn everyone night and day with tears" (Acts 20:31). He knew the importance of admonishment.

In 1 Corinthians 4:16 Paul says, "I beseech you, be ye followers of me." The person you are discipling is to follow your example. That means you have to be further along the path of spiritual development than he or she is. You have to be able to provide leadership. Now keep in mind that our Lord isn't asking for perfection, but direction. Paul said, "Be ye followers of me, even as I also am of Christ" (1 Cor. 11:1, emphasis added). You need to tell the person you are discipling, "I want you to follow me as I follow Christ." You don't say it proudly; you say it humbly, understanding your own weakness. And your example will be a great encouragement, because a perfect person would be too hard to follow.

Paul mentions another element of discipleship in 1 Corinthians 4:17: "For this cause have I sent unto you Timothy, who is my beloved son and faithful in the Lord, who shall bring you into remembrance of my ways which are in Christ, as I teach everywhere in every church." Paul sent Timothy to teach the Corinthians. In discipleship, there has to be an imparting of divine truth. People function on truth.

Discipling is a function that everyone must be involved in. It isn't optional. We're all to bring people to the knowledge of the Savior and go through the process of helping them mature. We're all to disciple whomever the Lord brings across our path. You will probably have different kinds of relationships with the people you disciple, but discipleship is nothing more than building a true friendship with a spiritual basis. It's not being friends with someone because you both like baseball, the same music, the same hobbies, or work at the same place. At the core of your friendship is an openness about spiritual issues. That's what carries a discipling relationship along.

When you disciple someone, you're basically teaching him to live a godly lifestyle. You're teaching him biblical responses. A person is spiritually mature when his involuntary responses are godly. That's how to know if the Spirit of God has control in someone's life. In discipleship you're to bring a person to the point where he doesn't have to figure out how to act right because he can react right spontaneously.

SHEPHERDING

God's people in the church need to care for one another and meet each other's needs. Three times Jesus asked Peter, "Lovest thou me?" (John 21:15-17). Peter responded every time, "Yea, Lord; thou knowest that I love thee." Jesus said, "Then feed My sheep." He was saying, "You're a shepherd, Peter. Take care of My people."

Shepherding involves feeding and leading the flock. First Peter 5 says, "Feed the flock of God which is among you, taking the oversight of it" (v. 2). Acts 20:28 says, "Take heed, therefore, unto yourselves, and to all the flock, over which the Holy Spirit hath made you overseers, to feed the church of God." We are all to care for one another: First John 3:17 says, "Whosoever hath this world's good, and seeth his brother have need, and shutteth up his compassions from him, how dwelleth the love of God in him?" How can you say you love God if you don't care about people? As you interact with others, take the time to find out about their hurts and needs. If you have insight that a wandering person needs, share it with him and lead him back. Everyone is to be in the shepherding process. First Peter 5:4 calls the Lord "the chief Shepherd." The implication is that we're His undershepherds. We're all involved in caring for the sheep.

Sometimes it's hard to shepherd people. Some people who have needs escape the notice of others and are overlooked. It always breaks my heart when someone tells me, "I was sick, and no one called me. No one cares." Sometimes I get letters from distraught people who say, "Such-and-such happened, and you didn't call us. You didn't care. No one from the church helped us." Sometimes people's expectations are too high; no one person can be everywhere at one time. But most of the time people are overlooked because no one makes himself available when a need arises. For example, when someone has a death in his family, everyone immediately swarms around that person to comfort and support him. But after the funeral, when the real depression hits, that person is often left alone. We lose our sensitive touch when it's most needed.

We need to be the kind of shepherd Jesus is. In John 10 He says, "I am the door of the sheep. . . . I am the good shepherd" (vv. 7, 11). Jesus was speaking of the way a shepherd cares for his sheep. When the sheep went into the fold at the end of a day, the shepherd would examine each one as it passed under the rod that he held across the entrance to the fold. If he found any bruises or scratches, he poured oil on them. That's what David was referring to in Psalm 23 when he said, "Thy rod and thy staff they comfort me. . . . Thou anointest my head with oil; my cup runneth over" (vv. 4-5). The shepherd is to care for his sheep.

There are some wonderful, quiet people in our church who don't get shepherded because they're quiet about their needs. There are others, however, who frequently fall into sin and who have shepherds hovering around them all the time trying to help them. It's very important for all of us to see ourselves as sheep and shepherds caring for one another. Church leaders can't be expected to handle all the shepherding needs themselves. We are accountable before God to care for one another. Grace Church is not my church; it's everyone's church. It's Christ's church.

The first thing I did when I starting pastoring at Grace Church was develop a way to shepherd our people. I knew we could feed them; I just wanted to make sure we could lead them because a shepherd feeds the flock *and* leads it to Christlikeness.

BUILDING UP FAMILIES

The family is God's designated unit for passing righteousness on from one generation to the next (Deut. 6:7, 20-25). Satan, however, attacks whatever God has ordained to preserve righteousness.

Satan attacks all three preserving forces in society: the government, the church, and the family. Wherever God has ordained a government that punishes evildoers and supports those who do right, Satan will assail it. Wherever there is a church that exalts Christ and proclaims the Word, Satan will attack. And he doesn't want families to pass on righteousness, so he tries to disintegrate them.

Satan is using the immoral, lust-filled society we live in to attack the family. He has made it hard for the family to survive. The church has to help preserve the family. We're committed to that at Grace Church; we teach and disciple children and young people. It's beautiful to see the adults of our church working with the younger people, because the younger people are responsible for preserving what they learn and giving it to the next generation. I want our young people to know what God's standards are for marriage and the family.

When people are filled with the Spirit of God, they submit to one another (Eph. 5:21–6:9). In a family situation, that means wives will submit to their husbands, and husbands will submit to their wives by loving them with a nourishing, cherishing, and purifying love. Children will submit to their parents, and parents will submit to the needs of their children by not provoking them to wrath but by nurturing them and bringing them up in the ways of Christ. Submission flows from Spirit-filled lives. The church is to make sure that families are controlled by the Spirit of God so they can experience blessedness from everyone's submission to one another. If everyone in a family is fighting for his own rights, then any potential for meaningful relationships is destroyed.

The families of a church should uphold each other. They should help each other with their children; they should pray for each other's children. What is your reaction when you see unruly children? Do you pray for them? Do you help other parents by teaching their children proper behavior? A church must care for its families.

TRAINING

The church is to equip people for ministry. Ephesians 4:11-12 says, "He gave some, apostles; and some, prophets; and some, evangelists; and some, pastors and teachers; for the perfecting of the saints for the work of the ministry for the edifying of the body of Christ."

We have courses in our church for training people to eventually become deacons and elders. We have courses in evangelism, missions, and youth work. We have a seminary on our campus and a Bible institute to train young people for ministry. We don't want to give people general information; we want to prepare them for a specific ministry.

GIVING

Giving has little to do with how much a person has (2 Cor. 8:1-5). Paul says in 2 Corinthians 9:6, "He who soweth sparingly shall reap also sparingly; and he who soweth bountifully shall reap also bountifully." Jesus said, "Give, and it shall be given unto you; good measure, pressed down, and shaken together, and running over" (Luke 6:38). God wants you to know you can trust Him with your money. It's the reverse of what He's doing to you: He gives you money and asks you, "Can I trust you with this money?" You must prove that He can trust you with the money He gives you by giving it back to Him.

How well do you manage God's possessions?

You need to realize that the things you have don't belong to you. When you trust them to God, you become free. Then all you have to do is manage those things. If you own something that someone else needs more than you do, give it to him. That's the spirit of Acts 2:44-45: "All that believed were together, and had all things common; and sold their possessions and goods, and parted them to all men, as every man had need."

Some people don't give at all. Some people give only token amounts. They'll throw a couple of dollars in the offering plate each Sunday. Usually those who give minimally do so because they're spending their money on earthly possessions. That's sad. I grieve for them. I want people to give generously so that they will be able to experience God's blessings. When King David wanted to buy a threshing floor from someone so that he could build an altar on it to the Lord, the threshing floor was offered to David for free. He replied, "Nay, but I will surely buy it . . . at a price; neither will I offer burnt offerings unto the Lord my God of that which doth cost me nothing" (2 Sam. 24:24). He wanted to offer God a costly offering, not a token one.

How committed are we to giving? One man told me about a church that is half the size of Grace Church, yet gives twice the amount of money to the Lord. He asked me, "Why is that?" I said, "I don't know. If they're giving for the wrong motives or if they are giving legalistically, their offerings are meaningless. But if they're giving abundantly from their hearts, then that's great!" I don't know what the answer to that situation is, but I do know this: many people at Grace Church aren't doing what they should do every week. First Corinthians 16:2 says, "Upon the first day of the week let every one of you lay by him in store, as God hath prospered him."

Giving is a function of the church. We are to give not just to support our own churches but to advance God's kingdom. Churches aren't supposed to amass a fortune. We are to be good stewards of the money God gives us for our own use and use the rest to reach people with the gospel.

FELLOWSHIP

Fellowship is essential. Fellowship means "a common life together." In a way, it sums up the other functions we've talked about.

Fellowship involves being together, loving each other, and communing together. Fellowship includes listening to someone who has a concern, praying with someone who has a need, visiting someone in a hospital, sitting in a class or a Bible study, and even singing a hymn with someone you've never met. Fellowship also involves sharing prayer requests.

Do you open your life to others? Do you share your problems with others who have problems so that you can minister to each other? Be committed to fellowship!

A Look at the Outside

Using the body analogy, we've looked at the skeleton, internal systems, and muscles of a church. Now let's talk about the epidermis. It's not important what the skin of a church is like. When we look at a church, we see what's on the outside, but God looks at the heart (cf. 1 Sam. 16:7). It's what's in a church's heart that gives it its character. It is important that a church have a skeleton: it must be committed to a high view of God, the absolute priority of Scripture, doctrinal clarity, personal holiness, and spiritual authority. A church must have internal systems—it must have certain spiritual attitudes. It must also be committed to certain functions. But when a church has all those things, it doesn't really matter what it looks like on the outside or how its programs take shape.

When God by His wonderful grace first brought me to Grace Church, I prayed, "Lord, I know that if we are what You want us to be, there will be no trouble ministering effectively." What is in our hearts is important, not what we are on the outside. Sometimes after pastors visit Grace Church, they try to implement what they see on the outside. But that won't work, because the flesh can't stand without a skeleton, and it can't live without the internal systems. Once a church has a skeleton, internal systems, and muscles, then the flesh will take form. The true beauty of a church comes from inside.

Our church is a unique place. Almost every Sunday at the reception we have for first-time visitors I meet people from other states. A typical conversation will go like this:

"We're from Michigan."

I say, "How nice! Are you visiting here?"

"No, we moved here."

I'll ask them why, and they say, "To come to this church." Then they say, "Do you know where we might be able to find a place to stay until we get a house and a job?" People just pack up and move to come to Grace Church! Sometimes they have children, too. Why do they do that? One reason they give is, "We believe that life centers on the church, not the job." That gives me a lump in my throat and helps me remember the tremendous accountability all of us in church leadership have before God to shape our churches into what He would have them be for His glory.

Chapter 4

The Head*

We have now come to the most important part in our study of a church's anatomy: the head. No body is complete without a head. The Head of the church is the Lord Jesus Christ. In Ephesians 4 Paul says, "We will in all things grow up into Him who is the Head, that is, Christ. From Him the whole body, joined and held together by every supporting ligament, grows and builds itself up in love, as each part does its work" (vv. 15-16; NIV**). Although we are to do everything we can in the church, it's the power of Christ that makes everything work. It is great comfort to know that when we fail, He succeeds. Christ is our Head; without Him we can do nothing (John 15:5).

A most helpful passage in examining our Lord's work for His church is the majestic benediction that concludes the epistle to the Hebrews: "Now the God of peace, that brought again from the dead our Lord Jesus, that great Shepherd of the sheep, through the blood of the everlasting covenant, make you perfect in every good work to do his will, working in you that which is well-pleasing in his sight, through Jesus Christ, to whom be glory forever and ever. Amen" (13:20-21).

---

* From tape GC 2029B.
** New International Version.

He Is the Savior

Three things in this text point to the saving work of Christ on behalf of His church.

HIS NAME

In Matthew 1:21 we read, "Thou shalt call His name Jesus; for he shall save his people from their sins." Jesus means "Jehovah saves." It is the Greek form of the Old Testament name *Joshua*. It is the name of One who saves. Hebrews 2:9-10 says, "We see Jesus, who was made a little lower than the angels for the suffering of death, crowned with glory and honor, that he, by the grace of God, should taste death for every man. For it became him, for whom are all things, and by whom are all things, in bringing many sons unto glory, to make the captain of their salvation perfect through sufferings." Jesus is the One who tasted death for every man. He became "the captain" [Gk., *archēgos*, "the pioneer" or "beginner") of salvation.

Acts 4:12 says, "There is no other name under heaven given among men, whereby we must be saved." Jesus' name speaks of His saving work.

HIS BLOOD

The Jewish people knew that sin had to be atoned for by blood. That's part of the message of the book of Hebrews. In Hebrews 9:18 we read, "Whereupon, neither the first testament was dedicated without blood." Every Jewish person knew that the ratification of the Old Covenant in Leviticus 17:11 was by blood. God required that there had to be bloodshed to deal with sin. Moses was God's agent to sprinkle the blood to ratify the Old Covenant: "When Moses had spoken every precept to all the people according to the law, he took the blood of calves and of goats, with water, and scarlet wool, and hyssop, and sprinkled both the book, and all the people, saying, This is the blood of the testament which God hath enjoined unto you. Moreover, he sprinkled with blood both the tabernacle and all the vessels of the ministry" (Heb. 9:19-21). There was blood everywhere: on the book of the law, on the people, on the Tabernacle, and on all the vessels in the Tabernacle.

All that bloodshed, however, was only symbolic of the blood that would be shed by Christ to bring peace between man and God. Hebrews 9:22 says, "Almost all things are by the law purged with blood, and without shedding of blood is no remission [forgiveness]." That's why Jesus had to shed His blood to ratify the New Covenant. He says in Matthew 26:28, "This is My blood of the new testament, which is shed for many for the remission of sins."

Notice that Hebrews 13:20 says, "The blood of the everlasting covenant." The Mosaic Covenant—the Old Covenant—was not everlasting. It was a temporary covenant, a shadow of things to come (Heb. 10:1). Jesus Christ made an everlasting covenant: "By one offering he hath perfected forever them that are sanctified" (Heb. 10:14). By one act of sacrifice, Christ brought everlasting salvation. Hebrews 9:12 says, "Neither by the blood of goats and calves, but by his own blood he entered in once into the holy place, having obtained eternal redemption for us." Whereas the priests of Israel had to repeatedly make sacrifices in the holy place, Christ made one sacrifice, and purchased eternal redemption for us (Heb. 10:11-12).

HIS RESURRECTION

When we think of Christ's resurrection, we tend to see it as a means to our own resurrection. But there's much more to it than that. The resurrection of Jesus Christ is the single greatest affirmation of the Father's approval of Jesus' saving work. When the Father raised Jesus from the dead, He was affirming that Jesus had accomplished what He had gone to the cross to do.

HE IS THE SHEPHERD

Hebrews 13:20 calls the Lord the "great Shepherd of the sheep." In contrast to all other shepherds, He is the Great Shepherd. Psalm 77:20 says, "Thou didst lead thy people like a flock by the hand of Moses and Aaron." Moses and Aaron were shepherds but not Great Shepherds. Jesus is called shepherd three times in the New Testament: In John 10:11 He's the "good shepherd," in 1 Peter 5:4 He's the "chief Shepherd," and in Hebrews 13:20 He's the "great Shepherd." Many times the Bible refers to ungodly people as sheep without a shepherd (Num. 27:17; 1 Kings 22:17; 2 Chron. 18:16; Ezek. 34:5, 8; Zech. 10:2; Matt. 9:36; Mark 6:34). Believers are sheep *with* a shepherd.

At one of our elders' meetings, we were discussing how we can develop a better way to shepherd people in our church. Some of the leaders were saying, "Certain people are not getting involved, and others are not following through on their responsibilities. We've lost contact with some people, and there are others who have been gone for a long time, and we're trying to track them down." When I leave a meeting like that, I think, "Lord, how are we going to keep track of the people we have? How can we better shepherd them?" We can all take comfort in this: the Great Shepherd is shepherding His sheep. Sometimes when a saved person doesn't get into a follow-up program, we act like he will lose his salvation. We say, "We have to help the Holy Spirit along. We can't just leave people up to the Lord. We've got to get them into a program!" It's good to watch over and help God's people, but we must remember that the Lord is the Shepherd.

I wouldn't be able to maintain my sanity if I felt I were ultimately responsible for Christ's sheep. My whole heart is in what I'm doing for His sheep, but not because I think it all depends on me. At Grace Church we serve the Lord with our whole heart. But when we run out of resources and don't know what to do to meet people's needs, we can say, "The Lord is the Great Shepherd."

In Hebrews 13:21 we read that the Great Shepherd makes "you perfect in every good work to do His will." He is equipping us to do His will. He's given us His Word (2 Tim. 3:16-17), and He's given us gifted men to help equip us (Eph. 4:11-12). We are perfected in another way: First Peter 5:10 says that after we have suffered a while, the Lord will make us perfect. He gives us trials so that the Word can work in our lives. John 15:2-3 says that the Word prunes us.

Our Lord not only equips us but also intercedes for us. Just as a shepherd would protect his sheep by fighting off a wolf, the Lord Jesus Christ fights off the adversary who constantly comes before the throne of God to accuse Christians. Satan accuses us as he accused Job (Job 1:7-12; 2:1-5). However, Jesus comes to our rescue. He is our defender, intercessor, advocate, and sympathizer. He is our High Priest.

John said, "If any man sin, we have an advocate with the Father, Jesus Christ the righteous" (1 John 2:1). In other words, when you sin and accusation is brought before the throne of God, Jesus stands as your advocate and says, "Father, My blood paid for that sin." That's why no sin can be charged against God's elect (Rom. 8:33-34). Is God going to charge your sin against you when He has already justified you?

The writer of Hebrews said, "We have not an high priest who cannot be touched with the feeling of our infirmities, but was in all points tempted like as we are, yet without sin" (Heb. 4:15). Christ knows exactly what we go through, so He is able to help us (Heb. 2:18). He is a perfect High Priest who ever lives to make intercession for us (Heb. 7:25). He experienced hunger, thirst, and fatigue. He was raised in a family. He loved, hated, and marveled. He was glad, sad, angry, sarcastic, and grieved. He was distressed over future events (such as His crucifixion). He exercised faith, read Scripture, and prayed all night. He poured out His heart over the pain of man and wept when His own heart ached. The Lord has been through all that we go through—and more. He's sympathetic, and He defends us. Christ is our faithful High Priest, always interceding for us.

As our Shepherd, He nurtures us, cherishes us, and equips us to do His will. He also intercedes as our High Priest on our behalf, making sure that no sin is charged against us. His blood keeps on cleansing us from all sin (1 John 1:9).

HE IS THE SOVEREIGN

Looking again at our text, Hebrews 13:20-21, notice the word *Lord* in verse 20. There are various meanings of the word, but when used in the New Testament in reference to the Son of God, it speaks of one who is in complete authority. He is the Lord—the Sovereign of His church. Ephesians 1:22-23 says that God "hath put all things under his feet, and gave him to be the head over all things to the church, which is his body, the fullness of him that filleth all in all."

Colossians 1:18-19 says the same thing: "He is the head of the body, the church; who is the beginning, the first-born [Gk., *prōtotokos*, "the preeminent one"] . . . that in all things he might have the preeminence. For it pleased the Father that in him should all fullness dwell."

The Lord manifests His sovereignty in the church in two ways.

HE RULES HIS CHURCH

As Lord of His church, He is its ruler. If anyone asks who is in charge of Grace Church, we tell him, "Jesus Christ." Ephesians 5:23 says, "Christ is the head of the church."

In Revelation 1:12-15 we see Christ moving among candlesticks, which represent His church. He has feet like fine bronze, and burning, penetrating eyes that search for the sin that needs to be removed from His church. That's why Jesus says in Matthew 18:20, "Where two or three are gathered together in my name, there am I in the midst of them." He wasn't talking about His presence at a prayer meeting. The context reveals He was talking about being with two or three witnesses that confirm the sin of someone in the discipline process. Jesus was saying, "Don't hesitate to discipline people in the church. When you've called together the right witnesses and affirmed the sin, I'm there in your midst disciplining with you." You are acting on behalf of Christ.

The New Testament teaches that Christ rules His church through a plurality of godly men, or elders. At Grace Church, we have about thirty elders, and our one goal is to do what Christ wants us to do. We know most of what He wants to do because it's written in the Bible.

When Scripture is silent about a certain issue, then it's up to us to discern the mind of God prayerfully, thoughtfully, and patiently. We wait until God shows us what He wants us to do. That's why we've always been committed to unanimous agreement on a matter. God only has one will, so we know we have to be unanimous.

HE TEACHES HIS CHURCH

The Lord's will is revealed through His Word and through human instruments, but He's the Teacher. He teaches through the Word and His Spirit. In John 15:26 Jesus says, "When the Comforter is come, whom I will send unto you from the Father, even the Spirit of truth, who proceedeth from the Father, he shall testify of me." In other words, "The Spirit will tell you what you need to know about Me." In addition, Jesus said, "I have yet many things to say unto you, but ye cannot bear them now. Nevertheless, when he, the Spirit of truth, is come, he will guide you into all truth; for he shall not speak of himself, but whatever he shall hear, that shall he speak; and he will show you things to come. He shall glorify me; for he shall receive of mine, and shall show it unto you" (John 16:12-14).

First John 2:20 says that we can draw on the Spirit for knowledge. Verse 27 says that we have an anointing from God; we don't need worldly, human teachers who don't know the Scriptures. Christ rules His church through His Word, the Holy Spirit, and gifted men of God. As a pastor, I'm not to give you my own opinion of things. I'm not to talk about social issues that aren't related to the Word of God. I'm to open the Word of God to you so that you may know the mind of God and the heart of the Savior. Christ is the Teacher. I'm only a waiter. I didn't cook the meal; I'm only supposed to deliver it to you hot without messing it up!

HE IS THE SANCTIFIER

According to Hebrews 13:21, Christ is "working in you." That is wonderful to know! He is the One who sets us apart from sin, purifies us, and leads us to give Him glory forever.

When you see a Christian in sin, I'm sure you feel concern for him. You want to see him get rid of his sin. Sometimes when you confront a person, the discipline process goes on and on. When you have a situation like that and your heart is grieved, the only comfort you have is knowing that Christ is the purifier of His church.

If the person you are disciplining is a Christian, Christ may purify His church by removing him. He may cause the death of an unfaithful believer, which is what Paul speaks of in 1 Corinthians 11:27-30 (cf. 1 John 5:16).

In John 10:27 Jesus says, "My sheep hear my voice, and I know them, and they follow me." I like that. We belong to Him. He's the builder, owner, purchaser, chief cornerstone, and foundation of the church. The church is His. It's being built, and He has promised that it cannot fail. Opposition, threats, carnality, human ineptitude, indifference, apostasy, liberalism, and denominationalism will not prevail against the church. Christ is building His church.

Ephesians 5:25-26 says, "Christ . . . loved the church, and gave himself for it, that he might sanctify and cleanse it with the washing of water by the word." Christ wants His church pure so that ultimately "he might present it to himself a glorious church, not having spot, or wrinkle, or any such thing; but that it should be holy and without blemish" (v. 27).

It's comforting to know that Christ hasn't left us with the responsibility of building His church. We're not doing anything Christ can't do. If Grace Church disintegrated today, the church of Jesus Christ would move ahead. Christ does not need us to build His church.

Then why are we to work so hard? Because there's nothing more marvelous, thrilling, glorious, and satisfying than to be a part of what Jesus Christ is building for His eternal glory.

PART TWO
The Dynamic Church

Upon this rock I will build My church; and the gates of Hades shall not overpower it.

Matthew 16:18; NASB

Chapter 5

The Pattern of the Early Church*

The description of the early church in Acts 2:42-47 gives us a basic outline of what God intends the church to be:

> [The early church] continued steadfastly in the apostles' doctrine and fellowship, and in breaking of bread, and in prayers. And fear came upon every soul; and many wonders and signs were done by the apostles. And all that believed were together, and had all things common; and sold their possessions and goods, and parted them to all men, as every man had need. And they, continuing daily with one accord in the temple, and breaking bread from house to house, did eat their food with gladness and singleness of heart, praising God, and having favor with all the people. And the Lord added to the church daily such as should be saved.

Those who love Jesus Christ constitute the true church, the Body of Christ. We belong to the collective Body of Christ, whether we're alive or in glory. The Greek word for church is *ekklēsia*, which means "an assembly of called-out ones." The church is made up of people called by God to be His children. We have become united with all other believers by faith in Christ.

* From tape GC 1237.

The world cannot detect the invisible church of real Christians. They see only the visible church, which includes those who only profess to be Christians. The Lord intended to establish a visible church for a testimony to the world. When we gather together on the Lord's Day, we are a testimony to the world that Christ has indeed risen. Some people say that we don't need any buildings or organizational structure at all. However, I don't think Christ would have agreed. In Matthew 18, for example, Christ implies that the church has a specific form since it meets in a given place: "If thy brother shall trespass against thee, go and tell him his fault between thee and him alone; if he shall hear thee, thou hast gained thy brother: But if he will not hear thee, then take with thee one or two more, that in the mouth of two or three witnesses every word may be established. And if he shall neglect to hear them, *tell it unto the church*" (vv. 15-17, emphasis added).

In the book of Acts the invisible church became more visible. Although the visible and the invisible church were initially the same entity, the picture changed as false believers began to associate with the church. The invisible church became visible as believers began to gather together. Originally, they met in homes. However, by the third century, the church was meeting in its own building as it continued to grow in numbers.

Let's examine three aspects of the church: its founding, its ministry, and its leadership. Although there are new ways to communicate, new methods to utilize, and new problems to deal with in the twentieth century, I believe the Lord intends the twentieth-century church to follow the same principles that the first-century church did.

THE FOUNDING OF THE CHURCH

The first local assembly met in Jerusalem. It consisted primarily of humble people: fishermen, farmers, and other poor people. There were also some people who were well off, as indicated by the fact that they were willing to share their goods with the tremendous number of needy people in the church.

The church at Jerusalem was born in a prayer meeting on the Day of Pentecost. The Spirit came and filled those who were waiting in an upper room. As a result, all the Christians experienced a dramatic manifestation of the unity of the Spirit and the love of Christ, causing the church to grow rapidly. In fact, it acquired three thousand new Christians on the first day (Acts 2:41).

Acts 2:42 delineates the basic ingredients of church life: "They continued steadfastly in the apostles' doctrine and fellowship, and in breaking of bread [communion], and in prayers." The only other thing you can add to that was preaching the good news of Jesus Christ. They proclaimed it in the streets, in the Temple, in homes, and everywhere they had an opportunity. As a result, "the Lord added to the church daily such as should be saved" (v. 47). They had all the ingredients they needed to have a functioning, God-blessed, Spirit-directed church.

Today churches often use gimmicks and entertainment to try to get people into church. That is a sign that the people aren't following the biblical pattern or depending on the Spirit's leading.

The Jerusalem congregation began in the energy of the Holy Spirit and continued in it. They were preoccupied with the Spirit's power and with ministering in Christ's name.

The twelve apostles led the early church until it spread out and elders and deacons were trained to lead and serve in other congregations. Since everyone was a new convert in the early church, God left the twelve with the Jerusalem church for at least seven years.

After some years had passed, the apostles decided that some of the men had developed to a place of spiritual leadership and maturity. They chose some to become evangelists and teaching pastors. One example is Philip, who started out as a deacon and wound up as a church-planting evangelist.

The apostle Paul, Silas, Barnabas, and others planted several independent churches. Since each church was ultimately led by the Holy Spirit, there were no denominations holding them together organizationally—they were one in the Spirit. The early Christians had a common bond. In Romans 16:16 Paul says, "The churches of Christ greet you." There was a oneness among the independent congregations. They were composed of Jews and Gentiles and all classes of believers: rich, poor, educated, and uneducated. Christians from a wide spectrum of society were functioning together as one. The only organizational structure they had was that which was instituted by the Holy Spirit.

The church has changed a great deal over the centuries. It has become complex and businesslike. Today it is a massive organization with denominations, commissions, committees, councils, boards, and programs. It quite often functions like a business rather than a body, a factory rather than a family, and a corporation rather than a community. Churches have become entertainment centers, giving performances to placid piles of unproductive churchgoers. Almost all such devices are geared to get people into the church but don't do anything with them once they come.

THE MINISTRY OF THE CHURCH

I would like to look at three New Testament epistles—1 and 2 Timothy and Titus—because they tell us what the ministry and the organizational structure of the church should be. Timothy and Titus were evangelists. In the early church an evangelist was a church planter who went to an area where there were no Christians, won some people to Christ, and established a congregation. Usually he would stay with that congregation for as long as a year, maybe even longer, until he had taught them sufficiently. When some of the people had matured, he would then appoint elders in that city to care for the church and teach it. Then he would move to another place and do the same thing all over again.

The basic task of the church is to teach sound doctrine. It is not to give one pastor's opinion, to recite tear-jerking illustrations that play on emotions, to raise funds, to present programs and entertainment, or to give weekly devotionals. In Titus 2:1 Paul writes, "Speak thou the things which become sound doctrine."

If the church of Jesus Christ is to be protected from false doctrine, the elders who lead it must be faithful to teach sound doctrine. Many other things are good, but they're not priorities. As a minister of Jesus Christ, I am first of all responsible to God for the purity of the church and its protection from false doctrine. All ministers of the gospel are answerable to Christ for how faithfully they protect and nurture the flock. Unfortunately, there are many pastors whose churches expect them to do everything under the sun except what Christ intends—teaching the Word of God. Their energies are dissipated into other duties rather than their prime duty.

Here are some other passages that enjoin biblical preaching:

> *2 Timothy 1:13-14*—"Hold fast the form of sound words, which thou hast heard of me, in faith and love which is in Christ Jesus. That good thing which was committed unto thee keep by the Holy Spirit, who dwelleth in us." The word *form* implies that the regular instruction in the church should be the teaching of sound words.
>
> *2 Timothy 2:1-2*—"The things that thou hast heard from me among many witnesses, the same commit thou to faithful men, who shall be able to teach others also." A pastor teaches his congregation sound doctrine so that they can teach it to others.
>
> *2 Timothy 2:15*—"Study to show thyself approved unto God, a workman that needeth not to be ashamed, rightly dividing the word of truth." The effective ministry centers on teaching doctrine, and the key is diligent study.

2 Timothy 2:24-25—"The servant of the Lord must not strive, but be gentle unto all men, apt to teach, patient, in meekness instructing those that oppose him, if God, perhaps, will give them repentance to the acknowledging of the truth."

2 Timothy 3:14-17—"But continue thou in the things which thou hast learned and hast been assured of, knowing of whom thou hast learned them, and that from a child thou hast known the holy scriptures, which are able to make thee wise unto salvation through faith which is in Christ Jesus. All scripture is given by inspiration of God, and is profitable for doctrine, for reproof, for correction, for instruction in righteousness, that the man of God may be perfect, thoroughly furnished unto all good works." If Christians are to become spiritually mature, church leaders must preach from all of Scripture.

2 Timothy 4:1-2—"I charge thee, therefore, before God, and the Lord Jesus Christ, who shall judge the living and the dead at his appearing and his kingdom: preach the word; be diligent in season, out of season; reprove, rebuke, exhort with all long-suffering and doctrine."

So the ministry of the church is simple: teaching sound doctrine. The only way we can ever please the Lord and obey the Spirit is to preach sound doctrine in the pattern of the early evangelists.

THE LEADERSHIP OF THE CHURCH

In the New Testament church leadership belonged collectively to a group of elders who were its leaders under the Spirit of God. One man was not responsible for doing everything, and that's how it should be. The pastor is not the professional problem-solver who runs around with an ecclesiastical bag of tools, waiting for the next problem to repair or the next squeaky wheel to grease.

An elder is also referred to as a "bishop" in the New Testament. *Elder* emphasizes his title, and *bishop,* meaning "overseer," refers to his duty. He oversees the flock. The New Testament describes it as a spiritual ministry that is concerned with two things: prayer and teaching God's Word.

DECISION-MAKING

The elders who rule in the local church are ultimately and primarily responsible to Christ—not to the congregation or some council. First Timothy 5:17 says, "Let the elders that rule well be counted worthy of double honor, especially they who labor in the word and doctrine." An elder is not necessarily involved in teaching doctrine;

there are other capacities in the design of the Spirit. All elders, however, are responsible for making decisions after prayer and Bible study so that decisions can be made with the mind of Christ in the energy of the Spirit. Only then can they lead the church with positive effects for the entire congregation. Ruling as an elder is a high calling.

As previously stated, at Grace Church we are committed to the idea that when a decision is to be made among the elders, it needs to be made unanimously by men who have the mind of Christ (cf. 1 Cor. 2:16). It is made by common consent after prayer, the study of the Word, and sometimes after fasting. Then in a unified way they are able to deal with problems in the church.

DEFENDING

Titus 1:9-11 says that an elder should be "holding fast the faithful word as he hath been taught, that he may be able by sound doctrine both to exhort and to refute the opposers. For there are many unruly and vain talkers and deceivers, especially they of the circumcision, whose mouths must be stopped, who subvert whole houses, teaching things which they ought not, for filthy lucre's sake." The elders are to keep false teachers out.

DISCIPLINING

The elders are to discipline Christians who fall into doctrinal error. Second Timothy 2:17-18 speaks of the destructive teaching of "Hymenaeus and Philetus, who, concerning the truth, have erred, saying that the resurrection is past already; and overthrow the faith of some." The presence of heretics in the church is a serious problem that must be dealt with.

First Timothy 1:20 records how Paul dealt with Hymenaeus and Alexander: "I have delivered [them] unto Satan, that they may learn not to blaspheme." When a person teaches doctrinal error, he is put out of the fellowship until he is willing to abandon his error. Then God can begin to restore him.

Elders were ordained in every city where there was a church (Titus 1:5). They were chosen out of the congregation. A church is strongest, I'm convinced, when its own people rise to leadership. The elders who are chosen have been qualified by the Spirit of God and are prepared to serve in the local church.

The highest position of authority in the church belongs to elders, who rule under Christ as undershepherds (1 Pet. 5:2-4). Elders are responsible for teaching doctrine, administrating, disciplining, protecting the flock, praying for the flock, and studying the Word of God. They are answerable to Jesus Christ for their ministry.

Chapter 6

Elders, Deacons, and Other Church Members*

The church is a living community of people redeemed by Jesus Christ. No one is more visible to the watching world than those who are in leadership over the church. They are the ones the world will point to as examples of what Christians are. We've seen in recent years how a handful of highly visible but disqualified men can sully the reputation of the entire church. Who can say whether some of these people are even genuine believers? Satan commonly sows tares (false believers) among the wheat (true believers; Matt. 13:36-43). Therefore it is important to carefully evaluate someone's life before he can be put in a position of Christian leadership.

ELDERS

Acts 14:21-23 records the ordination of elders in the early church: "When [Paul and Barnabas] had preached the gospel to that city, and had taught many, they returned again to Lystra, and to Iconium, and Antioch, confirming the souls of the disciples, and exhorting them to continue in the faith, and that we must through much tribulation enter into the kingdom of God. And when they had ordained elders in every church, and had prayed with fasting, they commended them to the Lord, on whom they believed."

*From tape GC 1208.

How does God reveal to the church who the elders should be so that the church can ordain them? This passage suggests that prayer and fasting are part of that process. But in the end, the church must determine whom God desires to serve as leaders based on a set of biblical qualifications that are clearly delineated. Elders are not chosen on the basis of their knowledge of the business world, their financial ability, their prominence, or even their innate ability to be leaders. They are chosen because God has called and prepared them for the leadership of the church. The men whom God selects will meet the qualifications.

First Timothy 3 lists what is required of an elder: "This is a true saying, If a man desire the office of a bishop, he desireth a good work. A bishop then must be blameless" (vv. 1-2). That requirement encompasses all others. What does it mean to be blameless? It doesn't mean that a man has to be perfect. If so, we would all be disqualified! It means that there must not be any great blot on his life that others might point to. Here are the characteristics of blamelessness Paul specifically lists:

> [He must be] the husband of one wife [faithful to his wife], temperate, sober-minded, of good behavior, given to hospitality, apt to teach [able to communicate his faith]; not given [addicted] to wine, not violent, not greedy of filthy lucre [money], but patient, not a brawler, not covetous; one that ruleth well his own house, having his children in subjection with all gravity [seriousness] (for if a man know not how to rule his own house, how shall he take care of the church of God?); not a novice [recent convert], lest being lifted up with pride he fall into the condemnation of the devil. Moreover, he must have a good report of them who are outside, lest he fall into reproach and the snare of the devil. (vv. 2-7)

Paul also wrote to Titus regarding the requirements for an elder: "For this cause left I thee in Crete, that thou shouldest set in order the things that are wanting, and ordain elders in every city, as I had appointed thee" (Titus 1:5). In Titus 1:6-9 we find instructions that echo the qualifications in 1 Timothy 3. First of all we read that an elder must be blameless and "the husband of one wife, having faithful children not accused of profligacy, or unruly" (v. 6). An elder must give evidence of having been effective in communicating his faith to his own family. Certainly you don't expect to see complete sainthood in children, but they are to follow their father's faith with a measure of godly conduct.

Verse 7 says that the bishop or elder "must be blameless, as the steward of God." He must realize that he is a steward who doesn't own anything, but merely manages the affairs of God for the Body of Christ. Also he must not be "self-willed, not soon angry, not given to wine" (v. 7). About the only thing people could drink in New Testament days was wine because pure water was difficult to obtain. The Greek term pictures one who stayed beside his wine a long time, evidence that the person had a problem with alcohol. Also an elder must not be "violent" or "given to filthy lucre" (v. 7). He doesn't react with his fists, and he doesn't pursue money as his primary goal.

On a positive note, verse 8 says that an elder should be "a lover of hospitality." He must be willing to open his home to strangers. Besides the evidence that a well-managed household gives of his ability to manage the church (1 Tim. 3:4-5), it sets a good example for strangers and makes them feel welcome. An elder needs to have a home that displays what Christian living is all about. Furthermore, he is to be "a lover of good [things or men], sober-minded, just, holy, temperate, holding fast the faithful word" (vv. 8-9). An elder should know his priorities and practice self-control as he lives by the standards of God's Word. A man who meets those qualifications has been given by God to the local church to rule and teach it, and is therefore worthy of honor.

Acts 20 gives us a look at the elders in Ephesus. In verse 28 Paul says, "Take heed, therefore, unto yourselves, and to all the flock, over which the Holy Spirit hath made you overseers." An elder who rules the church must evaluate not only his own life but also the spiritual needs of his flock. We need to take note of everyone in the flock that God has given us so we can recognize and specifically pray for their individual problems and needs.

Paul also exhorted the Ephesian elders "to feed the church of God" (v. 28). What is it that the church must feed on? The Word of God.

Peter said, "The elders who are among you I exhort, who am also an elder, and a witness of the sufferings of Christ, and also a partaker of the glory that shall be revealed: Feed the flock of God which is among you, taking the oversight of it" (1 Pet. 5:1-2).

Peter further said that oversight of the flock should not be done "by constraint [and] not for filthy lucre but of a ready mind" (v. 2). An elder shouldn't serve as though his responsibility were a distasteful task but willingly because it is a privilege. His desire shouldn't be to minister only to rich people who financially reward him but to minister eagerly to everyone. Verse 3 says, "Neither as being lords over God's heritage, but being examples to the flock." The best way to lead is not by being a dictator but by being an example. If you try to lead people without setting a pattern they can follow, they will resist your leadership. Leading by example is worth doing because of its reward, as verse 4 indicates: "When the chief Shepherd shall appear, ye shall receive a crown of glory that fadeth not away." That crown is promised to those who are given oversight of the church and who lead by the guidelines Peter established. The wonderful thing about getting that crown is that the elders who receive it will be able to cast it at the feet of Jesus Christ—the One to whom it really belongs (Rev. 4:10). [Note: for more information on elders, see appendixes 1 and 3.]

DEACONS

Acts 6 introduces us to a group whom many believe to be the first deacons. Though these men are never specifically called deacons, they are certainly an appropriate model for deacons. Apparently it was sometime after this that the office of deacon was officially recognized in the church.

In the earliest days of the church, the church at Jerusalem was led by the apostles. Eventually it was necessary for them to delegate some of their responsibilities to other mature Christian men. That enabled them to concentrate on prayer and teaching (v. 5).

Verse 1 says, "In those days, when the number of the disciples was multiplied, there arose a murmuring of the Grecians against the Hebrews, because their widows were neglected in the daily ministration." One of the responsibilities of the church was taking care of needy widows. Contention arose because the Grecian Christians thought that most of the daily provisions were going to the Jewish widows.

Therefore "the twelve called the multitude of the disciples unto them, and said, It is not fitting that we should leave the word of God, and serve tables" (v. 2). In other words, "We must concentrate on studying and communicating the Word of God. As things now stand, we have to serve meals and run over here and there, so we're neglecting the Word of God." They understood what their priority was.

The apostles then said, "Wherefore, brethren, look among you for seven men of honest report, full of the Holy Spirit and wisdom, whom we may appoint over this business" (v. 3). These men were responsible for handing out financial support and various provisions to individuals in need.

Acts 6:3 gives some basic qualifications the men were to have: they were to be "of honest report, full of the Holy Spirit and wisdom." Those fit well with the specific requirements for deacons found in 1 Timothy 3:8-9: "In like manner must the deacons be grave [serious minded], not double-tongued [telling a person one thing and another something else], not given to much wine, not greedy of filthy lucre, holding the mystery of the faith in a pure conscience." The "mystery of the faith" is that God became man in Jesus Christ (1 Tim. 3:16). Therefore, "holding the mystery of the faith in a pure conscience" means to live in a Christlike manner.

Furthermore Paul said that deacons should "first be proved; then let them use the office of a deacon, being found blameless. . . . Let the deacons be the husbands of one wife, ruling their children and their own houses well. For they that have used the office of a deacon well purchase to themselves a good standing, and great boldness in the faith which is in Christ Jesus" (vv. 10, 12-13). [Note: for more information on deacons, see Appendix 2.]

THE CONGREGATION

For those who have been saying, "That's right, deacons and elders, get to work"—now it's your turn! Whereas the basic task of church leadership is to teach sound doctrine and explain how to apply it, the basic task of the people is to be Spirit-filled as they learn doctrine and then apply what they learn. The congregation is the object of the leaders' ministry. Perhaps someday as a result of that ministry members of the church will become deacons and deaconesses, elders, or even evangelists and pastor-teachers. We all start at the same point: somewhere in the congregation. Those who are faithful with small tasks can be entrusted with larger responsibilities. Consider Philip: he was chosen to be a deacon and ended up as an evangelist. Similarly, Stephen—another of the original deacons—became a tremendous defender of the faith, even to the point of becoming the first Christian martyr. God might lift you to a place of leadership, possibly even to the point where you might be martyred for your faith in Jesus Christ.

The congregation is the part of the church that is to do "the work of the ministry" (Eph. 4:12). Hebrews 13:17 identifies the general obligation of a congregation: "Obey them that have the rule over you, and submit yourselves." Assuming that the leadership of the church is Spirit-directed, we are to obey them because they are ministering on behalf of Christ as His undershepherds. The congregation is to subject itself to their godly ministry, although they may not understand it all, and may even disagree sometimes with what the elders are attempting to do. The church's obedience is a living testimony to the world. There are many things that hurt a church and destroy its testimony. The primary one is poor leadership or false teachers who fail to build the church on the Word of God. Another thing that weakens a church is a congregation that won't follow its leadership. That causes church splits as well as other problems that are exposed to the full view of the world. Every church member must follow the design of the Spirit and be faithful and obedient.

THE MEN

What are the responsibilities of the men in the local assembly? Paul identified some of them for Timothy:

First, men are to provide for their families. First Timothy 5:8 says, "If any [man] provide not for his own [dependents], and specially for those of his own house, he hath denied the faith, and is worse than an [unbeliever]. If you can't show the world that you are faithful to do your most basic duty, then you are denying the very basis of what Christian love is all about. There are times when men get laid off from work, but that should only be a temporary condition, because God expects a Christian man to work so that he can provide for his family—not to be on welfare unless he has some kind of a physical incapacity. The church should care for a family in such a situation rather than letting it be supported by a working wife and mother.

Men are to serve their employers. First Timothy 6:1 says, "Let as many servants [employees] as are under the yoke [subject to the authority of an employer] count their own masters worthy of all honor, that the name of God and his doctrine be not blasphemed." Poor work habits discredit your Christian testimony. You need to serve your employer with honor whether he deserves it or not for the sake of how the world views Christianity.

Verse 2 says, "They that have believing masters, let them not despise them because they are brethren." If you've got a Christian boss, that doesn't mean you can goof off because he's in the church. Rather, "do them service because they are faithful and beloved, partakers of the benefit." If you've got a Christian boss, that means you should work all the more diligently—don't take advantage of his graciousness.

Titus 2:9-10 says, "Exhort servants to be obedient unto their own masters, and to please them well in all things, not answering again [talking back]; not purloining [pilfering], but showing all good fidelity [honesty], that they may adorn the doctrine of God, our Savior, in all things." When you live a godly life in front of your employer, God even becomes more beautiful to him because he can see Him manifest in your life.

Titus 2:2 tells older men to be "sober-minded, grave, temperate, sound in faith, in love, in patience." Older men in the church are responsible to teach the younger ones. They should be serious and dignified, know their priorities, and be self-controlled. They should also be strong in faith, love, and patience—three attitudes directed toward God, others, and troubles, respectively.

Paul told Titus to exhort young men "to be sober-minded, in all things showing thyself a pattern of good works; in doctrine showing uncorruptness, gravity, sincerity, sound speech, that cannot be condemned" (vv. 6-8). It's easy for young men to say things that are not worth saying. They need to consider their words carefully before speaking.

Finally, 1 Timothy 2:8 says that men should "pray everywhere, lifting up holy hands, without wrath and doubting." Men are to be in constant prayer, especially since it's so easy for men to be distracted by things of lesser importance.

THE WOMEN

Paul begins his charge to Christian women by encouraging them to dress modestly. First Timothy 2:9 deals with the issue of a woman's clothing and appearance, which is as applicable today as when it was first established: "In like manner . . . women [should] adorn themselves in modest apparel." That, of course, is a basic principle of the Word of God for the dress of any believer. The issue is modesty. The Bible doesn't say there is a three-inch-above-the-knee rule. But some things are obviously immodest.

Christians are to dress modestly, but that doesn't mean if you bring to church an unsaved friend who is immodestly dressed that the ushers should say, "Sorry, lady, you'll have to wait until the service is over—your dress is not appropriate." This guideline in 1 Timothy is for believers.

Women are to dress modestly "with godly fear" [lit., "with a sense of shame"] (v. 9). Paul is not talking about extreme psychological trauma; he is saying that a woman should have just enough shame to be modest.

The idea of "sobriety" (v. 9) is to avoid extremes. There's no place in the church for showing off one's apparel. That distracts from what the Spirit of God wants to accomplish in our lives.

The end of verse 9 says that women should not adorn themselves "with braided hair, or gold, or pearls, or costly array." In Paul's day, there were popular styles of braiding the hair. Women wound all kinds of pearls and gold in their hair. You can imagine a man sitting with the rest of the believers when some lady plops down in front of him with a whole treasure chest on her head. He would be sitting there thinking, *I'll bet that pearl is worth eighty-nine drachmas, and that one over there—look at the size of that one!* The whole purpose of being there would be forgotten.

That doesn't mean Christian women today can wear only cheap pearls and dime-store earrings. The point is that there is no place for a showy display in front of people who are trying to worship God. We are to be modestly attired so that we don't distract others from what God wants to do through His Spirit and His Word. A Christian woman shouldn't be adorned with immodest, extravagant apparel.

Verse 10 says that the life of a godly woman is characterized by "good works." If you're a godly woman, you will look like someone who cares about godly things, not someone who cares only about showing off. A godly woman isn't concerned about putting herself on display.

Paul then reminds the women of their responsibility to learn submissively. "Let the women learn in silence with all subjection" (v. 11). Should the church have women preachers? No. That's exactly what that verse forbids. In the public service, women are not to teach. They are responsible to teach other women only. Verse 12 is even more specific: "I permit not a woman to teach, nor to usurp authority over the man, but to be in silence."

Paul also urged women to live righteously. Titus 2:3 says that older women should be "in behavior as becometh holiness, not false accusers." The Greek word for "accusers" means "scandalmongers." It's easy for older people who have more time available to get caught up in talking about things that are going on, especially in modern times with the invention of the telephone. Information that begins as an innocent rumor can become a real problem.

Women are to be "teachers of good things, that they may teach the young women to be sober-minded, to love their husbands, to love their children, to be discreet, chaste, keepers at home, good, obedient to their own husbands, that the word of God be not blasphemed" (2:3-4). The pastor is not responsible to run around and teach everyone everything. That's the congregation's responsibility as God directs them to minister to others. Many young women wonder why their children are hard to discipline and have problems. A major reason is that many of them are never home with their children, teaching them spiritual principles that should be basic patterns for the rest of their lives. A godly woman has her priorities in order, teaching her own children as she herself is taught.

Chapter 7

A Look at the Thessalonian Model*

All the basic ingredients that our Lord wants in a church were found in the Thessalonian congregation. The epistle that Paul wrote to the Thessalonians lays out for us the pattern of the church that Christ builds. It contains no reference to the number of members. It doesn't tell us about their goals and objectives, their programming, the kind of sermons that were preached, or the music they sang. It doesn't tell us about their Sunday school, their worship services, or their high school camps. However, it does tell us about several spiritual elements.

The apostle Paul first preached the gospel to the Thessalonians during his second missionary journey. After he left them, he sent Timothy to find out how they were doing. When Timothy returned, he came with a fantastic report that we find in 1 Thessalonians 3:6-7: "When Timothy came from you unto us, and brought us good tidings of your faith and love, and that ye have good remembrance of us always, desiring greatly to see us, as we also to see you; therefore, brethren, we were comforted." The good news that Timothy reported to Paul prompted him to write this first letter to the Thessalonians.

I trust that as we look at some of the basic principles in the epistle to the Thessalonians, the Lord will help you to see what He desires from you and how your church can be what He wants it to be.

* From tape GC 1237.

A Saved Church

The church at Thessalonica was a saved church. That is significant because many churches today don't know the meaning of salvation. The Thessalonian church was an assembly of born-again Christians. That fact is verified by the terms Paul used in the first four verses of chapter one: "Paul, and Silvanus [Silas], and Timothy, unto the church of the Thessalonians which is in God, the Father, and in the Lord Jesus Christ: Grace be unto you, and peace, from God, our Father, and the Lord Jesus Christ. We give thanks to God always for you all, making mention of you in our prayers, remembering without ceasing your work of faith, and labor of love, and patience of hope in our Lord Jesus Christ, in the sight of God and our Father, knowing, brethren beloved, your election of God."

Paul could thank God for the Thessalonians because they were all "in the Lord Jesus Christ" (v. 1). They gave evidence of personally knowing the Lord Jesus Christ as their Savior. Therein lies the beginning of an effective church. The reason so many churches are ineffective is that there is a mixture of wheat and tares, even among the leadership. Having unregenerate people in places of responsibility works against God's purpose and confuses the church's message.

Let's look at Acts 17 to see how the church at Thessalonica began. Verse 1 says, "When they had passed through Amphipolis and Apollonia, they [Paul and his companions] came to Thessalonica, where was a synagogue of the Jews." When Paul entered a city to spread the gospel, he generally went to the synagogue first. He found the greatest opportunity there since he was Jewish himself. Furthermore, he realized that if he went to the Gentiles first, the Jews would not be willing to listen to what he had to say. So he initially preached in the synagogues to win some Jews to Christ so that he could gain support for reaching the city.

Verses 2-3 report the content of Paul's preaching: "Paul, as his manner was, went in unto them, and three Sabbath days reasoned with them out of the scriptures, opening and alleging that Christ must needs have suffered, and risen again from the dead; and that this Jesus, whom I preach unto you, is Christ." The Jewish people had difficulty accepting Jesus as the Messiah because He had once died. Most Jewish people did not understand the concept of a suffering Messiah, which was prophesied in such places as Isaiah 53 and Psalm 22. Therefore, Paul spent time showing them that the Messiah had to suffer to fulfill God's plan. As a result of Paul's preaching, "some of them believed, and consorted with Paul and Silas; and of the devout Greeks a great multitude, and of the chief women not a few" (v. 4).

From the very beginning, there was a tremendous response, even though Paul spent only three Sabbaths in Thessalonica. They would have been in bad shape had they not been led by the Holy Spirit. Since Paul was justly concerned for their welfare, he was overjoyed to learn from Timothy that they were having a dynamic impact on the surrounding area.

The key to the success of the Thessalonian church was its purity. If you read Acts 2, you'll find that at the birth of the church on the day of Pentecost, three thousand people believed the gospel and were baptized. Verse 42 says that "they continued steadfastly." Now that's a regenerated church! And because they were, they turned the city of Jerusalem upside down. They were making such an impact that the Jewish leaders were tearing their hair out, saying, "Ye have filled Jerusalem with your doctrine" (Acts 5:28). When you have a totally regenerated assembly of people moving through town in the power of the Holy Spirit, they are bound to make a great impact.

It was no different for the Thessalonians. Paul said, "For our gospel came not unto you in word only, but also in power, and in the Holy Spirit, and in much assurance, as ye know what manner of men we were among you for your sake" (1 Thess. 1:5).

A Surrendered Church

Verse 6 of chapter 1 says, "Ye became followers of us, and of the Lord." The genuine character of the church's salvation is apparent in that statement. The Greek word translated "followers" is *mimētēs*, from which the English word *mimic* is derived. The Thessalonian Christians weren't just talkers; they were imitators. They didn't merely talk about their Christian experience; they actually modeled their lives after Paul and his companions.

Not only are Christians to be collective representatives of Christ on earth but also individual representatives as each believer strives to be like Him. The pursuit of the Christian is to be like Christ. That's the key to unity in the church. If all of us were like Christ, we'd have no problem getting along with each other. But unfortunately, we are not always in tune with one another because we are not all following Christ. A. W. Tozer said that if a hundred pianos were merely tuned to each other, their pitch would not be very accurate. But if they were all tuned to one tuning fork, they would automatically be tuned to each other. Similarly, unity in the church isn't the result of running around and adjusting to everyone else. Rather, it is becoming like Jesus Christ. The Thessalonian church was surrendered to Christlikeness, which had been demonstrated in the lives of Paul, Silas, and Timothy.

A Suffering Church

First Thessalonians 1:6 says, "Ye became followers of us, and of the Lord, having received the Word in much affliction, with joy of the Holy Spirit." The Thessalonian church didn't have it easy. In fact, any church that is saved and surrendered to Christ is going to have a difficult time.

As soon as the Thessalonian assembly had begun, they experienced opposition. Acts 17 records what happened: "The Jews who believed not, moved with envy, took unto them certain vile fellows of the baser sort, and gathered a company, and set all the city in an uproar, and assaulted the house of Jason, and sought to bring them [Paul, Silas, and Timothy] out to the people. And when they found them not, they drew Jason and certain brethren unto the rulers of the city, crying, These that have turned the world upside down are come here also" (vv. 5-6). Persecution began immediately for that church.

First Thessalonians 2:14-16 reviews the persecution the church had experienced: "Ye, brethren, became followers of the churches of God which in Judea are in Christ Jesus; for ye also have suffered like things of your own countrymen, even as they have of the Jews, who both killed the Lord Jesus and their own prophets, and have persecuted us; and they please not God, and are contrary to all men, forbidding us to speak to the Gentiles that they might be saved, to fill up their sins always; for the wrath is come upon them to the uttermost."

The church that is saved and surrendered to Christ is going to antagonize the world. Consequently, suffering will come. Jesus put it this way: "If the world hate you, ye know that it hated me before it hated you. . . . If they have persecuted me, they will also persecute you" (John 15:18, 20).

In Colossians 1:24 we read that Paul was willing to suffer if it brought about the salvation of others: "[I] rejoice in my sufferings for you, and fill up that which is behind of the afflictions of Christ in my flesh." Paul meant that since the world couldn't directly persecute Jesus anymore, it would persecute His followers. The apostle was willing to suffer for the One who had suffered for him.

Wouldn't it be great to be persecuted for being Christlike because you've turned the world upside down? If unbelievers got irritated about your church (assuming that it wasn't for being unnecessarily offensive), it would probably mean that it was correctly preaching the gospel in a manner that exposes sin. The church that confronts the world is going to suffer. Tradition records that eleven out of the twelve apostles were martyred.

A SOUL-WINNING CHURCH

The Thessalonian church had a marvelous twofold testimony. The first way they spread the gospel was by living exemplary lives. Paul said of them, "Ye were an example to all that believe in Macedonia and Achaia" (1 Thess. 1:7). Other people could look at the Thessalonian church and say, "That's the way we ought to be living." Amazingly, it took the Thessalonians only two weeks to establish a lifestyle that was surrendered to Christ. Once they had done that, everything happened. It isn't the programs or creativity that gives a church a credible testimony. It is each member's Christlikeness.

The Thessalonians were like Jesus Christ. They set a pattern for everyone else, including believers. Chapter 1 shows how the believers in Macedonia and Achaia responded to the Thessalonians' testimony: "They themselves show of us what manner of entering in we had unto you, and how ye turned to God from idols, to serve the living and true God" (v. 9). Paul didn't have to tell others about the conversion of the Thessalonians because they told it with their lives. The latest news around town was "Have you heard what happened at Thessalonica? Many people turned to God from idols." The incredible thing was that Thessalonica was only fifty miles from Mount Olympus—the supposed residence of the Greek gods. Although they had been raised from their earliest years to believe in a plurality of gods, within three successive Sabbaths an entire community of people dropped their idolatrous system to serve the living God. That kind of turnaround makes news.

The second way of spreading the gospel is through a verbal witness of the Word. First Thessalonians 1:8 says, "From you sounded out the word of the Lord . . . in every place." The Greek word for "sounded out" is *exēchētai*, from which we get the English word *echo*. A Christian's testimony should never be independent of God's Word. It should be only an echo of God's truth. An echo always repeats what is originally spoken. God has put His voice in you—the Holy Spirit. He doesn't want you to create your own words; He wants you to echo His truth.

A SECOND-COMING CHURCH

Verse 10 says the Thessalonians had turned from idols to serve God "and to wait for His Son from heaven, whom he raised from the dead, even Jesus, who delivered us from the wrath to come." Jesus promised that He would come back and gather the faithful to be with Him forever (John 14:1-3). Consequently, the ideal church awaits His return.

Did you know that many churches aren't waiting for Christ's return? Peter said, "There shall come in the last days scoffers, walking after their own lusts, and saying, Where is the promise of his coming?" (2 Pet. 3:3-4). Some people today claim to be Christians, but they don't ever talk about the return of Christ. In fact, I heard a preacher say, "I never talk about the return of Christ—there's too much confusion on that issue." Maybe it's fortunate for the people in his church that he doesn't. There's no sense in adding more confusion to what already exists. But that doesn't excuse him from speaking the truth. Every church that is truly committed to being what God wants it to be must be aware that Jesus is coming.

Christians should be anxiously waiting for Christ's return. Anticipation of the future motivates us to live godly lives for His service in the present. The last recorded words of Jesus are these: "Behold, I come quickly, and my reward is with me, to give every man according as his work shall be" (Rev. 22:12).

Knowing that Christ is coming gives me a sense of urgency about sharing the good news with others. After His resurrection Jesus said, "Ye shall receive power, after the Holy Spirit is come upon you; and ye shall be witnesses unto me" (Acts 1:8). When He had ascended into heaven, two angels appeared and said, "This same Jesus, who is taken up from you into heaven, shall so come in like manner as ye have seen him go into heaven" (v. 11). Paul says in 2 Corinthians 5:11, "Knowing, therefore, the terror of the Lord, we persuade men." When I realize the impending judgment of God, I can't help but persuade men to be "reconciled to God" (v. 20).

A church that doesn't believe in the return of Jesus Christ has no sense of rewards or urgency to deliver the ungodly from judgment. The Lord wants us to remember His return.

A STEADFAST CHURCH

First Thessalonians 3:8 says, "Now we live, if ye stand fast in the Lord." Paul was saying, "When we got the message that you were standing fast in the Lord, we were really living! That report made our day!"

Standing fast in the Lord means two things: not wavering doctrinally and maintaining a steadfast love. A person can stand fast doctrinally but dry up spiritually. That is why a Christian needs to stand fast in terms of love. Unfortunately the church at Ephesus didn't. Our Lord reproved them, saying, "I have somewhat against thee, because thou hast left thy first love" (Rev. 2:4).

The Thessalonian church stood firmly on the Word of God. Paul said, "Our gospel came not unto you in word only, but also in power, and in the Holy Spirit. . . . And ye became followers of us, and of the Lord, having received the word in much affliction" (1:5-6). Paul also told them, "Ye received the word of God . . . not as the word of men but as it is in truth, the word of God" (2:13). And he said, "We were comforted over you in all our affliction and distress by your faith" (3:7). How exciting it is when a church doesn't waver from its doctrine or its commitment to love one another!

A SUBMISSIVE CHURCH

This final principle isn't as obvious as the others. In no other New Testament epistle does Paul make as many unqualified and undefended commands as in this one. For example, when Paul wrote to the Corinthians, it was necessary for him to defend his instructions because they did not have the submissive mentality of the Thessalonians (e.g., 1 Cor. 1:10–2:5; 2 Cor. 10:1–13:10).

However, Paul didn't have to reprimand or convince the Thessalonians of anything. In chapter 4 he says, "Study to be quiet, and to do your own business, and to work with your own hands, as we commanded you" (v. 11). Similarly, chapter 5 contains many brief, unqualified commands:

> We beseech you, brethren, to know them who labor among you, and are over you in the Lord, and admonish you, and to esteem them very highly in love for their work's sake. And be at peace among yourselves. Now, we exhort you, brethren, warn them that are unruly, encourage the fainthearted, support the weak, be patient toward all men. See that none render evil for evil unto any man, but ever follow that which is good, both among yourselves, and to all men. Rejoice evermore. Pray without ceasing. In everything give thanks; for this is the will of God in Christ Jesus concerning you. Quench not the Spirit. Despise not prophesyings. Prove all things; hold fast that which is good. Abstain from all appearance of evil. (vv. 12-22)

Paul didn't need to give a detailed explanation of his instructions to the Thessalonians because they were a submissive church. He didn't have to defend himself. Can you imagine a preacher getting up on Sunday morning and saying only, "My text for this morning is 1 Thessalonians 5:16—'Rejoice evermore!' Now let us pray. Next week we'll be taking verse 17"? If Paul said in the Corinthian assembly, "Pray without ceasing," it would have taken him three chapters to prove why they should! But that was not necessary with the Thessalonians' spirit of submission to the Word. That's what made the Thessalonian church unique.

Paul said, "Ye became followers of us, and of the Lord, having received the word in much affliction, with joy" (1:6). In the next chapter he said, "Ye received the word of God . . . not as the word of men but as it is in truth, the word of God" (2:13). And he said, "Furthermore, then, we beseech you, brethren, and exhort you by the Lord Jesus, that as ye have received of us how ye ought to walk and to please God, so ye would abound" (4:1). Paul was saying, "You readily opened your heart and accepted our instruction. So just keep on obeying it."

The primary role of a pastor is to lead his people to submit totally to the Word of God. If a pastor preaches on topics that are purely his own ideas without any biblical content, a church will never be trained to accept the Word of God when it is presented. Don't make that mistake.

Chapter 8

Marks of an Effective Church*

I have a great love for the church—not only Grace Community Church, but the church of our Lord Jesus Christ as a whole. I also have a great love for pastors and a burden that churches be shaped into what God wants them to be. When I recall the words of the apostle Paul to take care of the church that Christ "purchased with his own blood" (Acts 20:28), I am sobered by that tremendous responsibility.

There are reasons for a church's prospering spiritually and growing numerically. The following are principles that constitute the key ingredients in a successful church.

GODLY LEADERS

You cannot bypass the need for godly leadership and still receive God's blessing. There must be holy men and women who are in positions of responsibility in a church; there is no substitute for that. Paul repeatedly said that Christ is the head of the church (1 Cor. 11:3; Eph. 1:22; 4:15; 5:23; Col. 1:18). As its head, Christ wants to rule His church through holy people. Unholy people just get in the way.

It's amazing how most churches choose their leadership. They select people who are the most successful in business, who have the most to say, and who have the most money. One pastor confessed to

*From tape GC 1306.

103

me that one of the problems he had in working with his board was that half were Christians and half were not. That is a serious problem because Satan and Christ don't cooperate! A man is not to be a leader in the church because he is a successful businessman, has innate leadership ability, or is a supersalesman. He is to be a leader because he is a man of God. That is the beginning of effectiveness in the church.

God has always mediated His rule in the world through godly people. In the beginning, God mediated His rule through Adam. After the Fall, it was through human conscience. After the Flood, it was through government. Eventually, God began to mediate His rule through the patriarchs, the judges, and then kings, prophets, and priests. In the gospel accounts, He ruled through Christ. And now He rules through the church, whose leaders are representatives of Jesus Christ in the world.

The primary ingredient in church leadership is holiness. However, it takes time to develop holy leadership. It took God forty years to make Moses into the leader He wanted. Joshua was an understudy of Moses for years before he was ready to lead the Israelites into the Promised Land. It took years to prepare Abraham and David. It took time to get Peter, Philip, and Paul prepared for their far-reaching ministries. It takes time to make a man of God.

When Timothy stayed in Ephesus, he had the responsibility of bringing the church to spiritual maturity. He knew he couldn't do it alone and that he needed godly leaders. A church shouldn't accept just any volunteers; it should look for godly men. Titus faced the same challenge in Crete, and Paul gave him similar advice. In his pastoral epistles, Paul gave a profile of the kind of people that are to be leading the church. They are to be:

> *Above Reproach* (1 Tim. 3:2)—Leaders are to be unblamable, having nothing in their lives for which they can be rebuked.
> *Devoted to Their Wives* (1 Tim. 3:2)—They are to be one-woman men.
> *Temperate* (1 Tim. 3:2)—They are to be spiritually stable, having a clear, biblical perspective on life.
> *Prudent* (1 Tim. 3:2)—Sometimes that word is translated "sober-minded." It means they know their priorities.
> *Respectable* (1 Tim. 3:2)—Leaders are to have such well-ordered lives that they are honored for it.
> *Hospitable* (1 Tim. 3:2)—They are to love strangers, opening their homes to those in need.
> *Able to Teach* (1 Tim. 3:2)—That phrase is translated from the single Greek word, *didaktikos*. It is never used to speak of the gift of teaching or the office of a teacher. It is not saying that a lead-

er must be a great Bible teacher. It is saying that he must be teachable as well as able to communicate biblical truth to others. The word conveys not so much the dynamics of his teaching as his sensitivity to other people. He teaches with a meek and gentle spirit.

Self-controlled (Titus 1:8)—Leaders are not to be addicted to alcohol or drugs of any kind. They need to be in control of themselves.

Not Self-willed (Titus 1:7)—They should not be self-centered. A church can't have people in leadership who are concerned only about themselves. The most important thing about church leaders is that they be concerned about the people they are shepherding.

Not Quick Tempered (Titus 1:7)—Those in leadership cannot have a volatile temperament; they must be patient.

Not Pugnacious (Titus 1:7)—This literally means "not a fighter." A church doesn't want someone in leadership who solves problems with his fists.

Not Contentious (1 Tim. 3:3)—This attitude corresponds to the previous physical reaction. A contentious person likes to compete and debate.

Gentle (1 Tim. 3:3).

Not Materialistic (1 Tim. 3:3)—Church leaders should be free from the love of money (but that is not to say that they must be free from money itself).

Managing Their Households Well (1 Tim. 3:4)—Church leaders are required to keep their children under control with dignity. Many people keep their kids under control, but not many do it with dignity.

Having a Good Reputation Among Unbelievers (1 Tim. 3:7)— What does the world think of the church leaders? As they interact with the unsaved world, their integrity should be above reproach.

Loving What Is Good (Titus 1:8).

Just (Titus 1:8)—Church leaders are to be fair.

Devout (Titus 1:8)—They are to be holy in their daily lives.

Not New Converts (1 Tim. 3:6)—They are to be spiritually mature.

Those are the qualifications given in Scripture for leaders in the church. They indicate the kind of people that God wants to lead His church. If a church doesn't have people who measure up to God's standards, there will be problems from the beginning. In fact, having godly leaders is so important that when an elder sins, he is to be rebuked before the whole congregation (1 Tim. 5:20).

FUNCTIONAL GOALS AND OBJECTIVES

A church must have functional goals and objectives, or it will have no direction. If you don't know where you're going, you won't know when you've arrived. A church that lacks direction will have no sense of accomplishment.

We must first recognize the basic biblical goals of the church: winning people to Christ, and helping them mature. Underneath those overarching goals are more specific ones such as unifying families, preventing divorce, and educating children in the things of the Lord. Those are just a few of the many biblical goals we have.

In addition, we must have functional objectives. They are the stepping-stones we use to accomplish biblical goals. It isn't enough just to say that we must learn the Word of God. We must go a step further and provide some steps to attain that goal.

Functional goals and objectives are essential. A church can't be nebulous in its direction. It must give people goals and also objectives to reach them.

Discipleship

A church should emphasize discipleship. The design of the Christian church is not to have a professional preacher financed by laymen who are merely spectators. Every Christian should be involved in edifying other believers.

I was once asked when I do my pastoral visitation, which many pastors traditionally do in the afternoons after studying in the morning. Where does the Bible say that a pastor is supposed to do visiting all afternoon? One of the few things it does say about visiting is found in the book of James: "Pure religion and undefiled before God and the Father is this: to visit the fatherless and widows in their affliction" (1:27). Who is to be involved in pure and undefiled religion? Is it just the preacher? No. Every Christian is. If you have someone to visit, do so. Likewise, if I know someone who needs to be visited, I'll do the same. There's no sense in my visiting those whom you ought to visit, and your visiting those whom I ought to visit. As a pastor, I don't believe that I'm called to be the official visitor. Visitation—and the related ministry of discipleship—is everyone's responsibility.

When I disciple someone, there are basically three things I do. First, I *teach biblical truth*. I usually give them books to read and tapes to listen to that deal with specific topics I want them to understand. Besides teaching from the pulpit, I teach biblical truths on a personal level from the Word of God.

Second, *I apply Scripture to life*. You'd be amazed to know how many people learn principles that they never put into action. I ask questions that get the disciple to think through his own set of circumstances from God's perspective. I want him to interpret life spiritually. For example, a man I was discipling was panicky over the world situation. But as he began viewing the world from the standpoint of a sovereign God and not from that of a desperate human, the problem disappeared. Then he began saying, "Isn't it terrific to see what God is doing in the world?" Biblical truth must be taught and then translated into appropriate attitudes and actions.

Finally, I work with a disciple to *solve problems biblically*. Biblical problem-solving is a key to effective discipling. People learn best when they have a need to know. A good example is the way people listen to the stewardess giving safety instructions before takeoff. No one pays any attention to her (except the people who are on their first flight) because they've heard it all before and don't expect that they'll need to know it. However, if someone looked out the right side of the plane and saw flames coming from the engine as the stewardess said, "Please take your emergency card," everyone would grab them. And if there weren't enough cards, someone would get trampled trying to find one! The change in interest can be attributed to a sudden need to know. You always learn best when you *have* to know the answers. Effective discipleship involves giving someone biblical answers to problems that they're involved in and teaching them how to make applications in a crisis. You can't just give a disciple a lecture. You've got to know enough Scripture to give him answers when he needs them.

AN EMPHASIS ON PENETRATING THE COMMUNITY

A church that is effective and successful will have a strong emphasis on penetrating the community. We are to reach people for Christ.

In the first few chapters of Acts, we see that the early church blitzed their community. On the Day of Pentecost, three thousand people were saved, who in turn moved through Jerusalem like wildfire. That church grew so fast that the Jewish leaders said to the apostles, "Ye have filled Jerusalem with your doctrine" (5:28). Their message had penetrated the entire community.

For many Christians, the nearest they come to penetrating their community is driving to church in a car that has a fish sticker on the back window. We come to church and say, "I've done my duty to God." We try to live our testimony rather than speak it. But no one ever got to heaven just because someone lived his testimony in front of him. Sooner or later you've got to give them the words of the gospel. Penetrating the community involves reaching people for Christ.

The early Christians didn't isolate themselves in a corner and talk about doctrine. They got out and saturated their communities with the gospel.

Acts 13:44—"The next sabbath day came almost the whole city together to hear the word of God." The Christians of Antioch were so busy that when it came time for preaching, nearly the whole city showed up. That was typical of the early church.

Acts 14:1—"It came to pass in Iconium that they went both together into the synagogue of the Jews, and so spoke, that a great multitude, both of the Jews and also of the Greeks, believed." Paul and Barnabas confronted both Jews and Gentiles with the gospel.

Acts 16:5—Paul, Silas, and Timothy established the churches of Phrygia and Galatia "in the faith, and [they] increased in number daily."

Acts 17:3-4—Paul entered the Thessalonian synagogue, "opening and alleging that Christ must needs have suffered, and risen again from the dead. . . . And some of them believed . . . and of the devout Greeks a great multitude [believed]."

The most effective evangelism is done on a personal level in the area where you live.

Some people go wild on programs of evangelism. I went to a church banquet where the church was presenting its evangelistic program for the year. It was centered around a football theme with goal posts and a scoreboard set up in the auditorium. When anyone got saved, they kicked the ball over the goal post. Furthermore, to motivate people to evangelize, five footballs were hidden in the homes of five unsaved families. Whoever found the football won a prize. The church also had a hot-dog stand set up outside. They were even giving sweaters to kids who brought a certain number of people to church. I couldn't believe all the gimmicks they were using!

I can't help but think that such a program is the worst possible way to evangelize—giving people ulterior motives for winning someone to the Lord. How would the unsaved people feel who were brought partly so church members could win prizes?

The church doesn't need that kind of thing. If you try to motivate people to do things for selfish motives, what they do won't honor God. That's pharisaism. I'm not against having a visitation night or door-to-door evangelism, but the best way to penetrate the community is for Christians to reproduce themselves—then you don't need a program. Which would you rather have: a week of revival meetings once a year, or a congregation that evangelizes 365 days a year? One of the reasons we've never had a hellfire-and-damnation revival meeting is that I don't like to reduce the church to a once-a-year emphasis on evangelism. Evangelism ought to be going on all the time. It's important to evangelize on a personal level.

ACTIVE CHURCH MEMBERS

If the staff does everything, something's wrong with the church. The pastoral staff is to equip the saints to do the work of the ministry (Eph. 4:12). The ministry of the church extends to all believers, with each of us using the gifts God has given us for the edification of the Body (Rom. 12:6-8).

There's a story about baseball pitcher Dizzy Dean, whose career ended because his toe got hit by a line drive. That injury ruined his throwing motion because when he came off the rubber to pitch, he had to compensate by turning his foot the wrong way. Consequently he began overextending his arm, which eventually ruined it for pitching. The same is true spiritually in the church. Where there are non-functioning members, there will be adverse effects somewhere else in the Body. All the saints must be involved in ministering the gifts that God has given them.

When people in my church say to me, "We need such-and-such a program in our church," I say, "Good, if you feel that way, go ahead and do it." After I had responded that way for a few years, no one asked about starting a program unless he was serious. The church should emphasize ministry for every individual believer. Church leadership shouldn't recruit their members to do something out of a legal obligation that they are not really motivated or gifted to do. Rather, the leadership should develop its members along the lines that the Spirit has gifted them. Aggressive, active, ministering people make a successful church.

CONCERN FOR ONE ANOTHER

A dynamic church will be involved in the lives of its people. Many churches are simply places where people go to watch things happen. But the church cannot sit in isolation. Its members cannot merely come in, sit down, walk out, and say that they are involved in the church. Tremendous responsibilities are laid at the feet of all Christians to minister to other believers. The New Testament is full of exhortations about ministering our spiritual gifts and responding appropriately to others.

I was listening to a radio preacher scream at the top of his voice. He was in one of those "amen" congregations where you can hardly hear the preacher for all the people shouting back. For several minutes he kept saying, "When I was a boy, I remember when people went to church. What we need to do is go to church—we got to get

back to church." But those people were already there. They didn't
need to hear that! What he really needed to do was tell them what
they were there for.

We've heard other people say that America needs to get back to
church. However, America never found out what it was supposed to
do when it went, so it left. Now we want people to come back, but
we're still not telling them what to do when they get there!

Why do we go to church? Hebrews 10:24-25 says, "Let us consider one another to provoke unto love and to good works, not forsaking the assembling of ourselves together, as the manner of some is,
but exhorting one another." We don't attend church just to listen. We
should be encouraging one another to do good. Every Christian ought
to be like a battery that joins with other believers and corporately in-
creases the church's output.

The New Testament has much to say about the response of believers toward one another. Being concerned about others is an important theme in Scripture:

James 5:16—We are to confess our sins one to another.
Colossians 3:13—We are to forgive one another.
Galatians 6:2—We are to bear one another's burdens.
Titus 1:13—We are to rebuke one another.
1 Thessalonians 4:18—We are to comfort one another.
Hebrews 10:25—We are to exhort one another.
Romans 14:19—We are to edify one another.
Romans 15:14—We are to admonish one another, which refers to
            counseling with a view toward changing behavior.
James 5:16—We are to pray for one another.

All of those *one anothers* clearly indicate the responsibilities
that Christians have toward each other throughout their lives.

As I look at the life of our Lord Jesus Christ, I see Someone who
was involved with individuals. He was a caring, sensitive, loving
friend who personally interacted in the lives of others. He brought joy
to a wedding. He so freely associated with drunkards that people
started calling Him one too. He met with weak, unimportant people
and made them eternally important. He met with perverse and hostile
people and revealed a warmth that made Him approachable.

When Jesus arrived in the country of the Gadarenes near the
Sea of Galilee, He was met by a mad man who "cried with a loud
voice, and said, What have I to do with thee, Jesus, thou Son of the
Most High God?" (Mark 5:7). This man was demon possessed. He
"had his dwelling among the tombs; and no man could bind him, no,
not with chains; for he had been often bound with fetters and chains,

and the chains had been plucked asunder by him, and the fetters broken in pieces; neither could any man tame him" (vv. 3-4). Obviously people avoided him! But Jesus took care of him. After Jesus had cast the demons out, the villagers found the man "sitting, and clothed, and in his right mind" (v. 15). Jesus got involved in one man's life and transformed it. And that's only one of many examples.

The church must be a loving community that shares with one another. So often we think we've done our job if we've gone to church. We waltz into the building, sit down, listen, and get back in the car to go about our business. God help us if that's our perspective of what a church should be.

DEVOTION TO THE FAMILY

There was a time when the family functioned as a unit. Every member went to church together and even sat in the same pew every Sunday. Then as the church became program-oriented, everyone went off and did his own thing. Groups were formed to counteract the loss of identity in a rapidly growing technological society. Old people became known as senior citizens. Kids became identified with youth groups that, in many cases, set the pace for the rest of the church. After a while the church began to leave the parents behind. There needs to be a balance of emphasis on all family members.

Exodus 20:12 records the fifth of the Ten Commandments: "Honor thy father and thy mother, that thy days may be long upon the land which the Lord thy God giveth thee." The consequences of dishonoring one's parents give us an idea of how serious God is about it: "He that smiteth his father, or his mother, shall be surely put to death . . . and he that curseth his father, or his mother, shall surely be put to death" (Ex. 21:15, 17).

God wants order and respect in the family. Not only does He not want you to hit your parents, but He doesn't want you to curse them either. Have you ever heard young people who had bad things to say about their parents? That would have been worthy of death in the Old Testament. We must teach young people the responsibility they have toward their parents.

You may identify with the description of unruly children given in Proverbs 30. Verse 11 says, "There is a generation that curseth their father, and doth not bless their mother." In many cases, mothers and fathers don't deserve honor, but that doesn't excuse the children from not giving it. Verse 12 says, "There is a generation that are pure in their own eyes, and yet are not washed from their filthiness." They think they have no need for their parents' instruction and assume they have all the answers. But they don't realize how bad off they are. Verses 13-14 say, "There is a generation, oh, how lofty are their eyes! And their eyelids are lifted up [in pride]. There is a generation, whose teeth are like swords, and their jaw teeth like knives, to devour the poor from off the earth, and the needy from among men." When a prideful younger generation grows up, it takes advantage of others. We have seen evidence of that in America.

Verse 15 says, "The horseleach hath two daughters, crying, Give, give." A horseleach is an insect that leaches blood from horses. The verse compares a prideful generation to a horseleach, implying that it takes everything it can out of society yet never is satisfied.

Verse 17 says, "The eye that mocketh at his father, and despiseth to obey his mother, the ravens of the valley shall pick it out, and the young eagles shall eat it." That's strong language. When you read that you get the idea that God is serious about children honoring their parents.

One of the great disasters in the ministry concerns pastors who don't take care of their families because they are too busy with other things. Howard Hendricks, a professor at Dallas Theological Seminary, related a personal example. Someone called him and said, "Dr. Hendricks, we're having a Bible conference, and we want you to be our speaker. Can you come?" Hendricks said no, but the conference planner continued, "This is a crucial event for our whole community. Why can't you come? Do you have another appointment?"

Hendricks said, "No. I've got to play with my kids."

"You've got to play with your kids? Don't you realize that our people need your instruction?"

"Yes. But my kids also need me." Dr. Hendricks was right. If a man of his far-reaching influence ever lost the respect of his kids, the credibility of his ministry would be gone, besides his heart being broken. It's good to play with your kids if you want to avoid ending up like Eli.

Eli, the Old Testament priest, took care of everyone else's spiritual problems but apparently never took care of his own children. His sons, Hophni and Phinehas, turned out to be wicked men. In effect, God told Eli, "When I initiated the priesthood, I told Aaron and the others that they would be priests forever through the Aaronic lineage. But your sons have violated My law to such an extent that I'm going to call a halt to the priestly ministry of your family. To validate those words, Hophni and Phinehas are going to die the same day" (1 Sam. 2:27-34). Eli's heart was broken after hearing that. He had been so busy taking care of everyone else that he couldn't take care of himself and his family.

I'll never forget a story that I heard from a man who was constantly involved in evangelistic meetings. He overheard his boy asking a neighbor to play. The other boy said, "I can't do anything with you because I've got to go with my dad. We're going to go down to the park and play." The evangelist's son said, "Oh. My dad can't play with me; he's too busy playing with other people's children." The evangelist said few things ever affected him as much as overhearing that remark.

Christians have an obligation to their families. A strong Christian family should be a high priority. And there is a high price to pay if we don't make it a priority. Therefore we must strive to develop solid marriages and family-oriented ministries by teaching husbands to love their wives (Eph. 5:25), wives to submit to their husbands (5:22), children to obey their parents (6:1), and parents not to exasperate their children but to nurture them (6:4).

BIBLE TEACHING AND PREACHING

When W. A. Criswell went to First Baptist Church of Dallas, he was only the second pastor in its history. He had been preceded by another great man of God, George Truett. As Criswell took over the pulpit, he told the board that he planned to teach through the Bible verse-by-verse. They said, "You can't do that; you'll empty the place!" He didn't empty it, for that church became the biggest in America, with over 15,000 members. All those people came because he taught them the Word of God, and it changed their lives as they responded to it.

The proclamation of God's truth by preaching (Gk., *kērugma*) and teaching (Gk., *didachē*) changes men and women's lives. That is why dynamic churches are directed by a pulpit that teaches biblical truth and motivates Christians to apply it.

Some believe that preaching should make everyone feel good. Suppose a man has an unhappy life. He works hard for an unfair boss, he's henpecked at home, his kid is a delinquent, and he can't make the payments on his car. When he comes to church, he shouldn't be smashed from pillar to post. Therefore some think that preaching ought to emphasize positive thinking that assumes everything is wonderful and rosy.

I once saw on a Christian television program a preacher who said, "Oh, every day with Jesus is so happy! If you could only be as happy as I am!" That wouldn't go over very well with the wife who has just returned from the cemetery where she buried her husband, or with the mother whose little child has been diagnosed as having terminal leukemia. Every day is not a happy day. Every day is fulfilling and there is an abiding joy in the presence of Christ, but Christianity is not a slaphappy way of life. If all we do is come together and tell each other how wonderful life is, we're all lying.

Others think that preaching should be geared toward helping people solve their problems. We live in a world that is so psychologically oriented it seems we can hardly think without getting into clinical analysis. We can't objectively accept anything without analyzing it. That reasoning has carried over into the church and has developed what I call "problem-centered preaching." It is where the preacher states a problem and gives ten verses out of context on how to solve it, along with a few stories about some people who solved it.

A pastor isn't a glorified psychoanalyst, a grandfather, or a Santa Claus who pats you on the head and tells you everything is fine. The preacher's task is not only to educate Christians in the Word of God but also to encourage them to change their behavior in conformity to it. In fact, in many cases he should make them feel worse before they feel better because there has to be healing before there can be restoration. When I preach a sermon that convicts those who hear it, I know that the message is getting through. A church pulpit isn't primarily designed to help people make decisions about the details of everyday living. It is meant to teach the Word of God and identify sin so that they might change their behavior. Pacifying one's problems doesn't make a person feel better. Rather confessing and repenting of sin and changing one's life is what produces true joy.

A Willingness to Change

There's nothing sacred about tradition. A dynamic church should regularly burst out of old methods that are no longer effective. A church can become so comfortable with unchanging forms that its members lose sight of what they are there for.

The apostle Paul adapted to change. He taught from one to seven days a week. That intensity in preaching takes place today in some places in Africa, where many Christians meet together at daybreak on Sunday and return home when the sun goes down.

I've preached in black churches in the South where I'd finish one sermon and the congregation would say, "Brother, preach another one!" I'd turn the page in my notebook and take off on another passage. I have preached as many as three or four sermons in a row in situations like that. Contrast that with the more prevalent attitude of twelve o'clockitis: "It's twelve o'clock and the sermon is still going! Give me a break!"

Some people aren't very adaptable to change. Some would collapse if there were no Sunday morning worship. Suppose we said, "We won't be meeting on Sunday mornings anymore because of the energy crisis. Therefore we're going to meet for a while in different places around the city on Tuesday evening." That shouldn't be a major problem for any believer because every day is sacred to the Christian. We enjoy being together on the day of the week that commemorates our Lord's resurrection, but that shouldn't prevent us from changing when necessary.

There are three keys in helping a church maintain an attitude of flexibility.

First, *recognize that spiritual life takes precedence over structure.* What goes on in a Christian's life outside the church is more important than what goes on inside its walls. The church building is not God's house; the believer is (1 Cor. 6:19). Greek scholar Kenneth Wuest translates 2 Corinthians 6:16 as follows: "As for us, we are an inner sanctuary of the living God" *(The New Testament, An Expanded Translation* [Grand Rapids: Eerdmans,1980], p. 426).

Second, *be open to the Holy Spirit.* If the Holy Spirit is the One behind change, believers should be ready and willing to change.

Finally, *make sure that procedure follows needs.* To remain spiritually alive, a church must adapt to the needs of people. If society changes, then the church is going to have to be flexible so that it can minister effectively. A church must get rid of the attitude "We've never done it that way before."

GREAT FAITH

Great churches live on the precipice of faith where they can do nothing else but trust God. They are accustomed to the tension of trusting God and accepting the risk that is inseparable from faith.

Although faith is inseparable from risk, it is ironic that Christians generally dislike anything that is risky. Since Ephesians 3:20 says that God "is able to do exceedingly abundantly above all that we ask or think, according to the power that worketh in us," we need to believe Him for that. Hebrews 11 lists heroes of faith. They believed God and took risks. Daniel believed God and went into a lions' den. Abraham believed God when Sarah was too old to have a baby, and God delivered the promised child.

Christianity's approach is not "a bird in the hand is worth two in the bush." Christians should not be afraid of moving ahead with new ideas. A church may have all kinds of great plans, but if it can't trust God to supply the manpower and the money, it will never accomplish much. God never has a problem getting money for what He wants done. It's exciting to see faith work wonders.

SACRIFICE

A spirit of sacrifice is directly related to the previous point. The leadership of an effective church doesn't have to plead for its people to be involved or to give because the congregation's faith enables them to stretch themselves sacrificially. It shouldn't have a need for gimmicks, drives, or other artificial means of stimulating people to do what they ought to do. The church is to be characterized by a sacrificial spirit of giving, like that of the Macedonians, who showed their love by giving "beyond their ability" (2 Cor. 8:3; NASB). Paul commended the Philippian church for meeting his needs (Phil. 4:10, 14-16). He didn't have to ask them for anything because their love abounded to him in such a generous and tangible way.

WORSHIP

What ultimately makes a church great is its emphasis on worshiping God. A church can emphasize many things that are good. Some churches' entire orientation is around their theological distinctives. They claim to be the only ones who believe a certain way. Sometimes those distinctives are part of their title. They might be the First Sovereign, Premillennial, Pretribulational, Antiliberal, Proconservative, Uncompromising Church of Oak Street. Strong biblical theology is important, but there's more to the church than that.

When a church sets its complete focus on God and does everything it can to honor Him, it has a base for uncompromising integrity. It doesn't matter what makes the program or the church unique, or what theological distinctive is emphasized. What matters is what God requires.

May these twelve marks of an effective church be the basis for every Christian church that God may be fully honored.

Chapter 9

The Calling of the Church*

Grace Community Church has been the subject of much discussion throughout the years. Magazines have written articles about us. Doctoral students have written their theses on our church. Reports have tried to analyze us. We have been dissected, examined, studied, labeled, categorized, scrutinized, copied, blessed, cursed, endowed, publicized, and even sued. What has caused all that attention?

The key to understanding Grace Church is not to analyze its pastors, staff, programs, methods, elders, congregation, growth, size, or location. All those things are essential to what it is, but they are not the key. The issue is revealed in our very name, Grace Community *Church*. The world has such a difficult time understanding us because it doesn't understand what a church is. The term *church* sets us apart from all other human institutions. We are the church of the Lord Jesus Christ, purchased with His own blood. No other institution in the world owes its existence to such a fact.

Unfortunately the word *church* has lost its profound richness. Now it brings to mind a building of bricks and mortar on some corner. Or maybe we think of the church as an institutional hierarchy of religious orders. We need to go beyond the English to the Greek word.

"Church" is a translation of the Greek word *ekklēsia*. The term is derived from the verb root *kaleō*, which means "to call." That is a

*From tape GC 1284.

good definition for the church: We are the *called*. In fact, Romans 8:28 wonderfully defines the assembly of believers as "the called according to his purpose." We are a group summoned together by God for His purpose. We are not a human organization. We are not the result of man's ingenuity or power. We were not built by good, religious people. Rather, we have been called by God into existence.

That God calls believers is emphasized throughout the New Testament:

> *Romans 1:6-7*—Paul, writing to the church at Rome, said, "Among whom are ye also the called of Jesus Christ; to all that be in Rome, beloved of God, called to be saints."
>
> *1 Corinthians 1:2*—"Unto the church of God which is at Corinth, to them that are sanctified in Christ Jesus, called to be saints, with all that in every place shall call upon the name of Jesus Christ, our Lord."
>
> *1 Corinthians 1:26*—"For ye see your calling, brethren." Paul then went on to describe the character of those who make up the church.
>
> *Ephesians 4:1-4*—"Walk worthy of the vocation to which ye are called. . . . Ye are called in one hope of your calling."
>
> *1 Thessalonians 2:12*—"Walk worthy of God, who hath called you unto his kingdom and glory."
>
> *2 Timothy 1:9*—"[God] hath saved us, and called us with an holy calling, not according to our works but according to his own purpose and grace."
>
> *1 Peter 5:10*—"The God of all grace . . . who hath called us unto his eternal glory by Christ Jesus."

The entire church has been called into existence by God Himself. That helps to explain the church's overall success and blessing. However, the weaknesses and failures of the church are explained by the fact that God has chosen to work through human agents. When we succeed it is because of Him, not us. When we fail it is because of us, not Him. The main goal of the church is to let God work and build His kingdom as we obediently submit to His Word and Spirit. Ephesians 1 helps us to understand the extent of what it means to be called.

Called *Before:* Election

He hath chosen us in him before the foundation of the world . . . having predestinated us unto the adoption of sons by Jesus Christ to himself according to the good pleasure of his will . . . being predestinated according to the purpose of him who worketh all things after the counsel of his own will (Eph. 1:4-5, 11).

The church is not something that accidentally came into being. It is the result of God's predetermined, sovereign call.

The apostle Paul reiterates God's election in 2 Timothy 1:9: "[God has] saved us, and called us with an holy calling, not according to our works, but according to His own purpose and grace, which was given us in Christ Jesus before the world began."

In the hymn "The Inner Life" an anonymous lyricist wrote, "I sought the Lord and afterwards I knew, He moved my soul to seek Him, seeking me. It was not I that found, O Savior true. No, I was found by Thee." The church is fulfilling a predetermined destiny, a calling from beyond space and time. In God's mind, there is no time frame. Everything is an immediate eternal present. The church was as real to Him before the world began as it is now.

Before I came to Grace Church, I was being considered as a pastoral candidate for a large, well-known church. However, the leaders there concluded that I was too young and inexperienced for their church. Although I was open to wherever the Lord wanted me to go, I was disappointed. But God's plan wasn't for me to be there. Before the foundation of the world, God knew He would use Grace Church to redeem souls and that I would be part of that process. Every time I hear about someone being saved because of our church, I am thrilled by the realization that that is one more fulfillment of God's predestined plan.

CALLED OUT: REDEMPTION

In [Christ] we have redemption through his blood, the forgiveness of sins, according to the riches of his grace . . . in whom ye also trusted, after ye heard the word of truth, the gospel of your salvation; in whom also after ye believed, ye were sealed with that Holy Spirit of promise (Eph. 1:7, 13).

Paul identifies the church as those who have been graciously redeemed and forgiven. God has "delivered us from the power of darkness, and hath translated us into the kingdom of his dear Son" (Col. 1:13). We have been called out of sin, death, and the world's system into life (Rom. 6:8-11; 1 John 2:15-17). We are a redeemed community, born again by the Spirit of God.

Unredeemed people who assemble under a religious banner with the title of "church" are not part of the church that Christ is building. There are so-called churches all over the world that appear to be alive but are dead (Rev. 3:1). Rather than being called out from the world, they are part of it—in spite of their religious exercises.

Having a church membership that is truly saved is so important to me that I preached on that subject the first Sunday I pastored at Grace Church. My text was Matthew 7:21-23: "Not every one that saith unto me, Lord, Lord, shall enter into the kingdom of heaven. . . . Many will say to Me in that day, Lord, Lord, have we not prophesied in thy name? . . . And then will I profess unto them, I never knew you; depart from me." Perhaps you think I should have waited before I hit them between the eyes with a message like that! But I was concerned that some people there thought they were part of the church but really weren't. A church needs to understand from the very beginning what it is so that it can know what direction it should be going. As a result of that confrontive sermon, several couples left the church, and we discovered that at least one elder was not a Christian.

The title of that sermon was "How to Play Church." In Luke 6:46 Jesus says, "Why call ye me, Lord, Lord, and do not the things which I say?" Reminiscent of that verse is a painting in the cathedral of Lübeck, Germany, titled "The Lament of Jesus Christ Against the Ungrateful World." The corresponding text reads,

> You call Me master, and obey Me not;
> You call Me light, and see Me not;
> You call Me the way, and walk Me not;
> You call Me life, and live Me not;
> You call Me wise, and follow Me not;
> You call Me fair, and love Me not;
> You call Me rich, and ask Me not;
> You call Me eternal, and seek Me not.
> If I condemn thee, blame Me not.

I read about an old pastor who had been forced to retire because years of preaching had caused his voice to crack. Although a humble man, he was invited to a high-society luncheon by a friend. The person heading up the luncheon requested a famous actor who was present to recite something for the guests. Agreeing to do so, he asked if anyone had a specific request. The old pastor thought for a moment and said, "How about the Twenty-Third Psalm?" The actor replied, "That's an unusual request, but I happen to know it. I'll do it on one condition, though: you recite it after me." The old pastor hadn't bargained for that, but for the sake of the Lord, he agreed. The actor stood up and recited the Twenty-Third Psalm with the great intonation of his lyrical voice. When he finished, everyone applauded. The old pastor then stood up and went through the psalm in his humble way with a crackling voice. When he was done, there was not a dry eye in the room. Sensing the emotion of the moment, the actor stood up and said, "You clapped for me, but you wept for him. The difference is obvious: I know the psalm, but he knows the Shepherd."

If there's any one thing a church must be, it is an assembly of people who know the Shepherd. Anything less is not a church.

CALLED FROM: SANCTIFICATION

That we should be holy and without blame before him (Eph. 1:4).

Christians have been called from the world to pursue holiness. First Peter 1:16 says, "Be ye holy; for I am holy." We are called to be separated from the world. We are to be uncompromising. The Spirit has instructed us to keep ourselves "unspotted from the world" (James 1:27). The Lord desires a church "not having spot, or wrinkle, or any such thing; but that it should be holy and without blemish" (Eph. 5:27). In 2 Corinthians 11:2 Paul expresses his desire to present the church "as a chaste virgin to Christ." God has called us to holiness, Christlikeness, and virtue.

Christians are to manifest the holiness of our heavenly Father, our Savior, and the Spirit who dwells within us. We are to avoid complicity with the world (2 Cor. 6:17). We are not to practice the deeds of the flesh (Gal. 5:16-25; Col. 3:5). First John 2:15 warns us not to love the world's system, which is opposed to God. We have been called to holy lives. Therefore as a church we must emphasize the importance of humility, confession of sin, church discipline, and worship so that we might live in reverential fear of Him.

In 1 Thessalonians 5:23-24 Paul calls us to live holy lives with these words: "The very God of peace sanctify you wholly; and I pray God your whole spirit and soul and body be preserved blameless unto the coming of our Lord Jesus Christ. Faithful is he that calleth you, who also will do it." In our pursuit of holiness, we must first recognize the holiness of God and Christ to fear them. In the gospel accounts people often feared Jesus when His glory and holiness were revealed to them (Mark 9:5-6; Luke 5:8).

We are uniquely called according to God's purpose, and part of that purpose is to be holy.

CALLED TO: IDENTIFICATION

He hath chosen us in him . . . that we should be holy and without blame before him, in love having predestinated us unto the adoption of sons by Jesus Christ to himself. . . . He hath made us accepted in the Beloved (Eph. 1:4-6).

The prepositional phrases "in him," "before him," "to himself," and "in the Beloved" reveal that Christians are intimately identified with God and Christ. The church is unique. It is not a religious organization of people committed to a certain set of rules or trained in a certain mode of religion. We are in Christ and in God.

1 Thessalonians 1:1—This epistle begins, "Paul, and Silvanus, and Timothy, unto the church of the Thessalonians which is in God, the Father, and in the Lord Jesus Christ." The church is called to an intimate identification with God Himself.

1 John 1:3—Our personal union with God is a marvelous fellowship. According to John, "Our fellowship is with the Father, and with His Son, Jesus Christ." We are in an intertrinitarian fellowship.

John 17:22—Before His arrest, Jesus prays that believers might be one with Him as He and the Father are one.

1 Corinthians 6:17—"He that is joined unto the Lord is one spirit."

Romans 8:14-17—Christians have become intimately related to God, having been adopted as His sons. That makes us joint heirs with Christ. The church isn't a group that you join by signing your name. It isn't merely a society committed to a system of teaching.

Romans 6:4-5—When we are saved, we enter into a personal relationship with the living God through Jesus Christ. We are identified with Christ in His death and raised with Him in His resurrection so that we might "walk in newness of life" (v. 4).

Galatians 2:20—Paul said, "I am crucified with Christ: nevertheless I live; yet not I, but Christ liveth in me." That is a clear statement of the believer's spiritual union with Christ. I am not conscious of where John MacArthur ends and Jesus Christ begins. (But when I sin, I know I am responsible!) It should be natural for you to see God at work in your life, sensing His power, experiencing His answers to your prayers, following His guidance, and being refreshed by His comfort.

We don't believe God is a cosmic ogre waiting to step on us if we break one of His rules. Rather, we have an intimate love relationship with Him. We are called to a sweet intimacy with Jesus Christ—a personal, living relationship with God.

CALLED *UNDER:* REVELATION

In whom we have redemption through his blood, the forgiveness of sins, according to the riches of his grace, in which he hath abounded toward us in all wisdom and prudence, having made known unto us the mystery of his will (Eph. 1:7-9).

God has filled us in on great spiritual truths concerning life, death, God, man, and eternity. He also has given us prudence, which is practical wisdom concerning earthly things, such as solving problems.

Christians are called to submit to the Word of God—we don't chart our own course. When we meet together to plan, pray, and serve the Lord, one thing should be central in our minds: What does the Word of God say about the matter? That should be the focus of everything we do.

When I came to Grace Church, my candidating sermon was an exposition of Romans 7. Because I had a tremendous burden to explain that difficult chapter and was oblivious to all else, I spoke for one hour and thirty-five minutes. (My wife said, "Well, there goes that church. And if the word gets out, you'll never get any other church either!" Afterward, some of the people came up and said, "That's what we want—but could you shorten it a little bit?") One of the elders said, "We are ready to serve. We want to know what God wants us to do." That has been the commitment of Grace Church throughout its history. I discovered in those first few days that the people had a mind to submit to the authority of God's Word. Since that time the motto of the church has been "perfecting of the saints to do the work of the ministry" (Eph. 4:12).

Christians mature through the study and application of Scripture. The job of church leaders is to equip people with "the sword of the Spirit, which is the word of God" (Eph. 6:17). That means more than merely owning a Bible; rather, our people need to understand the Bible so they can use it as a weapon for good.

Called *With:* Unification

That in the dispensation of the fullness of times he might gather together in one all things in Christ (Eph. 1:10).

The ultimate purpose of God is to gather all things together at the completion of redemptive history. The church is the symbol of that now. We are called to be one in the family of God. I grew up in a day when spiritual isolation was common. Everyone kept his spirituality to himself. It was something you didn't talk about. Rather, you smiled the Christian smile, carried the zipper Bible, and went to Sunday school. People didn't let anything out or anyone into their inner selves. Fellowship for most Christians in that era was little more than red punch and stale cookies and ladies serving doughnuts and coffee! There was little depth to it. But we have been called into a marvelous fellowship of unity.

In Philippians 2:2 Paul says that Christians should be "of the same mind, maintaining the same love, united in spirit, intent on one purpose" (NASB). Our love for others must be based in humility. That's why Paul said, "Look not every man on his own things, but every man also on the things of others" (v. 4), which was beautifully exemplified by Christ, who humbled Himself (vv. 5-8). To achieve unity we must look out for one another, not just ourselves. That's why I don't preach a "self-help gospel," which says, "You're all right; think positive; be somebody." Show me a church where that kind of message is preached, and I'll show you a church that doesn't know the meaning of fellowship because everyone's there for himself—not for the benefit of anyone else. On the other hand, show me a church where they preach humility, and I'll show you a church where people can love each other.

Called Unto: Glorification

In whom also we have obtained an inheritance (Eph. 1:11).

Peter described our inheritance as being that which is "incorruptible, and undefiled, and that fadeth not away, reserved in heaven for you" (1 Pet. 1:4). Christians are committed to glorification. Our focus is future. We are not citizens of this world. Philippians 3:20 says, "Our citizenship is in heaven." We're not earthbound, tied to the evil world's system. We have been made heirs of a boundless, eternal inheritance. That's why I don't preach explicitly political or social messages that have only temporal relevance.

Colossians 3:1-2 says, "If ye, then, be risen with Christ, seek those things which are above . . . Set your affection on things above, not on things on the earth." We look for Jesus to return and His kingdom to be fully established. Consequently, we're not investing our lives and all our assets in this passing world. In the words of Hebrews 11, we look "for a city . . . whose builder and maker is God" (v. 10).

Called For: Proclamation

To the praise of his glory (Eph. 1:12).

We have been called to proclaim the glory of God's grace. The world should look at us and say, "Look at that group of people. What a gracious God they have!" God should be glorified in how we live and in what we say. In a sense we proclaim God's glory to Him and His holy angels, as well as to the world about us. We have been redeemed for His glory. Consequently, the world cannot understand us unless it understands the glory of God, for we are its primary manifestation. More than anything else, the glory of God has been the focus of my own heart, not to mention the greatest theme in the Bible. The glory of God serves as the most important checkpoint in my life. I ask myself only one question when I come to a crossroad: Will my decision glorify God? The church was established to be to the praise of His glory. Our Lord put it this way: "Let your light so shine before men, that they may see your good works, and glorify your Father, who is in heaven" (Matt. 5:16).

Chapter 10

The Lord's Work
in the Lord's Way[*]

Some Scriptures don't appear to have much spiritual value at first
glance. But a thorough study can often uncover valuable insights.
Much of 1 Corinthians 16 is that way:

> I will come unto you, when I shall pass through Macedonia; for I do
> pass through Macedonia. And it may be that I will abide, yea, and
> winter with you, that ye may bring me on my journey wherever I
> go. For I will not see you now by the way; but I trust to tarry a while
> with you, if the Lord permit. But I will tarry at Ephesus until Pente-
> cost. For a great door, and effectual, is opened unto me, and there
> are many adversaries. Now if Timothy come, see that he may be
> with you without fear; for he worketh the work of the Lord, as I also
> do. Let no man, therefore, despise him, but conduct him forth in
> peace, that he may come unto me; for I look for him with the breth-
> ren. As touching our brother Apollos, I greatly desired him to come
> unto you with the brethren, but his will was not at all to come at
> this time; but he will come when he shall have a convenient time
> (vv. 5-12).

It sounds as if Paul was being indefinite: "I'm going here; I might
go there. If Timothy arrives, take care of him. I wanted Apollos to
come, but he didn't want to." You might wonder how anyone could

* From tapes GC 1886-1887.

benefit from such seemingly insignificant material. The key to the text is the phrase "the work of the Lord." It first appears in verse 58 of chapter 15: "Therefore, my beloved brethren, be ye steadfast, unmovable, always abounding in the work of the Lord." And 16:10 says, "If Timothy come, see that he may be with you without fear; for he worketh the work of the Lord, as I also do." That helps reveal what Paul was talking about in the verses in between—the work of the Lord. He was saying, "You ought to be always abounding in the work of the Lord as Timothy and I are."

Paul said that those who do the Lord's work ought to be "unmovable, always abounding" in it. We ought to be overdoing it! When someone comes up to you and says, "You're doing too much," perhaps you're properly applying 1 Corinthians 15:58. Doing the work of the Lord is a vital responsibility.

What is the Lord's work?

To answer that question, you have to find out what work the Lord did when He was on earth. He basically did two things: He evangelized and He edified. Luke 19:10 says, "The Son of man is come to seek and to save that which was lost." That's evangelism. Acts 1:2-3 says, "Until the day in which [Jesus] was taken up [into heaven, He was] speaking of the things pertaining to the kingdom of God." That refers to the edification of Christ's disciples.

The work of the Lord is never described in the Bible as being easy. The words "work" and "labor" in verse 58 carry the idea of working to the point of exhaustion. Commentator G. Campbell Morgan said that Paul had in mind the "kind of toil that has in it the red blood of sacrifice, that kind of toil that wears and weakens by the way" (*The Corinthian Letters of Paul* [Old Tappan, N.J.: Revell, 1946], p. 207). Paul said this about Epaphroditus: "For the work of Christ, he was near unto death" (Phil. 2:30). That young man nearly worked himself to death. He is a good example of someone who was always abounding in the work of the Lord.

"Your labor is not in vain" when you abound in the Lord's work (v. 58). It won't be empty, pointless, useless, or unproductive. Rather, it will make a difference and produce fruit.

Many people are very busy around the church, but I'm not sure they're doing the Lord's work of evangelism and edification.

Christians have been called to do the Lord's work in the Lord's way. Recognizing that privilege ought to thrill us. Do you realize that the Almighty God, the ruler of heaven and earth, has said, "Would you be My personal envoy, taking My message to people around the world for as long as you live?" William Barclay has correctly said, "It is not the man who glorifies the work but the work which glorifies the man. There is no dignity like the dignity of a great task" *(The Letter to the Corinthians* [Philadelphia: Westminster, 1975], p. 165).

Paul, describing his work and that of Timothy and Apollos, gives us seven practical principles for doing the Lord's work as He wants it done.

A VISION FOR THE FUTURE

Anyone committed to the Lord's work and motivated to reach others will see many needs that haven't been met yet. So he will plan how to meet them. Such a person has a visionary perspective. He's never satisfied with what is already being done. He focuses on what isn't being done, and that's why he plans ahead, looking for new worlds to conquer. He faces the reality of unmet opportunity, waiting for new doors to open.

In 1 Corinthians 16:5 Paul says, "I will come unto you, when I shall pass through Macedonia; for I do pass through Macedonia." Apparently Paul wrote 1 Corinthians at the end of a three-year stay in the city of Ephesus. Timothy delivered the letter. According to 2 Corinthians 1:15-16, Paul had originally planned to follow Timothy to Corinth, then go to Macedonia, and return to Corinth. Although he had a plan, he changed it, deciding first to head straight to Macedonia, then to Corinth, and finally to Jerusalem.

In 1 Corinthians 4:18-19 Paul says, "Now some are puffed up [conceited], as though I would not come to you. But I will come to you shortly, if the Lord will." Paul wanted to go to the Corinthian church because it was struggling with internal problems. In verse 6 of chapter 16, he says in essence, "I've got to come and stay for the winter. Then you can give me some supplies so that I can continue on from there." Paul was planning ahead. He had a vision for what he needed to do in Macedonia and Corinth before returning to Jerusalem.

Romans 15 provides a glimpse of Paul's visionary strategizing. He wrote to the Roman Christians, saying, "Whenever I take my journey into Spain, I will come to you. . . . When, therefore, I have performed this, and have sealed to them this fruit, I will come by you into Spain" (vv. 24, 28). Paul had set his sights on Spain because no missionary had ever been there. Spain was in a blaze of glory at that time as part of the Roman Empire. Some of the greatest writers and orators were living in Spain. In fact, the great Stoic philosopher Seneca, who became the tutor of Nero and prime minister of the Roman Empire, was an influential man in Spain. No doubt Paul was excited about the impact that the gospel would have on such a place.

It is important to prepare for the opportunities God gives you. Some people say, "There is a lot to do in the future." But often they do nothing to get ready.

Nehemiah didn't approach King Artaxerxes and say, "I would like a ministry. Could you please find something for me to do with my people?" Instead he said, "My people have a problem: they need their city and its wall rebuilt. I want to do it and have already figured out how it can be done. I'm just waiting for your permission now." The king allowed Nehemiah to accomplish his plans.

If you're going to have a vision for the future, you need to strategize in the present to make the future a reality whenever God presents the opportunity. One reason some people never enter the ministry they are waiting for is that they have not planned for it. We also have to be working to prove ourselves useful in the present so that we're ready when the opportunity presents itself. We need to prove ourselves worthy.

William Carey, the great pioneer of modern missions, made and repaired shoes in England. While he worked at his trade, he wept and prayed over a map of the world that he kept before him in his shop. After years of studying and strategizing, he was sent by God to work in India. He opened that nation to the gospel for every missionary who's gone there since. God used a man with a vision for the future who was faithful in the present and proved himself capable.

What are you planning to do? Where's your vision? There's a whole world without God. What's your strategy to reach someone for Christ? To develop your spiritual gifts? To use your ministry to its fullest potential? If you aimlessly float from day to day, saying, "I'm just waiting for God to give me something to do," you'll never be given anything. However, if you're doing the Lord's work in the Lord's way, you will have a vision for the future.

A SENSE OF FLEXIBILITY

The future may not come together the way you think it will, so you've got to be flexible. Some people say, "I know exactly what God wants me to do. I have such-and-such a gift and such-and-such a talent; therefore, I should be doing this. And until such-and-such happens and I find something that exactly fits my list of expectations, I'm not going to do anything." That's poor reasoning in following God's will.

In 1 Corinthians 16:6-7 Paul says, "It may be that I will abide, yea, and winter with you, that ye may bring me on my journey wherever I go. For I will not see you now by the way; but I trust to tarry a while with you, if the Lord permit." Paul had the unsettled attitude of an adventurer: "When I come to see you, I think I might stay for the winter. When I'm done, I might go somewhere else. I'm not too sure, but I am going to stay if the Lord permits." I like Paul's style of planning. He had wonderful plans, but he remained flexible and gave God the right to change them midstream.

The Corinthians had accused Paul of being fickle. In response Paul wrote, "I was minded to come unto you before . . . and to pass by you into Macedonia, and to come again out of Macedonia unto you, and of you to be brought on my way toward Judea. When I, therefore, was thus minded, did I use lightness? Or the things that I purpose, do I purpose according to the flesh, that with me there should be yea, yea, and nay, nay?" (2 Cor. 1:15-17). In other words, "When my plans kept changing, was I being fickle? No, I did the best I could under the circumstances and needed to be ready to change my mind."

As we discovered previously, Paul learned flexibility early in his ministry. He had been to Phrygia and Galatia and was planning to go through the major cities of Asia Minor: Ephesus, Laodicea, Pergamum, Smyrna, Thyatira, Sardis, and Philadelphia. I'm sure he had his strategy all mapped out. However, look what happened: "When they had gone throughout Phrygia and the region of Galatia, [they] were forbidden by the Holy Spirit to preach the word in Asia" (Acts 16:6). Paul and his companions decided, "If we can't go south, we must go north. Let's go to Bithynia." But verse 7 says that "the Spirit allowed them not." Their only option was to go west.

They kept walking until they came to Troas, where "a vision appeared to Paul in the night: there stood a man of Macedonia, beseeching him, and saying, Come over into Macedonia and help us. And after he had seen the vision, immediately we endeavored to go into Macedonia, assuredly gathering that the Lord had called us to preach the gospel unto them" (vv. 9-10). What flexibility! They had their plans, and even though they were scuttled, they kept on moving. If you've ever tried to steer a car that's standing still, you know it's very difficult. But once it gets rolling, it's much easier to maneuver.

Did you know that David Livingstone, the world-renowned explorer and missionary to Africa, had originally set his heart on going to China? He was disappointed that he didn't get there, until he realized God's will was for him to go elsewhere. Livingstone ended up doing for Africa what Carey did for India: he opened it up to the missionaries who would follow him.

A COMMITMENT TO THOROUGHNESS

The work of the Lord must not be done superficially. In verse 6 Paul says, "It may be that I will abide, yea, and winter with you." Paul apparently did end up spending the winter with the Corinthians. He probably wrote his first letter to them in the spring from Ephesus, where he stayed until June. Then he went on to be with the Corinthians and spent the three winter months there. In verse 7 Paul says, "I trust to tarry a while with you." In other words, "I don't want to just pass through. I want to stay with you a while." Paul had a commitment to thoroughness in the ministry.

Our Lord said, "Go therefore and make disciples of all the nations . . . teaching them to observe all that I commanded you" (Matt. 28:19-20; NASB). You can't teach someone to follow everything that God has commanded without investing your life in that person. Discipling can't be done superficially. You can't make disciples by passing out tracts and beating it out of town! There's more to it than that.

Paul had no intention of making a quick stop in Corinth. He knew the needs were great, as evidenced by the contents of 1 Corinthians. He had spent eighteen months there the first time and now wanted to spend at least another winter there. He spent three years ministering in Ephesus. He went to Galatia on his first, second, and third missionary journeys because he wanted to accomplish a thorough work there. I'm in the pastorate because that's where I believe I can do the most thorough work. I traveled on the preaching circuit for two-and-a-half years before coming to Grace, and I spoke thirty-five to forty times a month. I'd present a church with biblical truth from one to four days and then leave town to go on to another church. That frustrated me because my messages were usually in the context of evangelistic meetings and were limited to topics such as prophecy, the Holy Spirit, and worldliness. Then Grace Church came into my life. The Lord fulfilled the desire of my heart to do something that was more thorough.

In Colossians 1:27-28 Paul states that God has made "known what is the riches of the glory of this mystery among the Gentiles, which is Christ in you, the hope of glory; whom we preach, warning every man, and teaching every man in all wisdom, that we may present every man perfect in Christ Jesus." Paul was saying, "We want to teach everything to everyone all the time, so that they may become mature." That's a commitment to thoroughness!

In praying to the Father, Jesus reported that He had done the work that the Father had given Him to do (John 17:4, 8). Jesus was thorough. His training of the twelve took Him three years.

As we prepare to serve Christ as His ambassadors, we must do so with a commitment to excellence. We ought to be doing it to the limit of our capacity. Then our labor will not be in vain.

A Commitment to Present Service

There are plenty of dreamers dreaming what they will do, but far fewer doers doing what they should do. If you want God to use you in the future, you need to be ministering in the present. Young men in seminary often have great expectations about the ministry they want to be part of. But what are they doing now? The present is the proving ground for the future. I'll never forget talking to a seminary student who was going to graduate in a month. He said, "I finished four years of seminary and have a great deal of information in my head. I'm going to be pastoring a church, but I don't have any idea of what's required of me!" A seminarian can't expect to be dropped out of heaven as a man with all the answers. He has to be a proved commodity.

I get letters almost every day from churches and organizations wanting us to recommend people for ministry. They almost always request someone who has proved to be effective. I can't say I blame them.

The Lord addressed the church at Philadelphia, by saying He was the One who "openeth, and no man shutteth; and shutteth, and no man openeth. . . . I have set before thee an open door, and no man can shut it" (Rev. 3:7-8). That church was very different from the dead church at Laodicea, which the Lord addressed next. Perhaps one of the things that can turn a Philadelphia into a Laodicea is a refusal to go through open doors.

An Acceptance of Opposition As a Challenge

If you find a place that doesn't have any problems, then you're not needed there. Accept opposition as a challenge. Paul said, "I will tarry at Ephesus until Pentecost. For a great door, and effectual, is opened unto me, and there are many adversaries" (1 Cor. 16:9). That would seem to be a good reason not to stay—but not to Paul! G. Campbell Morgan once said that if you have no opposition in the place you are serving, then you're serving in the wrong place *(The Corinthian Letters of Paul* [Old Tappan, N.J.: Revell, 1946], p. 213).

In effect Paul was saying, "I have to stay in Ephesus because I can't leave the troops alone; there's too much opposition here!" The city of Ephesus was rough. The temple of Diana was the center of organized idolatry characterized by sexual perversion involving priestesses who were prostitutes. In addition, there were certain Jewish exorcists who claimed to cast out demons. There was prejudice, superstition, racism, sexual vice, religious animosity, paganism, idolatry—everything that exists in any city in the world today. Most people would say, "I'm looking for a place that is somewhat tamer," but Paul accepted it as a challenge.

Paul went to Ephesus and taught the Word of God every day for more than two years (Acts 19:8-10). It is likely that those who were saved there were the ones who founded the other churches of Asia Minor mentioned in Revelation 2-3. Those who had practiced magical arts publicly burned their books (Acts 19:19), and so many people stopped buying idols of the goddess Diana that the craftsmen who made them angrily stirred up a demonstration (vv. 23-41). The gospel made quite an impact on Ephesus.

Paul looked back on the battle in Ephesus in 2 Corinthians 1: "We should like you, our brothers, to know something of what we went through in Asia. At that time we were completely overwhelmed; the burden was more than we could bear; in fact we told ourselves that this was the end. Yet we believe now that we had this experience of coming to the end of our tether that we might learn to trust, not in ourselves, but in God who can raise the dead" (vv. 8-9, Phillips). When you get into a desperate situation like that, you do not trust yourself. You turn to God. That's when His power begins to flow and the enemies begin to drop one by one!

In 2 Corinthians 4:10 Paul says, "Every day we experience something of the death of Jesus, so that we may also know the power of the life of Jesus in these bodies of ours" (Phillips). In other words, "We face death every day. In such severe opposition, where we have no resources and must depend on God, we see the power of Christ flow." That's the excitement and the adventure of the ministry— charging into battle and confronting opposition in the power of Christ. That's when God gives us the victory. Take up the challenge and find a difficult place to minister!

John Paton accepted an immense challenge. While he was a student at a Bible college in London, God called him to go to the cannibal-infested New Hebrides islands in the South Pacific. Some of us might have said, "Lord, You've got the wrong guy! Are You sure my gifts are fit for that? And besides, I graduated—I can make it in the ministry. No sense in my being someone's lunch after all the effort I've put in. I know a Bible college dropout who will never make it in the ministry. Send him there; they'll eat him and who will know? The guy will go down in history as having died a hero!"

But John Paton didn't argue with God. From the moment he and his wife set up a little hut on the beach, the Lord miraculously preserved them. Later, when the chief of the tribe in that area was converted to Christ, he asked John who the army was that surrounded his hut every night. God's holy angels had stood guard. After a short time, his wife gave birth to a baby, and both she and the baby died in childbirth. He was forced to sleep on the graves to keep the cannibals from digging up the bodies and eating them. In spite of the great challenge, he decided to stay. The adversaries were many, but that's where God wanted him.

A TEAM SPIRIT

Paul was a team-oriented leader. He didn't try to be a lone superstar. He depended on other people. In 1 Corinthians 16:10 he says, "Now if Timothy come, see that he may be with you without fear." According to 1 Corinthians 4:17 Paul was sending Timothy to Corinth, perhaps with this letter. He warned the proud and self-willed Corinthians not to intimidate Timothy, saying, "He worketh the work of the Lord, as I also do. Let no man, therefore, despise him, but conduct him forth in peace, that he may come unto me; for I look for him with the brethren" (16:10-11). Paul asked the Corinthians to respect his emissary, whom he hoped would bring back a good report. Even though Timothy was Paul's son in the faith (1 Tim. 1:2), Paul considered them equals. He was quick to stand up for his fellow worker. Even though Paul was a leader among leaders, he recognized that he was simply a co-worker in God's service. He had a great sense of teamwork.

When we see Paul doing the Lord's work, we always see him teamed with Silas, Barnabas, Luke, Aristarchus, Mark, or Timothy. One who does the Lord's work in the Lord's way realizes that he's just part of the fellowship and that it's his job to encourage and edify others.

God calls some people to lead and others to serve. Sometimes those who serve do so for their entire ministry. Other times they serve for a period of apprenticeship, and then the Lord calls them to lead on their own. But that sense of teamwork must be retained. Maybe we're called to support someone else or to lead on our own. Whatever it is, Jesus said to "love one another. By this shall all men know that ye are my disciples" (John 13:34-35). When the world sees the church working together as a team, they witness the validity of our faith.

A SENSITIVITY TO THE SPIRIT'S LEADING IN OTHERS

We should be sensitive to the Spirit's leading in others, as Paul was in the ministry of Apollos: "As touching our brother Apollos, I greatly desired him to come unto you with the brethren" (1 Cor. 16:12). Paul wanted Apollos to go along with Timothy to Corinth, apparently to straighten out the divisions that had centered on Paul and

Apollos in the church (1 Cor. 1:11-12). However, "His will was not at all to come at this time; but he will come when he shall have a convenient time" (16:12). Apollos said, "No, Paul, I can't go now. I'm busy with some other ministries." Note that Paul did not respond, "Don't you realize who the apostle to the Gentiles is? Don't you know who you are talking to? I am Paul, the one whom Christ appeared to on the road to Damascus!"

You can't force people to do the work of the Lord. An effective leader has to be sensitive to what God is saying to other members on the team. Don't dominate the team. Rather, patiently let the Spirit of God generate ministries among the rest.

May it be that all of us are always involved in the Lord's work. Then when the Lord Jesus comes to reward each one, He will be able to say, "Well done, good and faithful servant. You have fulfilled the work I gave you to do."

PART THREE

Qualities of an Excellent Servant

The king of the Gentiles lord it over them; and those who have authority over them are called "Benefactors." But not so with you, but let him who is the greatest among you become as the youngest, and the leader as the servant.

Luke 22:25-26; NASB

Shepherd the flock of God among you, exercising oversight not under compulsion, but voluntarily, according to the will of God; and not for sordid gain, but with eagerness.

1 Peter 5:2; NASB

Chapter 11

Understanding the Seducing Spirit*

The first five verses of 1 Timothy 4 are a stern warning about apostates. In verse 6 Paul says to Timothy, "If thou put the brethren in remembrance of these things, thou shalt be a good minister of Jesus Christ." To be an excellent servant of Christ, it is important that we have a good understanding of apostasy.

Second Chronicles 25 records the account of Amaziah, king of Judah. He was the son of Joash and the father of Uzziah, who was king during the time of Isaiah the prophet. Amaziah reigned in Jerusalem twenty-nine years. Verse 2 says, "He did that which was right in the sight of the Lord, but not with a perfect heart." He functioned in accord with the religion of Israel on the outside. He understood it and behaved by its ethics, but not with a willing heart. He practiced a heartless, external religion, not having a personal relationship with the living God. So he was soon lured into idolatry and began to worship the gods of Edom, to which he bowed down and burned incense (v. 14). His life ended tragically—he was murdered by his own people after turning away from the Lord (v. 27).

Departing from the faith happens today just as it did in the Old Testament and in the church at Ephesus, where Timothy was when Paul wrote this epistle. There are always people who understand the faith intellectually and behave according to the revelation of God but

*From tape GC 54-29.

have no heart for living to please God. Hebrews 3:12 says that those who depart from God demonstrate an unbelieving heart.

Paul states in 1 Timothy 4:1 that some—such as Judas, Demas, or the disciples of John 6 who walked no more with Christ—"shall depart from the faith" (Gk., *aphistēmi*, "to remove yourself from the position you originally occupied"). Apostasy isn't an unintentional departure or a personal struggle with doubt. It is deliberately abandoning truth for erroneous teaching. "The faith" refers specifically to the body of Christian doctrine, not the act of believing. Some will depart from "the faith which was once delivered unto the saints" (Jude 3). People who understand and outwardly affirm Christian doctrine but don't have a heart for God are prime candidates for being seduced by demons away from the faith.

An apostate is not someone who never knew the truth but someone who knew it and rejected it. He may have even been involved in various religious activities. But because he never truly knew God, he was lured away by the siren voices of the demons behind idols and false religious systems.

False religion propagates doctrine energized by seducing spirits. It is the playground of demons. Second Corinthians tells us that Satan and his angels disguise themselves as angels of light and become the purveyors of various religions (11:14-15).

The Lord Himself says in Leviticus 17:7 that whatever men sacrifice to idols is in fact being sacrificed to demons (cf. Deut. 32:17; Pss. 96:5; 106:36-37). In 1 Corinthians 10:20-21 Paul says that those who come to the Lord's Table and then worship at a pagan religious shrine are fellowshiping with both the Lord and demons.

False religious systems and the various idols that accompany them are focal points for demonic activity. We should not naively think that a false religion is simply a collection of misguided ideas. Realize that behind the scenes are fallen angels seducing people from the truth into eternal hell.

The Word of God clearly teaches that apostasy is a demonic seduction, that idol worship is actually worship offered to demons, and that false teachers are the agents of demons. The battle is fought by God and His truth against the devil and his lies. God calls people to Himself through the truth, and Satan tries to lure people away from truth with his hellish lies.

Scripture often exhorts the church to expose false teaching. That kind of confrontation is not popular today. Many churches, in the name of love, want to forget disagreements and avoid being critical at all costs. Nonetheless, there is a biblical mandate to deal with false teaching. The battle lines were drawn in Israel and in the early church, and they must be drawn today too. Like Timothy we must be warned and instructed to understand what is behind false teaching.

The theme of 1 Timothy 4:1-5 is this: "Some shall depart from the faith" (v. 1). Paul warned Timothy to expect apostasy and provided him with six characteristics of apostates so that he could identify and counteract them.

THE PREDICTABILITY OF APOSTATES

We should not be shocked to learn that some people will apostatize. The Spirit of God explicitly says that some will depart from the faith (v. 1).

Paul knew there would be apostates at the church in Ephesus because the Holy Spirit had revealed that fact to him earlier. Long before he had written this epistle to Timothy, Paul addressed the Ephesian elders with these words: "I know this, that after my departing shall grievous wolves enter in among you, not sparing the flock. Also of your own selves shall men arise, speaking perverse things, to draw away disciples after them" (Acts 20:29-30).

Such revelation about apostasy is not unique to the New Testament; the Holy Spirit had been warning about apostasy in the Old Testament as well. Many Scriptures in the Old Testament talk about Israelites (both individually and nationally) departing from the faith. Although many people belonged to the nation of Israel, that didn't mean they all believed in the God of Israel. Consequently, they were not part of the believing remnant of Israel (cf. Rom. 2:28-29). Through centuries of redemptive history the Spirit has indicated that some would depart from the faith (Deut. 13:12-15; 32:15-18; Dan. 8:23-25).

Several other New Testament passages mention those who will depart from the faith in the end times:

> *Matthew 24:5*—The Lord said, "Many shall come in my name, saying, I am Christ; and shall deceive many."
>
> *Mark 13:22*—In the same context Jesus said, "False Christs and false prophets shall rise, and shall show signs and wonders, to seduce, if it were possible, even the elect."
>
> *2 Thessalonians 2:3*—Paul informed us that before Christ comes in glory there will be a massive departure from the faith.
>
> *2 Peter 3:3*—Peter said there will come in the last times scoffers abandoning the faith to pursue their own lusts (cf. Jude 18).
>
> *1 John 2:18-19*—John said forerunners of the Antichrist will depart from the faith, revealing that they were never truly Christians to begin with.

Many people respond but momentarily to biblical truth, like the seed that fell on the rocky ground (Matt. 13:20-21). Because they have no root, no living union with God, they die. There are others whose spiritual pursuits are choked out by the cares of this world and the love of riches. Such people may hang around a while, but when their heart is not given to God, they are seduced away by demonic spirits through the human agency of false teachers.

THE CHRONOLOGY OF APOSTATES

"In the latter times" (1 Tim. 4:1) does not refer to a time in the distant future but to the church age, the time between the first and second comings of Christ. The apostle John said, "Little children, it is the last time" (1 John 2:18). Peter said Christ "was manifest in these last times for you" (1 Pet. 1:20). Hebrews 1:2 declares that God has "in these last days spoken unto us by his Son." Hebrews also states that "in the end of the ages [Christ] appeared to put away sin by the sacrifice of himself" (Heb. 9:26).

Those verses tell us that the last times began when Christ first appeared and initiated the messianic era. He is now building His kingdom in the hearts of men and will return to establish it on earth and then in the eternal state. So we are now living in the last times. It is in this dispensation, or age, that the apostasy Paul was referring to will occur.

THE SOURCE OF APOSTATES

The source of apostasy is demonic. Apostates listen to "seducing spirits" and the teachings of "demons" (1 Tim. 4:1). Paul described the supernatural battle with demonic forces when he said, "We wrestle not against flesh and blood, but against principalities, against powers, against the rulers of the darkness of this world, against spiritual wickedness in high places" (Eph. 6:12).

People with "an evil heart of unbelief [depart] from the living God" (Heb. 3:12) because they are lured away by demon spirits, even though they live under a facade of religion. Such people cannot be wooed by the Spirit of God because of their hardhearted unbelief. They therefore fall prey to Satan and his lies transmitted through his demons.

I often hear parents say, "Our child was raised in a Christian home, but when he went away to college, he was led astray by atheistic professors or religious cult leaders and now denies the faith." Such students aren't the victims of erudite and persuasive professors, religious leaders, or clever writers who subtly propagate falsehoods in textbooks. Ungodly philosophies and false religions are not merely human aberrations; they are the product of Satan himself.

We should be immensely cautious of exposing ourselves or anyone we love to false teaching. Many passages of Scripture warn us of the dangers of false teachers:

> *2 John 7, 10-11*—The apostle John gave us a warning about false teachers and how we should respond to them: "Many deceivers are entered into the world, who confess not that Jesus Christ cometh in the flesh. . . . If there come any unto you, and bring not this doctrine, receive him not into your house, neither bid him Godspeed; for he that biddeth him Godspeed is partaker of his evil deeds." Stay away from false teachers.
>
> *Jude 23*—Anytime you get near people who are under the influence of false teachers, you should yank them out of the fire, so to speak, exercising caution that you yourself don't get burned in the process.
>
> *Deuteronomy 13:12-17*—The Lord warned the nation of Israel about false prophets through Moses, saying, "If thou shalt hear a report in one of thy cities, which the Lord thy God hath given thee to dwell there, saying, Certain men, worthless fellows, are gone out from among you, and have withdrawn the inhabitants of their city, saying, Let us go and serve other gods, which ye have not known, then shalt thou inquire, and make search, and ask diligently; and, behold, if it be truth, and the thing certain, that such abomination is wrought among you, thou shalt surely smite the inhabitants of that city with the edge of the sword, destroying it utterly, and all that is therein, and the cattle thereof, with the edge of the sword. And thou shalt gather all the spoil of it into the midst of the street thereof, and shalt burn with fire the city, and all the spoil thereof every whit, for the Lord thy God, and it shall be an heap forever; it shall not be built again. And there shall cling nothing of the cursed thing to thine hand; that the Lord may turn from the fierceness of his anger, and show upon thee mercy, and have compassion upon thee." We know God is serious about false doctrine since He instructed the Israelites to go to the extreme of burning the city after slaying its inhabitants and cattle so it could never be rebuilt.

The phrase "seducing spirits" in 1 Timothy 4:1 refers to the source of false doctrines—supernatural demonic spirit beings who are fallen angels. "Seducing" is a translation of the Greek term from which we get our word *planet.* It conveys the idea of wandering and is applied to spirits that lead you to wander from the truth by seducing or deceiving you. Whereas the Holy Spirit guides us into truth (John 16:13), these spirits lead people into error. They are the principalities and powers that the church must wrestle against (Eph. 6:11-12).

The history of seducing spirits goes back to the Garden of Eden, where Satan seduced Eve into believing she was being cheated out of the best thing God had (Gen. 3:1-6). He seduced her to disobey God's instruction. Such seductions are chronicled throughout Scripture, all the way to the book of Revelation.

False teachers seduce people with the "doctrines of demons." The world is full of demonic teaching. Anything that contradicts the Word of God is ultimately a teaching from demons. False teaching doesn't come from clever men. It comes from demons. That's why exposing yourself to it is more dangerous than you might think.

Not all demonic teaching looks demonic on the surface, however. Some of it is so subtly disguised that we might not even recognize it as such, unless we look very closely.

THE CHARACTER OF APOSTATES

The doctrines of demons are dispensed through human agents "speaking lies in hypocrisy" (1 Tim. 4:2). Although the source is supernatural, the means of seduction is natural—occurring on the human level. The beginning phrase of verse 2 can best be translated "through the hypocrisy of men that speak lies." Demons may use men and women who appear to be well educated or religious. They may give the impression that their motives are pure and that they desire to help people. But the facade of religion serves only to hide the demonic error. Hypocritical teachers may seem to exalt God, but it is actually Satan whom they exalt. They are deceivers and liars who come masked in religious garb, possibly even teaching at a Christian church or school, or writing a book aimed toward a Christian audience. They find an audience and propagate their hellish doctrines under the direction of seducing spirits.

Some commentators believe the phrase "having their conscience seared with a hot iron" alludes to the ancient practice of branding slaves on their foreheads and therefore implies that such hypocrites are the devil's agents. Although that meaning makes sense, it seems better to regard the phrase as referring to more than just ownership by Satan. The conscience is the part of man that affirms or condemns an action, and thus it controls behavior. False teachers can practice their hypocrisy day after day because their consciences have been scarred beyond the ability to discern right and wrong. They have lost their sensitivity to truth and their integrity.

The Greek word for "seared" (*kausteriazō*) is the medical term Hippocrates used for the cauterizing process—the searing of body tissue or blood vessels with heat. False teachers have been scarred to the point where they can carry on their hypocritical lies with no compunctions.

I am very concerned about my responsibility to speak the truth of God. I regularly pray that every time I teach God's Word I would not utter anything that is untrue. My conscience demands that I deal with truth carefully because it is God's truth and men's souls are at stake. Yet some never investigate the accuracy of what they teach because their consciences have been desensitized to the truth by having been constantly abused. Their apostasy has scarred their consciences.

THE TEACHING OF APOSTATES

Apostates teach false standards of spirituality: "forbidding to marry, and commanding to abstain from foods" (v. 3). Those restrictions are just a sample of erroneous doctrines. Some false teachers taught that if you wanted to be spiritual you couldn't get married and you had to abstain from certain kinds of food. It is typical of Satan to take something that may be appropriate for certain people at certain times and make it mandatory for everyone. Paul honors singleness in 1 Corinthians 7, and Jesus acknowledges the place for fasting with the proper motives in Matthew 6. But the apostates Paul mentions in 1 Timothy 4 were requiring ascetic self-denial to attain spirituality. They thought salvation was based on what they denied themselves.

All false religions devise human means by which you become saved, either by things you do or don't do. They are all ultimately based on human achievement. Although ascetic practices may give the impression of spiritual sincerity, they aren't means to attain holiness.

As early as 166 B.C. the Essene sect of Judaism had been established in an isolated community by the Dead Sea. Its followers emphasized an ascetic lifestyle of marital and dietary abstinence. Such thinking may have found its way to Ephesus. More likely is that a precursor to Greek Gnosticism influenced the church at Ephesus. It held that spirit is good and matter is evil. So those who adhered to that philosophy denied themselves legitimate physical pleasures, such as marital relations and certain foods. They believed such abstinence would please their deities. That erroneous philosophy was probably what influenced the Corinthians on the topics of marriage (1 Cor. 7) and bodily resurrection (1 Cor. 15).

Such externalism is typical of false religion. Paul therefore emphasizes in 1 Timothy 4:3 that spirituality is not determined by which gifts God has given for man's enjoyment. In Colossians 2:16-23 he says, "Let no man, therefore, judge you in food, or in drink, or in respect of a feast day, or of the new moon, or of a sabbath day, which are a shadow of things to come; but the body [reality] is of Christ. Let no man beguile you of your reward in a voluntary humility and worshiping of angels . . . [or subject you] to ordinances (touch not; taste not; handle not; which all are to perish with the using) after the commandments and doctrines of men." Don't follow the ascetic approach of trying to earn acceptance before God. As a Christian you are already complete in Christ (Col. 2:10). True religion acknowledges that the Lord alone has accomplished our salvation. False religion says we've got to do it ourselves by self-denial and human achievement.

THE ERROR OF APOSTATES

Apostates do not understand basic facts about creation. "God . . . created [marriage and foods] to be received with thanksgiving by them who believe and know the truth" (1 Tim. 4:3). God created marriage when He provided a wife for Adam. Both Paul and Peter stressed the importance of a good marriage relationship (1 Cor. 7:1-5; Eph. 5:22-33; 1 Pet. 3:7). God provided a variety of foods for man's nourishment and enjoyment (Gen. 1:29; 9:3). In fact, when God created the earth, He declared the products of His handiwork "very good" (Gen. 1:31). It doesn't make sense to deny man what God created to be received with thanksgiving.

"Every creature of God is good, and nothing is to be refused, if it is received with thanksgiving" (1 Tim. 4:4). The Greek word translated "good" (*kalos*) means "inherently excellent." Marriage and food are inherently good and should not be rejected, but gratefully accepted.

"It is sanctified by the word of God and prayer" (v. 5). The phrase "the word of God" is used in the pastoral epistles to refer to the gospel of Jesus Christ. The message of salvation clarifies that all the dietary laws have been abolished. They were given for a brief time in Israel's history to develop the moral faculty of discernment in the Israelites and to make them distinct from other nations. But Christ came and fulfilled the sacrificial laws and made Jew and Gentile one in Him, so those dietary laws were set aside. They had a limited national purpose. To reimpose them is to manufacture a works-righteousness system and dishonor God by saying He created something evil.

If we understand that the gospel has freed us from dietary laws and if in prayer we offer God thanks, then we can receive any and all of His good gifts. Teaching mandatory celibacy and abstinence is demonic—it denies the goodness of God's creation and His desire for thanks and praise.

External self-denial is a severe error that is typical of false religions. The error of apostasy is thinking one can please God by following and teaching such pharisaical practices. Instead, that is displeasing to God and follows the lies of demons. Although King Amaziah of Judah did the right things on the outside, he never had a heart for God. That is the spirit of apostasy.

Chapter 12

Understanding the Duties of the Minister*

In 1 Timothy 4:6-16 the apostle Paul lists the qualifications of an excellent servant of Jesus Christ. The key phrase appears in verse 6: "Thou shalt be a good minister of Jesus Christ." In a sense, it is the underlying theme of the whole epistle, which was written to instruct Timothy on how to minister to the church at Ephesus.

The Greek word translated "good" could better be translated "noble," "admirable," or "excellent." It was used in 1 Timothy 3:1 to speak of the work of ministry, and here it is used to identify the kind of man God wants in ministry.

"Minister" is the translation of the Greek word *diakonos*, from which we get the English word *deacon*. It means "servant" and is used of those who hold the office of deacon in the church, as described in chapter 3. Although the word is not used here in a technical way to designate that office, it implies that anyone who serves in any capacity in ministry must see himself as a servant of the Lord Jesus Christ.

The word *diakonos* is different from the word *doulos*, which is also often translated "servant." Whereas *doulos* often refers to a slave under subjection, *diakonos* emphasizes a servant with a higher degree of freedom who yet serves willingly. The word conveys the idea of usefulness and implies that all Christians should seek to be useful in the cause of Christ. In 1 Corinthians 4:1-2 Paul says, "Let a man so

*From tapes GC 54-30–54-34.

account of us, as of the ministers of Christ, and stewards of the mysteries of God. Moreover, it is required in stewards, that a man be found faithful." We are called to be servants and stewards, managing that which belongs to God in a way that will bring honor to His name. Paul's instruction to Timothy is applicable for all who serve the Lord.

In 1 Timothy 4:1-5 Paul talks about doctrines of demons propagated by seducing spirits through lying hypocrites. Having warned Timothy that false teaching isn't human but demonic, he tells Timothy how to be a good and effective minister in the face of false doctrine. Yet in instructing Timothy how to deal with false doctrine, he majors on the positive, not on the negative. Rather than encouraging Timothy to develop a defensive ministry of refuting and denouncing error, Paul emphasizes taking the offensive approach by teaching the Word of God (vv. 6, 11, 13, 16). The church leader's ministry should primarily involve building up the people of God, not exclusively identifying and attacking error.

In verses 6-16 Paul gives eleven characteristics of being an excellent minister of Christ. They are practical and helpful objectives for everyone who desires to serve the Lord by leading His people.

THE EXCELLENT SERVANT WARNS PEOPLE OF ERROR

Although the ministry is not to be dominated by a negative approach, that doesn't mean there is no place for warning others about the destructiveness of false doctrine. Paul makes a transition from exposing demonic doctrines to explaining how to be an excellent servant of Jesus Christ by instructing Timothy to warn the church about such doctrines. "Put the brethren in remembrance of these things" (v. 6). It is necessary to remind Christians of error. Ministry demands warning.

The Greek word translated "put . . . in remembrance of" means to lay before. Its use here as a present participle indicates continually reminding people of the reality of false doctrine. It does not imply commanding people but giving them counsel and advice in a gentle, humble manner. A servant of Christ must teach people to be discerning by encouraging them to think biblically.

Identifying error is not to be the theme of the average pastor's ministry, but it should be a recurring reminder. When Paul met with the Ephesian elders he said, "I know this, that after my departing shall grievous wolves enter in among you, not sparing the flock. Also of your own selves shall men arise, speaking perverse things, to draw away disciples after them. Therefore, watch, and remember, that for the space of three years I ceased not to warn everyone night and day with tears. And now, brethren, I commend you to God, and to the word of his grace, which is able to build you up" (Acts 20:29-32). Paul continually made the Ephesians aware of error and pointed them to the positive solution, the Word. The truth supplies the foundation from which error can be dealt with properly.

Christians can avoid being "children, tossed to and fro, and carried about with every wind of doctrine" (Eph. 4:14) by being firmly grounded in the Word of God. First John 2:13-14 reinforces the fact that a believer learns to deal with satanic error by being strong in the Word, which is the sword of the Spirit. That's the only way to win against beings who disguise themselves as angels of light and ministers of righteousness (2 Cor. 11:14-15).

The church's failure to be discerning in this generation has allowed it to become infiltrated by all kinds of error. It is confused, weak, and in some cases apostate. Limp theology and convictionless preaching have replaced strong doctrine and clear exposition of Scripture. The legacy has been tragic. The church has been flooded with confusion, unbiblical psychology, occult influences, success-oriented philosophy, and prosperity theology.

The church must draw the lines between error and truth and build up its people in the Word of God. God holds pastors accountable to warn their people of spiritual danger. The Lord told Ezekiel, "Son of man, I have made thee a watchman unto the house of Israel; therefore, hear the word at my mouth and give them warning from me. When I say to the wicked, Thou shalt surely die; and thou givest him not warning, nor speakest to warn the wicked from his wicked way, to save his life, the same wicked man shall die in his iniquity, but his blood will I require at thine hand" (Ezek. 3:17-18). If spiritual leaders fail to do that, they will have to answer to God (Heb. 13:17). Although the church today seems to embrace everything, including error, the man of God must develop convictions based upon a biblical theology and continually warn his people of error. He is committed to protecting the flock, not petting the sheep.

The Excellent Servant
Is an Expert Student of Scripture

An excellent minister is also an expert student of Scripture: "Nourished up in the words of faith and of good doctrine, unto which thou hast attained" (v. 6). Sad to say, many Christian pastors have a minimal understanding of Scripture and little commitment to studying it. There was a day in the history of the church when the great students of Scripture and theology were pastors. Puritan ministers, rather than being just good communicators, were first and foremost students of God's Word. They worked at understanding, interpreting, and applying the Word of God with precision and wisdom.

The Greek word translated "nourished up" is a present passive participle, implying that being nourished with the Word of God is a continual process of feeding. That involves reading Scripture, meditating on it, interacting with it, and studying it until you've mastered the material.

It is essential that we be continually nourished by "the words of faith." That phrase refers to the body of Christian truth in Scripture. We are to master Scripture. We'll never accomplish that, but it is our pursuit. We are to be experts in that area, not just good communicators who tickle people's ears and make them think they heard something enjoyable (2 Tim. 4:3). We need to accurately interpret and defend the Word of God. Not only are we to be nourished directly by "the words of faith" but also by "good doctrine" (Gk., *kalē didaskalia*). "Good doctrine" encompasses teaching biblical truth and applying its principles. Spiritual growth is based upon our interaction with biblical truth.

> *1 Peter 2:2*—We grow spiritually as we study the Bible.
>
> *2 Timothy 2:15*—Paul said, "Study to show thyself approved unto God, a workman that needeth not to be ashamed, rightly dividing the word of truth." We are called—above and beyond all other elements in the ministry—to be expert students of the Word.
>
> *Ephesians 6:17*—We are to use "the sword of the Spirit, which is the word of God," with great precision.
>
> *Colossians 3:16*—We are to have the Word of Christ dwelling in us richly and deeply.
>
> *2 Timothy 3:16-17*—Since the Word of God "is profitable for doctrine, for reproof, for correction, for instruction in righteousness, that the man of God may be perfect, thoroughly furnished unto all good works," we must know it if we are to equip others spiritually.

To be able to think and speak biblically, a pastor must spend a large portion of his time interacting with the text of Scripture. It is an inexhaustible treasure that demands a lifetime just to begin to understand its riches. There is no virtue in being ignorant. Unfortunately we are a generation of people who do not like to think; we prefer to be entertained. Nevertheless we must commit ourselves to studying, understanding, and articulating the Word of God.

Sadly, there are many men who have no delight in their studies. They spend an hour now and then, or even no time at all. Many regard study an unwelcome task that interrupts an easy schedule of activity. They like to have guests as often as possible in their pulpits so they don't have to spend time studying, and they prefer the variety of administrative tasks and meetings. The minimal study that they do produces a weak sermon that fails to penetrate the hearts and minds of their listeners.

William Tyndale, the man responsible for getting the New Testament translated into the English language in 1525, was in prison facing martyrdom. He wrote a letter to the governor-in-chief, asking that these possessions be sent to him: a warmer cap, a warmer coat, and a piece of cloth to patch his leggings. Then he said, "But most of all I beg and beseech and entreat your clemency to be urgent with the commissary, that he will kindly permit me to have the Hebrew bible, Hebrew grammar, and Hebrew dictionary that I may pass the time in that study" (J. E. Mozley, *William Tyndale* [N.Y.: MacMillan, 1937], p. 334). Any seminary student who has struggled with Hebrew probably cannot relate to such a request! But later in life when you plunge more deeply into the Word of God, it's wonderful to be able to say that what you cherish most is what helps you understand the Word of God.

The Excellent Servant
Avoids the Influence of Unholy Teaching

"Refuse profane and old wives' fables" (v. 7). "Fables" is a translation of the Greek word *muthos,* from which the English word *myth* is derived. Second Timothy 4:4 says that some "shall turn away their ears from the truth, and shall be turned unto fables." Truth and fables are seen as opposites. The Christian is to be nourished by the truth and refuse that which opposes it.

The identification of fables with old women has a cultural meaning. The phrase was used in philosophical circles as a sarcastic epithet when one wanted to heap disdain on a particular viewpoint. It pictures a senile old lady telling a fairy tale to a child. It was applied to things lacking credibility.

The mind is a precious thing. God wants those who serve as spiritual leaders to have pure minds saturated with the truth of God's Word. There's no place for foolish myths or unholy contradictions to the truth. Yet somehow our society would rather believe stories than biblical truth. The mark of theological scholarship in some circles is no longer how well a man knows the Bible but how well he understands the speculations of the secular academic establishment.

When I was considering completing a doctoral degree in theology, the representative of the graduate program at the college looked over my transcripts and concluded I had had too much Bible and theology in my undergraduate work. So he gave me a list of two hundred books of preparatory reading before I could be admitted to the program. I checked out the list with someone who knew the various titles and learned that none of them contained anything but liberal theology and humanistic philosophy—they were full of profane old wives' fables passed off as scholarship! The college also required me to take a course called "Jesus and the Cinema." That involved watching contemporary movies and evaluating them according to whether they were antagonistic to or supportive of "the Jesus ethic." The divine Jesus had been reduced to an ethic! I met with the representative again and said, "I just want to let you know that I have spent all my life learning the truth, and I can't see any value in spending the next couple of years learning error." I put the materials down on his desk and walked away.

I'm grateful to God that since the beginning of my training my mind has been filled with the truth of God. My mind is not a battleground of indecision about what is true and what is false, over things "which minister questions rather than godly edifying" (1 Tim. 1:4). I can speak with conviction because there's no equivocation in my mind. I have avoided the plethora of supposed intellectuals and scholars who disagree with biblical truth. However, one man I knew had problems in that area. He entered a liberal seminary to prepare for ministry but came out a bartender. The confusion of liberalism had destroyed his motivation to serve God. Your mind is a precious thing, and it needs to be kept clear from satanic lies. The excellent minister maintains his biblical convictions and clarity of mind by exposing himself to the Word of God.

THE EXCELLENT SERVANT
DISCIPLINES HIMSELF IN PERSONAL GODLINESS

J. Oswald Sanders says in his book *Spiritual Leadership,* "Spiritual ends can be achieved only by spiritual men who employ spiritual methods" ([Chicago: Moody, 1980], p. 40). The issue in ministry is godliness. It isn't how clever you are or how well you communicate; it's whether you know the Word of God and are leading a godly life. Ministry is an overflow of the latter.

First Timothy 4:7 says, "Exercise thyself rather unto godliness." The English word *gymnasium* comes from the Greek word here translated "exercise" *(gumnazō),* used of those who trained themselves in athletic endeavors. It implies rigorous, self-sacrificing training. In Greek culture, the gymnasium was a focal point of the city for youths between the ages of sixteen and eighteen. Since athletic ability was highly esteemed, there was usually a gymnasium in every town. The cultic exaltation of the body resulted in a preoccupation with exercise, athletic training, and competition, not dissimilar to our own day.

Paul alluded to that cultural reality in exhorting Timothy to exercise himself for the goal of godliness, saying in effect, "If you're going to go into training, concentrate on training your inner nature for godliness." The Greek word for godliness is *eusebeia* and means "reverence," "piety," or "true spiritual virtue." "Keep yourself in training for godliness" would be an accurate way to translate Paul's exhortation to Timothy.

Paul understood the importance of discipline in the ministry: "I buffet my body and make it my slave, lest possibly, after I have preached to others, I myself should be disqualified" (1 Cor. 9:27; NASB). He told Timothy to "endure hardness as a good soldier of Jesus Christ. No man that warreth entangleth himself with the affairs of this life, that he may please him who hath chosen him to be a soldier. And if a man also strive for masteries, yet is he not crowned, except he strive lawfully" (2 Tim. 2:3-5). As a soldier endures hardship, makes sacrifices, and cuts himself off from the world to please the one who enlisted him; and as an athlete must diligently train and compete within the rules, so must a servant of God make sacrifices in disciplining himself and confining himself to God's standards.

Physical exercise profits little (v. 8). First, it benefits only the body and not the spirit. Second, it's good only for a short time. You could spend years getting yourself in shape, but as soon as you let up, you immediately start losing what you've worked so hard to achieve.

In contrast, "godliness is profitable unto all things, having promise of the life that now is, and of that which is to come" (v. 8). Godliness is profitable not only for the body but also for the soul. If you're going to make a New Year's resolution, don't resolve to go to the gym three times a week if you're not spending time in the Word of God every day and cultivating godliness. The present benefit of spiritual discipline is a fulfilled, God-blessed, fruitful, and useful life. And the blessings of godliness carry on into eternity.

"This is a faithful saying and worthy of all acceptance" (v. 9) is a formula Paul used four other times in the pastoral epistles (1 Tim. 1:15; 3:1; 2 Tim. 2:11; Titus 3:8). "Worthy of all acceptance" adds emphasis to his affirmation. It identifies a trustworthy statement or axiom that is patently obvious. The greater benefit of spiritual discipline is an obvious truth.

It is spiritually immature to preoccupy yourself with your body. Doing so betrays a limited perception of spiritual and eternal realities. It should be axiomatic in the church that Christians are a group of people who are in spiritual training to be conformed to the will of God, not a group of body worshipers.

The pursuit of the excellent minister is godliness. He uses all the means of grace available—prayer, Bible study, the Lord's Table, confession of sin, active service, accountability, and sometimes fasting —in the discipline of godliness.

Godliness is said to be at the heart of truth (1 Tim. 6:3). It comes through Christ (2 Pet. 1:3), yet we still must pursue it (1 Tim. 6:11). It causes trouble in a hostile environment (2 Tim. 3:12). And it blesses us eternally but not necessarily with temporal prosperity (1 Tim. 6:5-8).

The Excellent Servant Is Committed to Hard Work

Having called us to be godly, Paul now brings us back to earth. The ministry is a heavenly pursuit, but it is also an earthly task—it's hard work. "We both labor [strive] and suffer reproach" (v. 10).

In 2 Corinthians 5:9 Paul says, "We labor that, whether present or absent, we may be accepted of him." Then Paul gives two reasons for working hard. First, in verse 10 he says, "We must all appear before the judgment seat of Christ." We will stand before Christ and be eternally rewarded for the service we've rendered Him. The reward will be commensurate with the service we have rendered, whether good or useless (cf. 1 Cor. 3:11-15).

Then in verse 11 Paul says, "Knowing, therefore, the terror of the Lord, we persuade men." Here Paul was looking beyond himself to unregenerate people. They won't experience a time of reward; they'll face judgment. And since we know that, we should persuade them with the truths of the gospel that they might be saved and avoid judgment.

Paul worked hard because he knew his effort had eternal consequences—reward for himself and the possibility of changing the destiny of unbelievers. That is the perspective that propels the servant of God. There is an eternal heaven and an eternal hell.

In verse 10 "labor" (Gk., *kopiaō*) means "to work to the point of weariness." "Suffer reproach" (Gk. *agōnizomai*) means "to agonize in a struggle." We work to the point of weariness and exhaustion, often in pain, because we understand our eternal objectives.

J. Oswald Sanders wrote that if a man "is unwilling to pay the price of fatigue for his leadership it will always be mediocre" *(Spiritual Leadership* [Chicago: Moody, 1980], p. 175). He also said, "True leadership always exacts a heavy toll on the whole man, and the more effective the leadership is, the higher the price to be paid" (p. 169). We will not mitigate that price because we understand the urgency of our ministry. Weariness, loneliness, struggle, rising early, staying up late, and forgoing pleasures are all part of ministry.

In 1 Corinthians 9 Paul says, "Necessity is laid upon me; yea, woe is unto me, if I preach not the gospel! . . . So fight I, not as one that beateth the air; but I keep under my body, and bring it into subjection" (vv. 16, 26-27). That describes Paul's tremendous effort and commitment to a ministry with eternal consequences. In 2 Corinthians 11:24-27 Paul tells of the many times he was beaten with rods and a whip, and endured weariness, suffering, pain, agony, and shipwreck. He endured all those perils because he was totally committed to the ministry at hand. Why? Because he had eternity in view. He realized that the destiny of souls hung in the balance.

"Because we trust in the living God" (v. 10) literally means, "We have set our hope on the living God." Missionaries who preach the gospel of Jesus Christ through the years deprive themselves of almost every earthly pleasure because their hope is set on the living God. They believe He will provide life for them beyond this life. None of us should try to amass a fortune here so we can indulge ourselves before we leave. Our hope is set on the future.

Note that Paul speaks of God as "the Savior of all men, specially of those that believe" (v. 10). In what sense is God the Savior of all men? How is He especially the Savior of those who believe? Many suggestions have been made. The key to interpreting this phrase is to keep it in context.

When Paul preached to the learned men of Athens on Mars' Hill, he said that God is not "worshiped with men's hands, as though he needed anything, seeing he giveth to all life, and breath, and all things . . . for in him we live, and move, and have our being. . . . For we are also his offspring" (Acts 17:25, 28). In a general sense God is the provider and sustainer of life for all people.

During a storm at sea, Paul said to the crew, "Take some food; for this is for your health" (Acts 27:34). The Greek word normally translated "salvation" is here translated "health." Paul wasn't talking about spiritual salvation but about physical health.

In James 5:15 James writes, "The prayer of faith shall *save* the sick" (emphasis added). So the Greek words translated "salvation" or "save" aren't limited to describing the salvation of the soul. They can speak of deliverance from disease or trouble, or of sustenance from food.

That is the analogy Paul is using in I Timothy 4:10. We have seen God's sustaining and providing power on a worldwide basis. We have seen His great temporal provision for all people. But that provision is especially glorious for the believer because it is not only temporal but also eternal.

Paul's argument is this: we labor and strive in the ministry because we believe the consequences are eternal. We have set our hope on a living God, and we know He will save the souls of those who believe because we have seen His sustaining power at work in the world. That's why we work hard.

I remember reading about a man named Thomas Cochrane as he was being interviewed for the mission field. He was asked, "What portion of the field do you feel yourself specially called to?" He answered, "I only know I wish it to be the hardest you could offer me." The Lord's work is not for people who are looking for ease and comfort. Yet it is eternally rewarding for those who set their hope on eternity.

Richard Baxter wrote that ministerial work "must be managed laboriously and diligently, being of such unspeakable consequence to others and ourselves. We are seeking to uphold the world, to save it from the curse of God, to perfect the creation, to attain the ends of Christ's redemption, to save ourselves and others from damnation, to overcome the devil, and demolish his kingdom, and set up the kingdom of Christ, and attain and help others to the kingdom of glory. And are these works to be done with a careless mind or a slack hand? Oh see then that this work be done with all your might! Study hard, for the well is deep, and our brains are shallow" (*The Reformed Pastor* [London: James Nisbet, 1860], pp. 164-65).

Our whole work is a labor but not human labor: Paul said his goal was to "present every man perfect in Christ Jesus" (Col. 1:28). Then he said, "For this I also labor [Gk., *kopiaō*, "agonize"], striving according to his working, which worketh in me mightily" (v. 29). Our work isn't performed in the flesh. Through the Spirit the Lord energizes those who serve Him.

THE EXCELLENT SERVANT TEACHES WITH AUTHORITY

"These things command and teach," Paul instructed Timothy (v. 11). The Greek word translated "teach" in verse 11 refers to passing on information, in this case passing on instruction or doctrine. It is to be done in the form of a command.

There is much popular, entertainment-oriented preaching today, but not much that is powerful or transforming in nature. Are the weak suggestions from the pulpit these days really what God wants?

According to Acts 17:30 God "*commandeth* all men everywhere to repent" (emphasis added).

Matthew 7:28-29 says, "It came to pass, when Jesus had ended these sayings [the Sermon on the Mount], the people were astonished at his doctrine; for he taught them as one having authority." Paul told Timothy many times to be authoritative. In 1 Timothy 1:3 he says, "Charge some that they teach no other doctrine." Then he said, "These things command" (5:7). In 5:20 Paul urges Timothy to rebuke people publicly. Then in 6:17 he gives him commands to give to rich people in the church. In Titus 2:15 he says, "These things speak, and exhort, and rebuke with all authority. Let no man despise thee." That doesn't mean we are to be abusive or ungracious. But we are to confront people when they disobey God's Word.

The faithful servant is bold. He challenges sin head on. He confronts unbelief, disobedience, and lack of commitment. God said of Jesus, "This is my beloved Son . . . hear ye him" (Matt. 17:5). The excellent servant carries on that directive, commanding all men to repent and listen to Jesus Christ.

Our authority has a foundation. First, you must know what you believe about the Bible. If you're not sure it's the Word of God, you won't be authoritative. Next you have to know what God's Word says. If you're not sure what it means, you can't be authoritative. Then you must be concerned about communicating it properly because you care that His Word is upheld. Finally, you should care about people's response to His Word.

Our teaching should be filled with commands, not just sentimental pleadings. Instead of trying to sneak up on people with God's truth, we need to speak forth the Word of God and let it do its work.

THE EXCELLENT SERVANT IS A MODEL OF SPIRITUAL VIRTUE

Paul wrote Timothy, "Let no man despise thy youth, but be thou an example of the believers, in word, in conduct, in love, in spirit, in faith, in purity" (v. 12). The Greek word translated "example" is *tupos*, which means model, image, or pattern. To use a pattern in making a dress, the dressmaker will lay the pattern on top of the material and cut the material to match the pattern. An artist uses a model so that he can reproduce it in his painting. When you set an example, you are giving people a pattern to follow. Someone once said, "Your life speaks so loud I can't hear what you say." Your lifestyle is your most powerful message.

A friend of mine recently visited his alma mater, a well-known seminary in our country. He had noticed that the majority of the graduates appeared to lack an understanding of true godliness. He suggested they add a class on personal holiness. One of the professors told him, "That wouldn't have any academic credibility." But academic credibility is not the main issue in ministry. Give me a godly man, and I'll show you someone you can pattern your life after. Give me a man whose head is full of knowledge but without virtue in his life, and I'll show you a man you'd better run from. He will confuse you, and you'll begin to act like him, having all the right doctrine and none of the right behavior. That kind of dichotomy is deadly and frightening.

The New Testament is replete with injunctions for setting a pattern of godly living. Note these commands from the apostle Paul:

1 Corinthians 4:16—"I beseech you, be ye followers of me." You might think Paul was being egotistic. He wasn't—he was simply exhibiting the character of a godly man who knew he was to be an example. Obviously he knew he wasn't perfect, but it was his objective—as much as was humanly possible—to be what the people were to be. No man in ministry should aim for less than that. The Greek word translated "followers" is *mimētēs*, from which the English word *mimic* is derived.

1 Corinthians 10:31, 33; 11:1—"Do all to the glory of God. . . . Even as I please all men in all things, not seeking mine own profit, but the profit of many, that they may be saved. Be ye followers of me, even as I also am of Christ."

Philippians 3:17—"Be followers together of me, and mark them who walk even as ye have us for an example."

Philippians 4:9—"Those things which ye have both learned, and received, and heard, and seen in me, do."

1 Thessalonians 1:5-6—"Our gospel came not unto you in word only, but also in power, and in the Holy Spirit, and in much assurance, as ye know what manner of men we were among you for your sake. And ye became followers of us, and of the Lord."

2 Thessalonians 3:7, 9—"Ye yourselves know how ye ought to follow us; for we behaved not ourselves disorderly among you . . . but to make ourselves an example unto you to follow us."

2 Timothy 1:13—"Hold fast the form of sound words, which thou hast heard of me."

The author of Hebrews said, "Remember them who have rule over you, who have spoken unto you the word of God, whose faith follow" (13:7). When you minister in the church, you are to lead a life that others can follow. That's a tremendous challenge, which is why James said, "Be not many teachers, knowing that we shall receive the greater judgment" (James 3:1). It's a serious matter to be guilty of teaching error or living hypocritically. A man's life must match his message. Tragically, that principle is violated constantly in the ministry.

Timothy was young, probably under forty, and was therefore subject to a certain amount of questioning. So Paul told Timothy that he had to be respected if people were going to follow him. But since he was young, Timothy would have to earn that respect. How was he going to do that? By being "an example [to] the believers, in word, in conduct, in love, in spirit, in faith, in purity" (1 Tim. 4:12).

IN WORD

The conversation of the servant of God is to be exemplary. In Matthew 12:34 Jesus says, "Out of the abundance of the heart the mouth speaketh." Whatever comes out of the mouth reveals what is in a person's heart. That's why Jesus said, "By thy words thou shalt be justified, and by thy words thou shalt be condemned" (v. 37).

Ephesians 4 tells us what our speech should be like. Verse 25 says, "Putting away lying." A servant of the Lord should never speak any falsehood. He shouldn't talk out of both sides of his mouth—telling one thing to one person and another to someone else. Then Paul says, "Speak every man truth with his neighbor" (v. 25). You should speak the truth to everyone. The credibility of a leader is destroyed when people compare notes about the lies he has told them.

In verse 26 Paul says, "Be ye angry, and sin not." There's a place for holy wrath and righteous indignation but not for the sin of anger —especially the smoldering kind that lasts into the next day and longer. No excellent servant is to reach the point where he is so upset that his words are bitter, vengeful, or ungracious. His speech is to "be always with grace, seasoned with salt" (Col. 4:6).

Verse 29 says, "Let no corrupt communication proceed out of your mouth." The speech of a believer should never be less than pure. It is embarrassing to hear someone who claims to serve Jesus Christ speak ungodly words. That just reveals a dirty heart. There's no place for corrupt or filthy communication in the Christian life.

Speech that glorifies God "is good to the use of edifying, that it may minister grace unto the hearers" (v. 29). There's a place for fun and joy, for "a merry heart doeth good like a medicine" (Prov. 17:22). But there's no place for perverse talk, angry speech, or a lying tongue.

IN CONDUCT

You are to be a model of righteous living—a person who lives out his convictions based on biblical principles. The things you do, the places you go, the things you possess—every aspect of your life is a sermon. That sermon either contradicts or substantiates what you say.

What do you spend your time, money, and energy on? The life-style propagated by the world today is completely incompatible with the standards of Scripture. Many families disintegrate because both spouses want to work so they can buy a bigger house or a bigger car. They devote what little spare time they have to firming up their bodies instead of building up their souls, their families, or their children. And the church, instead of maintaining a contrasting lifestyle, too often mimics the world's perspectives.

IN LOVE

Ministering in love doesn't necessarily mean you're to be a hand-shaker and a back-slapper. The apostle Paul and Epaphroditus showed their love to the church by hard work (1 Thess. 2:7-12; Phil. 2:27-30). Sometimes I ask myself, *Should I stay and spend myself at Grace Church, or move on to another ministry?* Yet I know God has called me to give my life to the people of this church. That's how my love for the brethren is expressed. We all are to offer self-sacrificing service on behalf of others.

IN FAITH

The Greek word translated "faith" in 1 Timothy 4:12 could be translated "faithfulness," "trustworthiness," or "consistency." Timothy was to be consistent, faithful, and trustworthy in his ministry. People can follow that kind of leader. In 1 Corinthians 4:2 Paul says, "It is required in stewards, that a man be found faithful." Consistency separates those who succeed from those who fail.

Paul had the reputation of being faithful. So did his co-laborers. Epaphras (Col. 1:7) and Tychicus (Col. 4:7) were just two of many faithful servants of Christ.

IN PURITY

The Greek word translated "purity" (*hagneia*) refers not only to sexual chastity but also to the intent of the heart. If your heart is pure, your behavior will be pure as well.

History has shown us that a ministry can be devastated by sexual impurity on the part of its leaders. Men in leadership are vulnerable in that area when they let their guard down. We all must maintain absolute moral purity.

THE EXCELLENT SERVANT
HAS A THOROUGHLY BIBLICAL MINISTRY

"Till I come," Paul told Timothy, "give attendance to reading, to exhortation, to doctrine" (v. 13). The Greek verb translated "give attendance" is *prosechō*. It is a present active imperative, a continuing command. Paul is commanding Timothy to continually give attention to reading, exhortation, and teaching. It was to become Timothy's way of life. Commentator Donald Guthrie tells us that the verb "implies previous preparation in private" (*The Pastoral Epistles* [Grand Rapids: Eerdmans, 1978], p. 97). The same verb is used in Hebrews 7:13 of the priests who were continually devoted to their service at the altar. So Timothy was to center his ministry on reading, exhortation, and teaching.

READING

In verse 13 a definite article appears in the Greek text before the word translated "reading." Timothy was to give attention to "the reading." In the services of the early church a time was set aside for the reading of Scripture. It was followed by an exposition of the text.

That model of expository preaching comes from Nehemiah 8:8: "They read in the book in the law of God distinctly, and gave the sense, and caused them to understand the reading." Scripture needs to be explained so people can understand it. Obviously the further we are removed culturally, geographically, linguistically, philosophically, and historically from the original text of Scripture, the more necessary it becomes to research those facts. That's the challenge for the Bible teacher, and it's where his effort is needed.

EXHORTATION

If the reading and exposition of Scripture tell us what it means, what is exhortation all about? It is a call for people to apply it. To exhort is to warn people to obey with a view toward judgment. We are to encourage people to respond properly, telling them about the blessing or the consequences of their actions. It is always binding on a person's conscience to amend certain behavior.

DOCTRINE

The Greek word translated "doctrine" *(didaskalia)* means teaching. That means systematically teaching the Word of God in both group and individual settings. *Didaskalia* appears fifteen times in the pastoral epistles. That gives us some idea of its importance to the life of the church. No wonder the pastor must be "apt to teach" (1 Tim. 3:2). Since the church's ministry revolves around teaching the Word of God, how could anyone ever hope to lead in a church if he's not a skilled teacher?

First Timothy 5:17 says, "Let the elders that rule well be counted worthy of double honor, especially they who labor in the word and doctrine." The harder a man works in teaching God's Word, the more honorable he is. It's sad to realize that many men in ministry have been diverted away from the most important pursuit.

We need to be relentless teachers. Puritan clergyman John Flavel wrote, "It is not with us, as with other labourers: They find their work as they leave it, so do not we." Picture the cabinetmaker who leaves his unfinished work and comes back to it the next morning to find it exactly as he left it. Flavel continues, "Sin and Satan unravel almost all we do, the impression we make on our people's souls in one sermon, vanishes before the next" (*The Works of John Flavel,* vol. 6 [London: Banner of Truth, 1968], p. 569).

We fight the unraveling process all the time. That's why I repeat much of what I teach. Every good pastor and teacher knows that people forget what he teaches, so he must be repetitive. But he also realizes that people become familiar with what he teaches. When they realize they are being taught something they have already heard, they think they know it and become bored by it. The challenge for the teacher is to repeat his teaching in such a manner that the people think he is teaching them something new. It would be easy for me to pack up a hundred sermons, go out on the road, and preach them over and over again. The challenge for me is to stay in the same place, say the same things over and over, yet have people think I'm teaching them something they've never heard. If you study the Bible, you'll find that Scripture does the same thing. Its principles are repeated over and over in different contexts and through different narratives.

THE EXCELLENT SERVANT FULFILLS HIS CALLING

In 1 Timothy 4:14 Paul writes, "Neglect not the gift that is in thee, which was given thee by prophecy, with the laying on of the hands of the presbytery." Some people go into the ministry but bail out because they weren't called there in the first place. But sometimes people who are called into the ministry bail out, and that is a defection from where God intends them to be.

"Neglect not the gift" may indicate that Timothy was about to neglect his ministry or had already begun to neglect it. He may even have been close to a point of departure—a point where people can't handle the internal and external pressure of their situation. The Greek verb translated "neglect not" is a present active imperative. It is a command with a view toward continual behavior. The Greek word translated "gift" is *charisma*, a reference to a gift of grace from God. Every believer is given a gift, which is a means or channel by which the Spirit of God ministers to others. Comprehensive lists of all the gifts are in Romans 12 and 1 Corinthians 12, with references in Ephesians 4 and 1 Peter 4.

I like to think of spiritual gifts as divine enablements. They are given to us by the Spirit of God with a sovereign design. The church is made up of many people. It functions like a body, and every person is a part of the body. The spiritual gifts we've been given blend together to enable the Body to function properly. Timothy had the gift of teaching. That's why Paul told him to teach, preach, command, and exhort. He was to do the work of an evangelist, making full proof of his ministry (2 Tim. 4:5). He was gifted in the areas of evangelism, preaching, teaching, and leadership—all blended together as his own unique spiritual gift.

Each of us has one spiritual gift, a blend of the different gifts the Spirit has put together for each of us. Like a painter who is able to create an infinite number of colors by mixing any combination of the ten or so colors he carries on his palette, so the Spirit of God blends a little of one gift with a little of another to create the perfect combination within you. As a result, you have a unique position in the Body of Christ, with an ability to minister as no one else can.

In verse 14 Paul says Timothy's gift was given to him by prophecy. That's the objective affirmation of Timothy's call to the ministry. I don't believe he received the gift through the prophecy, but I do believe there was a public affirmation of his gift by direct revelation from God.

I should add that Timothy's experience is not normative. I'm not in the ministry today because God gave me a revelation. Timothy's gift was affirmed in the apostolic era. Today, the objective confirmation would come from providence, not direct revelation. How God arranges your circumstances and opportunities, and how He leads and directs people you meet, are often the ways He affirms your call. I've had young men ask me if I think they should go to seminary. One said, "I feel so compelled to preach, but I don't know whether I should go." I said, "Do you have an opportunity to go to seminary?" He said he did. I asked him, "Can you afford to go?" He said he could. Then I asked, "Do you have a good seminary you can go to?" Once more he answered in the affirmative. So I said, "Does that sound like the Lord may be arranging the circumstances providentially?" He realized that

that probably was true. So when you feel compelled to do something and the opportunity presents itself, that may be God's providential affirmation.

"The laying on of the hands of the [elders]" (v. 14) was the collective affirmation of Timothy's call. The church affirmed Timothy's gift. I'm sure that happened during the time described in Acts 16:1-5.

When the elders laid hands on Timothy, the church was affirming that Timothy was the right man. And Timothy's own desire to preach and teach affirmed his calling. That's the way God continues to call people into ministry. The person first must desire to minister. Next there must be the confirmation of the providence of God through circumstances. And finally, a collective assembly of spiritual leaders must put their hands on him, thus recognizing he is qualified. So Paul encouraged Timothy to fulfill the call of God and not neglect the gift that was confirmed in him.

There are many people in the ministry who serve for a while but quickly fade away. They're like shooting stars or short candles. In contrast, I am in awe of those who are faithful to minister the Word of God right to the end of their lives. I call them spiritual marathon ministers. They may have a small congregation, they may be unknown, but they remain faithful and fulfill their calling. In a spiritual sense, they die with their boots on.

You'll never be able to evaluate the ministry of John MacArthur until all the evidence is in. The true mark of an excellent servant of Jesus Christ is that he fulfills his calling to the end. He's internally driven by the passion of his heart, and he's externally compelled by the opportunities God has given him and the confirmation of godly men. I remember very well the day I knelt for godly men to put their hands on me to set me apart for the ministry. I have a certificate in my office with the names of those who confirmed I should do the work of the ministry for life. Fulfilling the call is a vital part of being the kind of servant God wants you to be.

THE EXCELLENT SERVANT
IS TOTALLY ABSORBED IN HIS WORK

"Meditate upon these things," Paul told Timothy, "give thyself wholly to them" (v. 15). An excellent minister is single-minded, as opposed to the double-minded man, who is unstable in all his ways (James 1:8). The Greek word translated "meditate" (*meletaō*) conveys the idea of thinking through beforehand, planning, strategizing, or premeditating. When a minister is not doing the work of the ministry, he's to be planning it.

"Give thyself wholly to them" literally reads "be in them" in the Greek text. We're to be wrapped up in ministry, totally absorbed in it. It doesn't take much of a man to be a minister, but it does take all of him. An excellent minister is totally absorbed in his work.

A minister can't have a double agenda. He can't divide his efforts between being in the ministry and becoming a tennis pro, a golf pro, making money, or developing a business on the side. People who fall into that trap never realize their full potential because they have too many things to distract them and drain their energy. A good servant of Christ must bury himself in his ministry, like Epaphroditus, who nearly died fulfilling his ministry (Phil. 2:25-27).

In 2 Timothy 4:2 Paul tells Timothy to "preach the Word; be diligent." Greek scholar Fritz Rienecker tells us that the word translated "diligent" *(ephistēmi)* is a military word. It means to stay at your post, to stay on duty *(A Linguistic Key to the Greek New Testament* [Grand Rapids: Zondervan, 1980], p. 647). A servant of God is never off duty; he is always at his post. My dad used to tell me that a preacher ought to be ready to preach, pray, or die at a moment's notice.

Paul told Timothy to "be diligent in season, out of season" (2 Tim. 4:2). A servant of Christ is on duty when it's convenient and when it's not. I remember going home one Sunday night very tired. All I wanted to do was get something cold to drink and sit in a chair and rest. I had no sooner sat down when the phone rang. A family was having major problems. I spent forty minutes on the phone, during which time the food my daughter had prepared for me became inedible. As soon as I hung up the phone it rang again, and it was a bigger disaster this time. I suppose that's the Lord's way of letting me know that I'm always on duty. That's how it is in ministry—you have to be totally absorbed in it.

THE EXCELLENT SERVANT
IS CONTINUALLY PROGRESSING IN HIS SPIRITUAL GROWTH

"That thy profiting may appear to all" (v. 15) suggests that Timothy's spiritual progress should have been obvious to everyone. That implies he hadn't yet reached perfection. A minister should not try to convince his people that he has no flaws; instead he should allow them to see his growth. The standard for a servant of Christ is high, and we all fall short of it. Even Paul said, "Not as though I had already attained. . . . I press toward the mark" (Phil. 3:12, 14). Paul had his faults; he wasn't perfect (Acts 23:1-5). People need to see our integrity and humility. I'm not perfect, but I hope I'm progressing.

The Greek word translated "profiting" *(prokopē)* is used in a military sense to speak of an advancing force. It was used by the Stoics to refer to advancing in knowledge (Rienecker, p. 628). It was used of a pioneer cutting a trail by strenuous effort and advancing toward a new location. We are to be advancing toward Christlikeness, and we need to let people see that.

People sometimes point out to me that what I've said on one tape doesn't agree with what I said on a later tape. My response to them is that I'm growing. I didn't know everything then, and I don't know everything now.

Humanly speaking, no one is fit for the task of ministry. The Lord knows that; the same Lord who gave us high standards knows we can never meet them on our own. Yet when we yield to the Spirit of God and depend on Him for what we can never accomplish on our own, His power will work through us.

Paul concludes 1 Timothy 4 by saying, "Take heed unto thyself and unto the doctrine; continue in them" (v. 16). "Take heed" means pay attention. Timothy was to focus on two things: his conduct and his teaching. Those two things are the heart of the ministry. The eleven qualities we've seen in this passage can be summed up in those two commands.

Scripture repeatedly affirms that those who are genuinely saved will continue in the faith. Paul assured Timothy that his continuing in personal holiness and accurate teaching would move him along the inevitable path of final and glorious salvation: "For in doing this thou shalt both save thyself and them that hear thee" (v. 16). His perseverance would be the proof that his faith was genuine.

If we persevere in godliness and truth, our lives will affect others; we'll bring them the message of salvation. We don't actually do the saving, but we are used by God as we preach the Word of God and live godly lives. All the qualifications of an excellent servant ultimately result in the salvation of souls. That is our purpose in life and the reason we remain in the world after we've been redeemed. If all God wanted was our worship, He could take us to heaven at the moment of our salvation. But He wants us to bring the message of salvation to lost people. That's the sum of ministry. It's a high, holy, and glorious calling!

Chapter 13

Shepherding the Flock of God*

I exhort the elders among you . . . shepherd the flock of God . . . exercising oversight not under compulsion, but voluntarily, according to the will of God; and not for sordid gain, but with eagerness; nor yet as lording it over those allotted to your charge, but proving to be examples to the flock. And when the Chief Shepherd appears, you will receive the unfading crown of glory.

1 Peter 5:1-4; NASB

Peter wrote those words to Christians living in a culture that was thoroughly familiar with sheep and shepherding. Unfortunately, much of the rich meaning of his analogy is lost on those of us who live where flocks of sheep are an unfamiliar sight. Perhaps a careful look at the role of shepherds and the nature of sheep will illuminate some helpful principles of church leadership for us.

My initial exposure to sheep came when I was in high school. I took a summer job as a shepherd, which sparked my interest in sheep. Throughout the years of my ministry I have studied shepherding, but my understanding of it greatly increased when I visited Australia and New Zealand in 1988. In addition to spending time with some lifelong shepherds, I studied the writings of one of the foremost shepherds in New Zealand. What I learned was enlightening.

* From tape GC 60-46.

Shepherds Are Rescuers

A sheep is a beautiful, gentle, humble, and—contrary to popular opinion—intelligent animal. But unlike other animals, it has no sense of direction and no instinct for finding its way home. A sheep can be totally lost within a few miles of its home. Lost sheep usually will walk around in endless circles, in a state of confusion, unrest, and even panic.

Within its range of familiar territory, a sheep does fine. It knows its own pasture and the place where it was born and suckled by its mother. It will invariably rest in the same shade every day and sleep in the same fold. It will stay in the home range more than any other grazing animal. But if it wanders from familiar surroundings, the results can be disastrous.

When Jesus saw the spiritually disoriented, confused, and lost crowds, He likened them to sheep without a shepherd (Matt. 9:36). The prophet Isaiah described lost men as those who, like sheep, have gone astray, each turning to his own way (Isa. 53:6). Like lost sheep, lost people need a rescuer to lead them to the safety of the fold.

Shepherds Are Leaders

Sheep are innate followers and are easily led astray. In New Zealand about forty million sheep are led to slaughter each year. A specially selected castrated male sheep aptly called the "Judas" sheep leads the unwitting sheep to the killing floor. Unaware of what is about to happen, the sheep blindly fall in behind the Judas sheep and follow him to their deaths.

Sadly, unfaithful or false shepherds can lead sheep astray as well. In Jeremiah 23:1-2 the Lord pronounces judgment against the unrighteous rulers of Judah, whom He likened to unfaithful shepherds:

> Woe to the shepherds who are destroying and scattering the sheep of My pasture. . . . You have scattered My flock and driven them away, and have not attended to them; behold, I am about to attend to you for the evil of your deeds. (NASB)

Shepherds Are Guardians

OF THE SHEEP'S DIET

Sheep spend most of their lives eating and drinking, but they are indiscriminate about what they consume. They don't know the difference between poisonous and nonpoisonous plants. Therefore their diet must be carefully guarded by the shepherd.

Once they graze through one range, they are unable to move to a new range on their own. If not led to green pastures, they continue to eat the stubble of the old pasture until nothing remains but dirt. Soon they run out of food altogether and starve to death.

Drinking presents other challenges. Sheep must have clear water that is not stagnant or filled with potential disease. It can't be too cold, too hot, or too fast-flowing. It must be nearby and easily accessible. They must be led, as the psalmist said, beside still waters (Ps. 23:2).

Most animals are able to smell water at a distance, but not sheep. If they wander too far from their own pasture, they can sense no water hole, though it may be near.

OF THE SHEEP'S PURITY

Young lambs are cuddly, soft, clean, white, wooly animals that are fun to hold and to feed from a bottle. But that soon changes as they grow. Older sheep are rarely white and almost never clean. They are stained and greasy because their wool contains an immense amount of lanolin, which attracts and holds dirt, weeds, seeds, and almost everything else blowing around in their environment. Because they have no capacity to clean themselves, they remain dirty until the shepherd shears them.

Also, if they feed on wet grass, they can develop severe diarrhea, which hardens as it mixes with the greasy wool. That can kill the sheep by stopping the normal elimination process or by giving flies a place to lay their eggs, which hatch into maggots. The shepherd must dip the sheep to keep them clean. Sometimes he must shear the rear part of the sheep to clear away the matted wool and droppings.

Wet ground also poses a threat. It must be fertile and productive, but not swampy. If the sheep spend too much time in wet terrain, they can develop foot rot or dangerous abscesses under their hooves.

Most diseases that afflict sheep are highly contagious. Parasites, infection, and other ailments spread quickly from sheep to sheep, making it urgent that the shepherd be on guard at all times so that he can diagnose and treat a sheep's infirmities before an epidemic ravages the flock.

SHEPHERDS ARE PROTECTORS

Sheep are almost entirely defenseless. They can't kick, scratch, bite, jump, or run. They need a protective shepherd to be assured of survival. When attacked by a predator, they huddle together rather than run away. That makes them easy prey.

If a full-wooled sheep falls on its back, often it is unable to roll back onto its feet. In most cases it will simply give up and die unless a shepherd comes to its aid.

When a sheep lies on its back for a long time, its circulation is cut off. If the shepherd sets it back on its feet before circulation is restored, the sheep will fall over again. The shepherd might have to carry it for an hour or more before it is able to walk again on its own.

Shepherds Are Comforters

Sheep lack the instinct for self-preservation. They are so humble and meek that if you mistreat them, their spirit is crushed, and they may simply give up and die. The shepherd must know his sheep's individual temperaments and take care not to inflict excessive stress on them.

A Day in the Life of a Shepherd

Such vulnerable animals require wise, sensitive, protective, and self-giving shepherds. The following is a beautiful portrayal of one such shepherd:

> With a spring in his step and an eye to the sky, at sunrise, he makes straight for the sheep fold. As soon as he rattles the gate, he gives his morning call, greets the sheep, often by name, every sheep is on its feet. They spring toward the gate, with expectancy written on their faces and in their eyes, another great day on the range with their loving shepherd leading the way to fresh grass and cool water.
>
> How they eagerly bound through the gate, one after another, the younger lambs and yearlings with a skip and a bound of sheer joy, pleasure, and playfulness, the older sheep in a more sedate and dignified manner, as if reserving their energy for the demands of the long day ahead.
>
> The sun peeps over the hilltop horizon to make jewels of the dew on the bushes, the ground grass and tussocks. The air is clear, brisk, and bright. The wind has not yet arrived and there is a sense of peace all around. As the flock strings out, all is joy, abounding life, and togetherness.
>
> The sheep follow after as the shepherd leads them along a different course in a new direction to feed on a fresh range that has not been grazed for months. The leaders are at first unsettled and seem to want to return to the old paths and the well-trodden ways, but they reluctantly follow the lead of their shepherd as he directs them to fresh, clean pastures and sweet grazing.

As they enter this new range, all is action. The flock comes alive. Each of the sheep tries to outstep the others in a search of the first morsel—a sweet wildflower, a ripe seed head, a rich bottom clover, or a ground-hugging plant. Each tender morsel is nipped off on the move, a bite at every stride. What a joy to observe a flock of hungry sheep graze the fresh, sweet pastures.

It doesn't last long. The first pangs of hunger are soon satisfied, and the mob aligns itself behind the active leaders. The lambs are ready for their morning treat: mother's milk. This wonderful mother gives all to her twin lambs, as they grow bigger and fatter, while she becomes thinner, and until they almost lift her off the ground as they bunt and bump to bring down the sweet milk. No wonder she often lags a bit and appears exhausted, having to meet the insatiable demands of these ravenous "younguns" that never seem to get enough.

The leaders are either alone or have only one lamb to tend to. Often they are barren ewes, wethers [castrated sheep], or rams, with nothing to hold them back. They are often more selfish than the other sheep, who are making many sacrifices. They hurry on, run ahead, push and jockey for position, demanding the first and best morsel for themselves.

The shepherd is well aware of their behavior and knows all about it. Many times he will deliberately let them charge ahead and up a barren rock plateau, while he turns the tail of the mob and the stragglers into a path leading to the sweet side valley and into the rich pasture. Gradually he goes back to the greedy sheep and the leaders who are stringing out the flock and taking them in the wrong direction. The shepherd takes his time to turn them and to bring them back to join the others, being sure they have had ample time to nourish themselves on the first fruits.

As the day grows hotter and the sun climbs to its zenith in the clear, bright sky, the mob starts to search for shade—the shade of any tree or bush or overhanging rock—and each sheep shows signs of thirst with the drooping ear and the licking of lips.

The shepherd knows the range. He has walked the sheep paths long before any of his flock were born. He knows where the green pastures are and he knows where the fresh springs of water are. The way is not always easy.

Sometimes the sheep must be forced and persuaded to move down a steep, rocky path. It is often difficult going. They would much rather climb than to descend. It is their natural inclination. The rocky path is narrow. The rocky path is perilous. The rocky path hurts their tender feet. There is unnecessary crowding—and there is dust and there is heat.

Finally, they come to the low plateau and the lower ground. At last, around the bottom bluff, the spring gently gurgles, making a still pond of crystal clear water. The leaders call to the others, signaling the discovery of the water, and within a few minutes, all is contentment. Thirst is replaced with refreshment.

And what a sight! Each sheep takes its turn. Each sheep sips, rather than gulps. There's no charging in, no shoving aside, no forcing itself ahead of the other. They wait politely one for another. They often take time to wet their silky muzzles, swish, and toss their heads, drinking slowly with no haste and great contentment.

Then it is siesta time, the sheep in the cool shade of boulders and bushes and trees, and the shepherd in the shade of a high point, where he can survey all the flock as they settle down for a 2 or 3 hour nap. At last the rams, the wethers, and the older sheep have found rest and relaxation. At last the lambs have quieted down, and are willing to leave their mother-ewes alone and undisturbed. A time for quiet. A time for rest. A time for meditation. A time for chewing the cud. No noise. No predators. No perils. No dangers. At last, near the soil, the grass, the water, the best part of the day. What a sanctuary for sheep and shepherd, and under his watchful eye.

It is mid-afternoon, and the first to move is the shepherd. The shadows are beginning to grow longer. The heat of the day is passed. And it is time to retrace steps back to home and to the sheepfold. The flock is slow to stir from its siesta. The sheep would remain where they were all day and into the twilight if the shepherd would let them, but it is time to depart and begin the journey homeward.

The leaders of the flock are started back first, along the path that leads homeward, and up the steep path. The rest slowly follow. On regaining the tops, the afternoon winds begin to stir. The stir becomes a strong wind and a gale, directly in the face of the flock, the dust flying and the hot air whistling straight into their faces.

How the flock dislike wind in their face! Always on the range they immediately turn their backs to the wind. But now they must take the wind head on. Why? Why doesn't the shepherd let us go before it, turn our back to it, or lead us some other way? The answer is, although it be difficult, although it be hard, it is the way home to the sheepfold. If they linger, if they dawdle, if they are not there by sunset, the flock will become scattered, sheep will lose their way, and they will become prey for predators, for thieves, for robbers—who prefer the darkness to the light because their deeds are evil.

It is not an easy end to the day. Many problems have been faced, many dangers anticipated, many needs met, and the shepherd has had to be vigilant all the day long.

When the way is hard, the flock may often become quite unsettled, even when it's on its way home. The shepherd observes a poor old ewe, limping along at the tail of the mob. He goes to her and finds a small hard stick between her hooves. He takes the ewe in his arms, holds her gently and reassuredly, and carefully removes the offending hurt. He rubs in some soothing salve, lifts her to her feet, and moves her into the homeward path.

A count of the flock reveals that one sheep is missing. He looks far and wide, and then retraces the path of the sheep, looking for the one that is lost. He searches high and low, and there, in the thicket of a thorn bush is the hogget [a young sheep], caught and unable to escape. Gently he works the yearling loose and carries it over his shoulders the half mile to rejoin the procession home.

When he catches up with the flock and returns the lost sheep, the shepherd spots two big rams fighting it out for leadership and dominance within the flock. Hurriedly the shepherd parts them and teaches them who's really the boss—the shepherd himself.

While the shepherd was gone, a ewe has become cast in a hole and her lamb separated off on the other side of the mob. Both are in great distress. The shepherd goes into action, lifting the ewe back on to her feet, reassuring her, walking her through the mob, while she calls for her little lamb. Finally they are soon reunited—with joy abounding.

The sun is setting amidst the colourful clouds in the western sky—"red sky at night, shepherd's delight"—there is promise of a wonderful day tomorrow.

The last mile, the easy mile, is a well-worn path back to the sheepfold. It has been traveled many times and on many days. The sheep sense familiar territory, their home field and their home fold. The shepherd precedes them, and stands at the sheepfold with the gate wide open. He calls them in, "come unto me . . . and ye shall find rest." The mob with little prompting streams through the portal to rest, to protection, and to contentment.

Here, in the sheepfold, no more dangers or perils. There are no rocky paths. There are no predators. There is no blazing sun, no dry grass, no dust, no wind, no thorns, no crying, no pain. Rather there is sweet straw, pure water, high walls around the sanctuary, protection against all dangers, sweet peace, sweet rest, and sweet fellowship—until the shepherd comes to awaken them again to a bright, new morning.

The shepherd knows his flock. The shepherd knows the correct number, and all are present and accounted for. All are in and he shuts the door. No one can enter and no one can leave. He alone has the power to open it again.[1]

THE CHIEF SHEPHERD

Jesus is the perfect example of a loving shepherd. He epitomizes everything that a spiritual leader should be. Peter called Him the

1. W. G. Bowen, *Why the Shepherd* (New Zealand: W. G. Bowen, n.d.), pp. 79-83. Quoted here by permission of the author.

"Chief Shepherd" (1 Pet. 5:4). Jesus called Himself the "Good Shepherd," who lays down His life for the sheep (John 10:11). In John 10:27-28 He says, "My sheep hear My voice, and I know them, and they follow Me; and I give eternal life to them, and they shall never perish; and no one shall snatch them out of My hand" (NASB). He is our great Rescuer, Leader, Guardian, Protector, and Comforter.

FROM ANALOGY TO REALITY

Elders are under-shepherds who guard the flock under the Chief Shepherd's watchful eye (Acts 20:28). Theirs is a full-time responsibility because they minister to people who, like sheep, often are vulnerable, defenseless, undiscerning, and prone to stray.

Under-shepherds must feed the sheep with God's Word and lead them by example. They must keep the sheep from straying from the fellowship or wandering off into some pasture that is harmful to them. They must protect them from any Judas sheep leading them into doctrinal error and spiritual disaster. They must "admonish the unruly, encourage the fainthearted, help the weak, [and] be patient with all" (1 Thess. 5:14; NASB).

Shepherding the flock of God is an enormous task, but to faithful elders it brings the rich reward of the unfading crown of glory, which will be awarded by the Chief Shepherd Himself at His appearing (1 Pet. 5:4).

APPENDIXES

Appendix 1

Answering the Key Questions About Elders*

A distinctive of the ministry at Grace Community Church over the years has been an emphasis on the leadership of elders. We have been blessed by the Lord with a group of consecrated men who, through unyielding commitment to the will of God, have provided strong and unified leadership to the Body. Their leadership, based on the biblical pattern, is a vital key to the blessing Grace Church has experienced in terms of growth and influence.

Twentieth-century American evangelicalism, with its heritage of democratic values and long history of congregational church government, tends to view the concept of elder rule with suspicion. Some have been vocal in characterizing it as a new and subversive concept, threatening the very life of the church. At our semiannual Shepherds' Conferences, invariably the most popular seminars are those that deal with the issue of elders. Pastors want to know what elder rule is, if government by elders genuinely strengthens the church, and how they can implement it in their churches.

Proper biblical government by elders does strengthen the church, and the biblical norm for church leadership is a plurality of God-ordained elders. Furthermore, it is the only pattern for church

---

* Unless otherwise noted, all Scripture references in this appendix are from the *New American Standard Bible.*

leadership given in the New Testament. Nowhere in Scripture do we find a local assembly ruled by majority opinion or by one pastor.

I am confident that a return to the biblical pattern of leadership would do much to revitalize the contemporary church. The strength, health, productivity, and fruitfulness of any church directly reflect the quality of its leadership.

Under the plan God has ordained for the church, leadership is a position of humble, loving service. Those who would lead God's people must exemplify purity, sacrifice, diligence, and devotion. And with the tremendous responsibility inherent in leading the flock of God comes potential for either great blessing or great judgment. Good leaders are doubly blessed; poor leaders are doubly chastened, for "from everyone who has been given much shall much be required" (Luke 12:48). James 3:1 says, "Let not many of you become teachers, my brethren, knowing that as such we shall incur a stricter judgment."

Biblically, the focal point of all church leadership is the elder. It is the elders who are charged with teaching, feeding, and protecting the church, and it is the elders who are accountable to God on behalf of the church. Yet as I meet elders and pastors from across the country, I find that many understand neither the gravity nor the potential of their role. Being uncertain of their function or their relationship to the Body, they are greatly hindered in their ability to minister effectively. With that in mind, let me suggest eleven key questions, the answers to which are fundamental to a biblical understanding of the ministry of elders.

WHAT IS THE PROPER
UNDERSTANDING OF THE TERM *ELDER*?

The term *elder* is of Old Testament origin. The primary Hebrew word for *elder (zaqen)* was used, for example, in Numbers 11:16 and Deuteronomy 27:1 of the seventy tribal leaders who assisted Moses. There it refers to a special category of men who were set apart for leadership—much like a senate—in Israel. Deuteronomy 1:9-18 indicates that they were charged with the responsibility of judging the people. Moses communicated through them to the people (Ex. 19:7; Deut. 31:9). They led the Passover (Ex. 12:21) and perhaps other elements of worship.

Later the elders of Israel were specifically involved in the leadership of cities (1 Sam. 11:3; 16:4; 30:26). Still, their function was decision making—applying wisdom to the lives of the people in resolving conflicts, giving direction, and generally overseeing the details of an orderly society.

The Old Testament refers to them as "elders of Israel" (1 Sam. 4:3), "elders of the land" (1 Kings 20:7), "elders of Judah" (2 Kings 23:1), "elders . . . of each city" (Ezra 10:14), and "elders of the congregation" (Judg. 21:16). They served in the capacity of local magistrates and as governors over the tribes (Deut. 16:18; 19:12; 31:28).

Another Hebrew word for *elder* is *sab*, used only five times in the Old Testament, all in the book of Ezra. It refers to the group of Jewish leaders in charge of rebuilding the Temple after the Exile.

The Greek word for *elder* (*presbuteros*) is used about seventy times in the New Testament. Like *zaqen*, which means "aged" or "bearded," *sab*, which means "gray-headed," and our English word *elder* (*presbuteros*) has reference to mature age. For example, in Acts 2:17 Peter quotes Joel 2:28: "Your old men shall dream dreams." The Hebrew word used for "old men" in Joel is *zaqen*, and the Greek word used in Acts is *presbuteros*. Used in that sense, *elder* does not constitute an official title; it simply refers to an older man.

In 1 Timothy 5:2 the feminine form of *presbuteros* is used to refer to older women. There, older women are contrasted with younger ones: "[Appeal to] the older women as mothers, and the younger women as sisters, in all purity." In that context, the term also signifies only mature age, not an office in the church.

First Peter 5:5 contains a similar usage: "You younger men, likewise, be subject to your elders." There, as in 1 Timothy 5:2, the word is used to contrast age and youth. In such a context, *presbuteros* is generally understood to mean only "an older person," not necessarily an officeholder. That is the primary meaning of the term in general Greek usage.

In the time of Christ *presbuteros* was a familiar term. It is used twenty-eight times in the New Testament to refer to a group of ex officio spiritual leaders of Israel: "the chief priests and elders" (Matt. 27:3), "the rulers and elders of the people" (Acts 4:8). In each of those instances and every similar usage, *presbuteros* refers to recognized spiritual leaders in Israel who aren't defined as priests of any kind. They seem to be the Sanhedrin, the highest ruling body of Judaism in Jesus' time.

Matthew 15:2 and Mark 7:3, 5 use the phrase "tradition of the elders." In these cases *presbuteros* refers to an ancestry of spiritual fathers who passed down principles that governed religious practice. They were the teachers who determined Jewish tradition. In that sense, *elder* is equivalent to *rabbi* and may or may not signify official status.

There are twelve occurrences of *presbuteros* in the book of Revelation. All of them refer to the twenty-four elders who appear to be unique representatives of the redeemed people of God from all ages.

How Is the Term *Elder* Used in Reference to the Church?

The New Testament church was initially Jewish, so it would be natural for the concept of elder rule to be adopted for use in the early church. *Elder* was the only commonly used Jewish term for leadership that was free from any connotation of either the monarchy or the priesthood. That is significant because in the church, each believer is a co-regent with Christ, so there could be no earthly king. And unlike national Israel, the church has no specially designated earthly priesthood, for all believers are priests. So of all the Jewish concepts of leadership, the elder best fits the kind of leadership ordained for the church.

The elders of Israel were mature men. They were heads of families (Ex. 12:21); possessors of strong moral character; God-fearing men of truth and integrity (Ex. 18:20-21); full of the Holy Spirit (Num. 11:16-17); capable men of wisdom, discernment, and experience; impartial and courageous men who could be counted on to intercede, teach, and judge righteously and fairly (Deut. 1:13-17). All those characteristics were involved in the Jewish understanding of the term *presbuteros*. The use of that term to describe church leaders emphasizes the maturity of their spiritual experience, as shown in the strength and consistency of their moral character.

Presbuteros is used nearly twenty times in Acts and the epistles in reference to a unique group of leaders in the church. From the beginning it was clear that a group of mature spiritual leaders was to have responsibility for the church. The church at Antioch, for example, where believers were first called "Christians," sent Barnabas and Saul to the elders at Jerusalem with a gift to be distributed to the needy brethren in Judea (Acts 11:30). That demonstrates that elders existed in the church at that early time and that the believers at Antioch recognized their authority.

Since the church at Antioch grew out of the ministry at Jerusalem, elders probably existed there as well. In fact, it is likely that Paul himself functioned as an elder at Antioch before he stepped out in the role of an apostle. He is listed in Acts 13:1 as one of that church's teachers.

Elders played a dominant role in the Council of Jerusalem as recorded in Acts 15 (see vv. 2, 4, 6, 22-23, and 16:4). Obviously they were influential in the foundational life of the early church.

As Paul and Barnabas began to preach in new areas and as the church began to extend itself, the process of identifying church leaders became more clearly defined. And throughout the New Testament, as the church developed, the leaders were called elders.

As early in the biblical narrative as Acts 14, we see that one of the key steps in establishing a new church was to identify and appoint elders for church leadership. Verse 23 says, "When they had appointed elders for them in every church, having prayed with fasting, they commended them to the Lord in whom they had believed."

Nearly every church we know of in the New Testament is specifically said to have had elders. For example, Acts 20:17 says, "From Miletus he sent to Ephesus and called to him the elders of the church." It is significant that the church at Ephesus had elders because all the churches of Asia Minor—such as those listed in Revelation 1:11—were extensions of the ministry at Ephesus. We can assume that those churches also identified their leadership by the same terms that were set as the pattern in Ephesus—a plurality of elders.

Peter wrote to the scattered believers in Pontus, Galatia, Cappadocia, Asia, and Bithynia, saying, "I exhort the elders among you . . . shepherd the flock of God" (1 Pet. 5:1-2). Those territories were not cities; Peter was writing to the number of churches scattered all over Asia. All of them had elders.

How Is the Elder Related to the Bishop and the Pastor?

Bishops and pastors are not distinct from elders; the terms are simply different ways of identifying the same people. The Greek word for *bishop* is *episkopos*, from which the Episcopalian Church gets its name. The Greek word for *pastor* is *poimēn*.

The textual evidence indicates that all three terms refer to the same office. The qualifications for a bishop, listed in 1 Timothy 3:1-7, and those for an elder, in Titus 1:6-9, are unmistakably parallel. In fact, in Titus, Paul uses both terms to refer to the same man (1:5, 7).

First Peter 5:1-2 brings all three terms together: "Therefore, I exhort the elders [*presbuteros*] among you, as your fellow-elder and witness of the sufferings of Christ, and a partaker also of the glory that is to be revealed, shepherd [*poimainō*] the flock of God among you, exercising oversight [*episkopeō*] not under compulsion, but voluntarily, according to the will of God."

Acts 20 also uses all three terms interchangeably. In verse 17 Paul assembles all the elders [*presbuteros*] of the church to give them his farewell message. In verse 28 he says, "Be on guard for yourselves and for all the flock, among which the Holy Spirit has made you overseers [*episkopos*], to shepherd [*poimainō*] the church of God."

In general usage I prefer the term *elder* because it seems to be free of the many connotations and nuances that have been imposed on both *bishop* and *pastor* by our culture.

Episkopos, the word for *bishop*, means "overseer" or "guardian." The New Testament uses *episkopos* five times. In 1 Peter 2:25 Jesus Christ is called the *episkopos* of our souls. He is the One who has the clearest overview of us, who understands us best. He is the Shepherd and Guardian of our souls. The other four uses of *episkopos* refer to leaders in the church.

Episkopos is the secular Greek culture's equivalent to the historic Hebrew idea of elders. Bishops were those appointed by the emperors to lead captured or newly founded city-states. The bishop was responsible to the emperor, but oversight was delegated to him. He functioned as a commissioner, regulating the affairs of the new colony or acquisition. Thus *episkopos* suggested two ideas to the first-century Greek mind: responsibility to a superior power, and an introduction to a new order of things. Gentile converts would immediately understand those concepts.

It is interesting to trace the biblical uses of *episkopos*. It appears in the book of Acts only once, near the end (Acts 20:28). Of course, at that time, there were relatively few Gentiles in the church, and so the term was not commonly used. But apparently as Gentiles were saved and the church began to lose some of its Jewish flavor, the Greek culture's word *episkopos* was used more frequently to describe those who functioned as elders (1 Tim. 3:1).

The New Testament bishop, or overseer, is responsible for teaching (1 Tim. 3:2), feeding, protecting, and generally nurturing the flock (Acts 20:28). Biblically, there is no difference in the role of an elder and that of a bishop; the two terms refer to the same group of leaders. *Episkopos* emphasizes the function; *presbuteros* the character.

Poimēn, the word for *pastor* or *shepherd*, is used a number of times in the New Testament, but Ephesians 4:11 is the only place in the King James Version where it is translated "pastor." Every other time it appears in the Greek texts it is translated "shepherd."

Two of the three times *poimēn* appears in the epistles, it refers to Christ. Hebrews 13:20-21 is a benediction: "Now the God of peace, who brought up from the dead the great Shepherd [*poimēn*] of the sheep through the blood of the eternal covenant, even Jesus our Lord, equip you in every good thing to do His will." First Peter 2:25 says, "You were continually straying like sheep, but now you have returned to the Shepherd [*poimēn*] and Guardian [*episkopos*] of your souls."

In Ephesians 4:11, *pastor (poimēn)* is used with the word *teacher*. The Greek construction there indicates that the two terms go together—we might hyphenate them in English ("pastor-teacher"). The emphasis is on the pastor's ministry of teaching.

Poimēn, then, emphasizes the pastoral role of caring and feeding, although the concept of leadership is also inherent in the picture of a shepherd. The emphasis of the term poimēn is on the man's attitude. To qualify as a pastor, a man must have a shepherd's caring heart.

So the term elder emphasizes who the man is. Bishop speaks of what he does. And pastor ("shepherd") deals with how he ministers. All three terms are used of the same church leaders, identifying those who feed and lead the church, but each has a unique emphasis.

WHAT IS THE ROLE OF AN ELDER?

As the apostolic era came to a close, the office of elder emerged as the highest level of local church leadership. Thus it carried a great amount of responsibility. There was no higher court of appeal and no greater resource to know the mind and heart of God with regard to issues in the church.

First Timothy 3:1 says, "It is a trustworthy statement: if any man aspires to the office of overseer [episkopos], it is a fine work he desires to do." In verse 5 Paul says that the work of an episkopos is to "take care of the church of God." The clear implication is that a bishop's primary responsibility is to be caretaker for the church.

That involves a number of specific duties. Perhaps the most obvious is the function of overseeing the affairs of the local church. First Timothy 5:17 says, "Let the elders who rule well be considered worthy of double honor." The Greek word translated "rule" in that verse is proistēmi, used to speak of the elders' responsibilities four times in 1 Timothy (3:4-5; 5:12, 17), once in 1 Thessalonians 5:12 (where it is translated "have charge over"), and once in Romans 12:8, where ruling is listed as a spiritual gift. Proistēmi literally means "to stand first," and it speaks of the duty of general oversight common to all elders.

As rulers in the church, elders are not subject to any higher earthly authority outside the local assembly. Their authority over the church is not by force or dictatorial power but by precept and example (Heb. 13:7).

Nor are the elders to operate by majority rule or vote. If all the elders are guided by the same Spirit and all have the mind of Christ, there should be unanimity in the decisions they make (1 Cor. 1:10; Eph. 4:3; Phil. 1:27; 2:2). If there is division, all the elders should study, pray, and seek the will of God together until consensus is achieved. Unity and harmony in the church at large begin here.

The elders are responsible to preach and teach (1 Tim. 5:17). They are to determine doctrinal issues for the church and have the responsibility of proclaiming the truth to the congregation. First Timothy 3:2, listing the spiritual qualifications of the overseer, gives only one qualification that relates to a specific *function*: he must be "able to teach." All the other qualifications are personal *character qualities*.

Titus 1:7-9 also emphasizes the significance of the elder's responsibility as a teacher: "The overseer must . . . be able both to exhort in sound doctrine and to refute those who contradict." Already the threat of false teachers was so great that a key qualification for leadership was an understanding of sound doctrine and the ability to teach it.

"Exhort" in that verse is the Greek word *parakaleō*, which literally means "to call near." From its use in the New Testament, we see that the ministry of exhortation has several elements. It involves persuasion (Acts 2:4; 14:22; Titus 1:9), pleading (2 Cor. 8:17), comfort (1 Thess. 2:11), encouragement (1 Thess. 4:1), and patiently reiterating important doctrine (2 Tim. 4:2).

The elders are a resource for those who seek partnership in prayer. James wrote, "Is anyone among you sick? Let him call for the elders of the church, and let them pray over him, anointing him with oil in the name of the Lord" (James 5:14).

Acts 20:28 says that another function of an elder is shepherding: "Be on guard for yourselves and for all the flock, among which the Holy Spirit has made you overseers, to shepherd the church of God." That involves feeding and protecting the flock. Verses 29-30 emphasize that the protecting ministry of the overseer is to counter the threat of false teachers.

The elder acts as a caring and loving shepherd over the flock but never in Scripture is it spoken of as "his flock," or "your flock." It is the "flock of God" (1 Pet. 5:2), and he is merely a steward—a caretaker over the possession of God.

Elders, as the spiritual overseers of the flock, are to determine church policy (Acts 15:22); oversee (Acts 20:28); ordain others (1 Tim. 4:4); rule, teach, and preach (1 Tim. 5:17); exhort and refute (Titus 1:9); and act as shepherds, setting an example for all (1 Pet. 5:1-3). Those responsibilities put elders at the core of the New Testament church's work.

Understandably, elders cannot afford to allow themselves to be consumed with business details, public relations, minor financial matters, and other particulars of the day-to-day operation of the church. They are to devote themselves first of all to prayer and to the ministry of the Word, and select others to handle the lesser matters (Acts 6:3-4).

WHAT ARE THE QUALIFICATIONS OF AN ELDER?

First Timothy 3 and Titus 1 identify the qualifications of an elder. First Timothy 3:1-7 says,

It is a trustworthy statement: if any man aspires to the office of overseer, it is a fine work he desires to do. An overseer, then, must be above reproach, the husband of one wife, temperate, prudent, respectable, hospitable, able to teach, not addicted to wine or pugnacious, but gentle, uncontentious, free from the love of money. He must be one who manages his own household well, keeping his children under control with all dignity (but if a man does not know how to manage his own household, how will he take care of the church of God?); and not a new convert, lest he become conceited and fall into the condemnation incurred by the devil. And he must have a good reputation with those outside the church, so that he may not fall into reproach and the snare of the devil.

The single, overarching qualification of which the rest are supportive is that he is to be "above reproach." That is, he must be a leader who cannot be accused of anything sinful. All the other qualifications, except perhaps teaching and management skills, only amplify that idea.

An elder must be above reproach in his marital life, his social life, his family life, his business life, and his spiritual life. "The husband of one wife" (lit. "a one-woman man") does not mean simply that he is married to one woman—that would not be a spiritual qualification. Rather, it means an elder is to be single-minded in his devotion to his wife. If he is not married, he is not to be a flirtatious type. "Temperate" speaks of a balanced, moderate life. "Prudent" is another word for "wise." "Respectable" means he has dignity and the respect of his peers. "Hospitable" means that he loves strangers—not necessarily that he has a lot of dinner parties but rather that he is not cliquish. "Able to teach" is *didaktikos*, or "skilled in teaching." In addition he is "not addicted to wine" (Timothy himself apparently drank none, 1 Tim. 5:23); and not "pugnacious" (not one who picks fights or is physically abusive), but "gentle, "uncontentious," and "free from the love of money."

All those must be proved qualities and abilities, and the first place he must manifest them is in his home. He must manage his own household well and keep his children under control with dignity. "Household" in verse 5 probably refers to an extended household, including servants, lands, possessions, and many in-laws and other relatives. Those were elements of a household in the first century, and a great deal of leadership skill and spiritual character were required to manage them well. If a man could not manage his household, how could he be charged with managing the church?

The qualifications of an elder, then, go far beyond good moral characteristics. An elder must be demonstrably skilled as a teacher and manager. If anything in his life signifies a weakness in those areas, he is disqualified. If he is in debt, if his children are rebellious, or if his business affairs are not above reproach, he cannot be an elder.

He clearly cannot be a new convert, for it takes time to develop spiritual maturity and to examine a man's life and evaluate his qualifications. In addition, elevating a new convert to a position of leadership can tempt him to become conceited.

To wrap all that up, an elder must have an impeccable reputation with those outside the church as well as those within.

In Titus 1:5-9 Paul lists similar qualifications:

> For this reason I left you in Crete, that you might set in order what remains, and appoint elders in every city as I directed you, namely, if any man be above reproach, the husband of one wife, having children who believe, not accused of dissipation or rebellion. For the overseer must be above reproach as God's steward, not self-willed, not quick-tempered, not addicted to wine, not pugnacious, not fond of sordid gain, but hospitable, loving what is good, sensible, just, devout, self-controlled, holding fast the faithful word which is in accordance with the teaching, that he may be able both to exhort in sound doctrine and to refute those who contradict.

Most of those qualifications echo the ones given in 1 Timothy. Again Paul says that an elder is to be a one-woman man, having children whose lives are not characterized by rebellion or dissipation, which is sinful indulgence. In other words, his children are not rebelling against him or against the values of a righteous home and family, and they are not living lives of profligacy.

The overseer must be "above reproach as God's steward." That implies again that he has already proved himself in the ministry. He is "not self-willed," seeking his own agenda. He is "not quick-tempered," "not addicted to wine," and "not pugnacious," or violent. He does not seek to get money through illicit or questionable means. He is "hospitable," fond of what is good and "sensible," or discreet. He is righteous, devoted to God, and "self-controlled."

In addition to all that, he must demonstrate skill in handling the Word of God so he can both "exhort in sound doctrine" and "refute those who contradict" it.

Notice the parallels and the differences in the two listings. (For a more thorough discussion of the specific characteristics, see appendix 3.)

1 Timothy 3	Titus 1
• above reproach (v. 2)	• above reproach (v. 6)
• the husband of one wife (v. 2)	• the husband of one wife (v. 6)
• temperate (v. 2)	• self-controlled (v. 8)
• prudent (v. 2)	• sensible (v. 8)
• respectable (v. 2)	
• hospitable (v. 2)	• hospitable (v. 8)
• able to teach (v. 2)	• able both to exhort in sound doctrine and to refute those who contradict (v. 9)
• not addicted to wine (v. 3)	• not addicted to wine (v. 7)
• not pugnacious (v. 3)	• not pugnacious (v. 7)
• gentle (v. 3)	
• uncontentious (v. 3)	
• free from the love of money (v. 3)	• not fond of sordid gain (v. 7)
• ruling his household well (v. 4)	• above reproach as God's steward (v. 7)
• having children under control with dignity (v. 4)	• having children who believe and are not accused of dissipation or rebellion (v. 6)
• not a new convert (v. 6)	
• good reputation outside the church (v. 7)	
	• not self-willed (v. 7)
	• not quick-tempered (v. 7)
	• loving what is good (v. 8)
	• just (v. 8)
	• devout (v. 8)

CAN WOMEN SERVE AS ELDERS?

No provision is made for women to serve as elders. First Timothy 2:11-12 says, "Let a woman quietly receive instruction with entire submissiveness. But I do not allow a woman to teach or exercise authority over a man, but to remain quiet." In the church women are to be under the authority of the elders, excluded from teaching men or holding positions of authority over them.

The reason women must submit to the leadership of men is not cultural, nor does it reflect a Pauline prejudice, as some claim. Rather, it is rooted in the order of creation: "For it was Adam who was first created, and then Eve" (v. 13). The Fall of man confirmed that order: "And it was not Adam who was deceived, but the woman being quite deceived, fell into transgression" (v. 14).

The balance of influence comes through the woman's responsibility of bearing and nurturing children (v. 15).

How Are Elders to Be Ordained?

The New Testament clearly indicates that elders were uniquely set apart or appointed to their office. The term normally used for the appointing of elders in the New Testament is *kathistēmi*, which means "to ordain." The concept of ordination implies official recognition by the leadership of the church and a public announcement setting men aside for special ministry.

In 1 Timothy 4:14 Paul says to Timothy, "Do not neglect the spiritual gift within you, which was bestowed upon you through prophetic utterance with the laying on of hands by the presbytery." That laying on of hands comes from the Old Testament sacrificial system. When a sacrifice was given, the hands of the offerer were placed upon the sacrifice to show identification. So the laying on of hands became a means by which one could identify himself with another.

In the same way, the New Testament ordination ritual demonstrated solidarity between the elders and the one on whom they laid their hands. It was a visible means of saying, "We commend you to the ministry. We stand with you, support you, and affirm your right to function in a position of leadership in this church."

Paul, however, warned Timothy, "Do not lay hands upon anyone too hastily and thus share responsibility for the sins of others; keep yourself free from sin" (1 Tim. 5:22). That emphasizes the seriousness of the statement of solidarity. If you lay hands on a man who is sinning and thereby ordain him to the pastorate, you have entered into his sin. If you don't want to be a participant in sin, don't fail to seek the mind of the Lord in the process.

A man should be considered for ordination only after he has proved himself suitable for a ministry of leadership through a period during which he is *tested*. Then he may be *tempered* for a time, during which he is observed functioning in a limited position of delegated oversight. If he demonstrates capability in leadership and loyalty to the message, he can be publicly acknowledged as one who is to be *trusted* in the service of leadership. The church should have men in all places of the proving process as it looks toward its future needs.

Biblically, the laying on of hands was done by the recognized leaders of a church. It was their way of identifying themselves with those who were becoming leaders. But the process of identifying leaders may also have involved the congregation. Acts 14:23 says, "When they had appointed elders for them in every church, having prayed with fasting, they commended them to the Lord in whom they had believed." The word for "appointed" in that verse is *cheirotoneō*, which literally means "to choose by raising hands." It is the same word used to describe how votes were taken in the Athenian legislature. It came to mean "to appoint."

Some think that the use of *cheirotoneō* implies that a congregational vote by show of hands was taken. That is forcing the word. The context of Acts 14:23 indicates that only Barnabas and Paul (the antecedents of the pronoun *they*) were involved in the choosing.

Second Corinthians 8:19 uses *cheirotoneō* to describe an unnamed brother "appointed by the churches" to travel with Paul. The plural *"churches"* indicates that he was selected not by a single congregational vote but rather by the consensus of the churches of Macedonia—probably as represented by their leaders.

So using the term *cheirotoneō* in an exaggerated literal way is not sufficient to support the idea of the election of elders by congregational vote, although the assent of the congregation may be implied.

Acts 6:5 is often submitted as proof for congregational selection: "The statement found approval with the whole congregation; and they chose Stephen, a man full of faith and of the Holy Spirit, and Philip, Prochorus, Nicanor, Timon, Parmenas and Nicolas, a proselyte from Antioch." Note, however, that those chosen were not called elders. They were servers whose task was to free the apostles for spiritual leadership. And the people brought them to the apostles for approval—not the reverse (v. 6). The congregation acknowledged them to be godly and qualified men, but the apostles appointed them to their task.

The New Testament church is seen in transition. Patterns of church leadership developed as the first-century church matured. We can trace three steps in the process of ordaining leaders. Initially it was the apostles who selected and ordained elders (Acts 14:23). After that, elders were appointed by those who were close to the apostles and involved in their ministry. For example, Paul specifically charged Titus with the ordaining of elders (Titus 1:5). In the third phase, the elders themselves ordain other elders (1 Tim. 4:14). Always the ultimate responsibility for appointing elders belonged to church leadership.

Today there are no apostles, but the biblical pattern still holds. Church leaders—whether they be called elder, bishop, pastor, missionary, evangelist, apostolic representative, or whatever—should have the responsibility of identifying and ordaining other elders.

Those who would be elders must desire to serve in that capacity. First Timothy 3:1 says, "It is a trustworthy statement: if any man *aspires* to the office of overseer, it is a fine work he *desires* to do" (emphasis added). The starting point in identifying a potential elder is the desire in the heart of the individual. First Peter 5:2 says, "Shepherd the flock of God among you, exercising oversight not under compulsion, but voluntarily, according to the will of God."

In other words, we are not to go out and recruit men to become elders. One who is qualified to be an elder will be eager to teach the Word of God and lead the flock of God, without any thought of gain at all. He will desire the office, pursue being set apart, and devote himself to the Word. No one will have to talk him into it; it is his heart's passion.

Furthermore, he serves "voluntarily, *according to the will of God*" (emphasis added). His service as an elder is a calling from God. The desire to serve as an elder is in his heart because God put it there.

If a man has the desire, feels he is called, and has all the qualifications, there is still one thing necessary before he can be ordained. The elders must together seek God's will and affirm that He is in the decision. Acts 14:23 describes the process the apostles followed in selecting elders: "When they had appointed elders for them in every church, having prayed with fasting, they commended them to the Lord in whom they had believed." Before they appointed any elders, they gave themselves over to prayer and fasting. They viewed the eldership with great seriousness as the very highest calling.

Acts 20:28 affirms the Holy Spirit's work in the selection of elders: "Be on guard for yourselves and for all the flock, among which *the Holy Spirit has made you overseers*" (emphasis added). In response to His call, God plants in a man's heart a passion for the ministry and then confirms it by the leading of the Holy Spirit in the hearts of the leadership through prayer and fasting.

When in my youth I sensed God's call to the pastorate, I spent years seeking God to affirm that call in my heart before starting to prepare for ministry. Every elder ought to view his calling as serious, for it is. A man should not become an elder just because he has a vague notion that he would like to use his gifts and abilities to help the church. He should be motivated by a burden that causes him to seek God earnestly.

Acts 13:2 says that the instructions from the Holy Spirit to set apart Paul and Barnabas came "while they were ministering to the Lord [worshiping] and fasting." The call of God is not to be taken lightly, and the will of God is not to be sought superficially. God's will in the matter of ordaining of church leaders will be expressed through the collective sense of God's working among the leadership. They must be sensitive to it. The church is where the call is confirmed.

So elders are a group of specially called and ordained men with a great desire to lead and feed the flock of God. They are initiated by the Holy Spirit, confirmed by prayer, and qualified through the consistent testimony of a pure life in the eyes of all.

ARE ELDERS TO BE SUPPORTED FINANCIALLY BY THE CHURCH?

Even in the early church, some elders were paid by the church for their labor. First Timothy 5:17-18 says, "Let the elders who rule well be considered worthy of double honor, especially those who work hard at preaching and teaching. For the Scripture says, 'You shall not muzzle the ox while he is threshing,' and 'The laborer is worthy of his wages.'" "Honor" in verse 17 is the Greek word *timē*, which, as the context shows, refers to financial remuneration.

In 1 Corinthians 9:1-9 Paul says,

> Am I not free? Am I not an apostle? Have I not seen Jesus our Lord? Are you not my work in the Lord? . . . My defense to those who examine me is this: Do we not have a right to eat and drink? Do we not have a right to take along a believing wife, even as the rest of the apostles, and the brothers of the Lord, and Cephas? Or do only Barnabas and I not have a right to refrain from working? Who at any time serves as a soldier at his own expense? Who plants a vineyard, and does not eat the fruit of it? Or who tends a flock, and does not use the milk of the flock? I am not speaking these things according to human judgment, am I? Or does not the Law also say these things? For it is written in the Law of Moses, "You shall not muzzle the ox while he is threshing." God is not concerned about oxen, is He?

In other words, it is bound into the very nature of the ministry that those who minister should be supported. Soldiers are supported by the government. Farmers eat of their harvest. Shepherds drink milk from the flock. Even oxen get fed through the work they do. So the pastor is to be supported by the church. He adds in verse 13, "Do you not know that those who perform sacred services eat the food of the temple?" Just as the priests lived off the offerings of the people, so those who minister under the New Covenant should be supported by those to whom they minister.

Nevertheless, Paul also establishes the fact that such subsidy is optional. It is a right, not a mandate. In verse 6 he says, "Do only Barnabas and I not have a right to refrain from working?" He and Barnabas were supporting themselves through work outside the scope of the church. They had given up their right to refrain from working. As ministers they had the right to be supported by the church, even if they chose not to exercise that right. Their working was from choice, not necessity, because they wanted to offer the gospel without charge (v. 18), and they did not want to place the burden of their support on the church (1 Thess. 2:9).

Every elder has the same right. If the Lord called him to be an elder and the church has recognized his calling, he has the right to be supported by the church. If he senses the leading of the Spirit of God to seek subsidy so that he can be more free to do what God has put in his heart to do, the church is obligated by the recognition of his pastorate to support him.

But the "tentmaking" role is also an option. If an elder chooses to gain income in another way, that is within the latitude of Scripture. Elders may choose to support themselves by working outside the church, as did Paul, for a number of reasons. They may not wish to put the burden of their support on the church. They may feel their testimony has a greater impact if they do not seek support. In a church with a plurality of elders, it is likely that some will support themselves and others will be supported by the church. Either way it does not affect the man's status as an elder.

The terms *lay* and *clergy* are nonbiblical. That doesn't mean they aren't helpful. In certain circumstances it may be useful to distinguish between those whose full support comes from their service to the church and those whose main source of income is another occupation, but in Scripture no such artificial distinctions are drawn. There are not different classes of saints, and in terms of position there is biblically no difference between a lay elder and a pastor. Each elder is charged with the oversight, care, feeding, protection, and teaching of the flock. All the elders together constitute the leadership and example for the rest of the church. All have been ordained by the church, called by God, and set apart by God to a shepherding function as defined in the Scriptures. They are all called to the same level of commitment and to the same office. Subsidy should not be a divisive issue. Every elder has the option to receive support or to support himself—whichever reflects God's will for him.

In fact, those who choose not to accept support from the church may have an advantage they could not enjoy if they were paid by the church. They are in a position to display to the world their testimony of being above reproach. They are more exposed to unbelievers in the workplace and are on the cutting edge in a different dimension of life, able to interface with people whom the church might otherwise have no contact with. They may bring a greater amount of credibility to the entire group of elders. So an elder's subsidy is optional; his spiritual qualifications are not.

IS THE PASTORATE A TEAM EFFORT?

All the biblical data clearly indicates that the pastorate is a team effort. It is significant that every place in the New Testament where the term *presbuteros* is used it is plural, except where the apostle John uses it of himself in 2 and 3 John and where Peter uses it of himself in 1 Peter 5:1. The norm in the New Testament church was a plurality of elders. Nowhere in the New Testament is there reference to a one-pastor congregation. That is not to say there were none, but none are mentioned. It is significant that Paul addressed his epistle to the Philippians "to all the saints in Christ Jesus who are in Philippi, including the overseers [pl., *episkopoi*] and deacons" (1:1).

Some have said that Revelation 1 supports the one-pastor concept. There the apostle John speaks of "the angels (Gk., *angeloi*) of the seven churches" (v. 20). *Angelos* can mean "messenger," and those who argue for the single-pastor church say that the messengers here and in chapters 2-3 are the pastors of the churches. However, there are some problems with that interpretation: first, *angelos* is nowhere used to refer to a pastor, elder, or bishop in the New Testament, and every other time *angelos* appears in the book of Revelation, it refers to angels.

Second, even if it could be demonstrated that these angels were pastors, that still does not prove that they were not representatives of a group of pastors. The clear New Testament pattern for church government is a plurality of elders. Acts 14:23 says, "When they had appointed elders for them in every church, having prayed with fasting, they commended them to the Lord in whom they had believed." Titus 1:5 says, "For this reason I left you in Crete, that you might set in order what remains, and appoint elders in every city as I directed you." It may be that each elder in the city had an individual group in which he had oversight. But the church was seen as one church, and decisions were made by a collective process and in reference to the whole, not the individual parts.

Much can be said for the benefits of leadership made up of a plurality of godly men. Their combined counsel and wisdom helps assure that decisions are not self-willed or self-serving to a single individual (cf. Prov. 11:14). In fact, one-man leadership is characteristic of cults, not the church.

DOES GOVERNMENT BY ELDERS
ELIMINATE THE ROLE OF A SPECIAL LEADER?

A plurality of elders does not eliminate the unique role of a special leader. Within the framework of elders' ministries is great diversity as each man exercises his unique gifts. Some demonstrate special giftedness in the areas of administration or service; others evidence gifts of teaching, exhortation, or other abilities. Some are highly visible; others function in the background. All are within the plan of God for the church.

The twelve disciples are a good example of how diversity functions in a unified system. The disciples were all equal in terms of their office and privileges. With the exception of Judas, they all will reign on equal thrones, all to be equally respected and honored (Matt. 19:28). And yet within the twelve, there was a tremendous amount of diversity.

Scripture records four lists of the disciples (Matt. 10:2-4; Mark 3:16-19; Luke 6:14-16; Acts 1:13). Each list divides the twelve into three groups of four names, and the three sub-lists always contain the same names, although the order is altered. Generally, the names appear in descending order, beginning with those who were most intimate with Christ, and always ending with Judas Iscariot.

The first four always listed are Peter, James, John, and Andrew. We are more familiar with them because they were closest to Christ and the gospels tell us more about them. The second group is Philip, Matthew, Nathaniel, and Thomas; and the last group includes James, Thaddeus, and both Judases.

It is significant that although the order of sub-lists differs from one account to the other, the first name in each group always remains the same. In the first group the leading name is always Peter. The first name in the second group is always Philip. And James always leads the listing of the third group.

Apparently each of the groups had a recognized leader. His position as leader was not necessarily by appointment but because of the unique influence had had on the rest of the group. Peter, the name at the first of every list, became the spokesman for the entire group, as we see repeatedly throughout Scripture. Almost every time the disciples wanted to ask Jesus a question, Peter was the mouthpiece.

They had an equal office, equal honor, and equal privileges and responsibilities. They were all sent out two by two. They all preached the kingdom. They all healed. They all had access to Jesus. Whereas none of them was less than the others in terms of office or spiritual qualification (except for Judas), some of them stood out over the others as leaders among leaders.

A position of leadership does not imply spiritual superiority. It seems unlikely that Peter was the most spiritually qualified of the disciples. Perhaps James and John came to Jesus to ask for the highest places because they thought Peter was not qualified. Even though he was a leader, he certainly was not spiritually superior to the others. It could be that James the Less was the most spiritual of all. He may have had marvelous gifts that we don't read about because Peter, as the spokesman for the group, was so dominant. We don't know. But it does no disservice to the equality of the twelve that one of them provided leadership to the group.

The same phenomenon can be observed in the book of Acts. James was apparently regarded as a leader and spokesman for the entire church (Acts 12:17; 15:13). Although he was not in any kind of official position over the other elders, they seemed to look to him for leadership, at least in the church in Jerusalem. Peter was present, yet James was in charge. Their roles clearly differed. But no one was the leader of everything.

Peter and John are the two main characters in the first twelve chapters of Acts. Yet there is no record that John ever preached a single sermon. Again, Peter did all the talking. It wasn't that John didn't have anything to say; when he finally got it out, he wrote the gospel of John, three epistles, and the book of Revelation. But Peter had unique gifts, and, in the plan of God, Peter was to be the spokesman. John's was a supporting role—not a less important role but a different one.

Beginning in Acts 13, Paul and Barnabas became the dominant characters. And although Barnabas was probably the leading teacher in the church before Paul came, Paul totally dominated the duo. The Greeks even named him Mercury because he was the chief spokesman. Barnabas undoubtedly did some teaching and preaching, but his sermons are not recorded. His role in their joint ministry was different—less visible, perhaps, but no less important.

Every ministry we see in the New Testament is a team effort. That does not eliminate the unique roles of leadership. But it does mean there's no place for a dictatorial, self-styled leader like Diotrephes, who loved to be first (3 John 9).

What Is the Elders'
Relation to the Congregation?

Elders are called and appointed by God, confirmed by the church leadership, and ordained to the task of leadership. To them are committed the responsibilities of being examples to the flock, giving the church direction, teaching the people, and leading the congregation. Scripture implies that anyone at a lower level of leadership should be under the elders' authority.

Because they share unique responsibility and position in the church, elders are worthy of great respect. First Thessalonians 5:12-13 says, "We request of you, brethren, that you appreciate those who diligently labor among you, and have charge over you in the Lord and give you instruction, and that you esteem them very highly in love because of their work."

The Greek word translated "appreciate" in that passage means "to know intimately." Along with the rest of this passage, it implies a close relationship involving appreciation, respect, love, and cooperation. That great feeling of appreciation is to arise "because of their work." We are to respect them because of the calling they are fulfilling—not only because of their diligent labor and the task they have but because that calling is so noble.

Hebrews 13:7 says, "Remember those who led you, who spoke the Word of God to you; and considering the result of their conduct, imitate their faith." That emphasizes both the elder's responsibility to live as an example, manifesting virtue in his life, and the church's duty to follow their example.

Verse 17 adds another dimension of the congregation's duty toward their spiritual leaders: "Obey your leaders, and submit to them; for they keep watch over your souls, as those who will give an account. Let them do this with joy and not with grief, for this would be unprofitable for you." In other words, the congregation is spiritually accountable to the elders, and the elders are accountable to God. The congregation should submit to the elders' leadership and let the elders be concerned with their own accountability before the Lord. And if the congregation is submissive and obedient, the elders will be able to lead with joy and not with grief, which is ultimately unprofitable for everyone.

That does not mean, however, that if an elder sins openly his sin should be ignored. First Timothy 5:19-21 says,

> Do not receive an accusation against an elder except on the basis of two or three witnesses. Those who continue in sin, rebuke in the presence of all, so that the rest also may be fearful of sinning. I solemnly charge you in the presence of God and of Christ Jesus and of His chosen angels, to maintain these principles without bias, doing nothing in a spirit of partiality.

An accusation of sin against an elder is not to be received lightly. Nor is it to be overlooked. Elders are to be disciplined for sinning in the same way anyone else in the church would be. In no way are they to receive preferential treatment.

The testimony of the church is most visible in the lives of the elders. If they ignore the biblical mandate for holiness, the church will suffer the consequences. Equally, if the church is not submissive to the leadership God has ordained, its testimony will suffer, its effectivenes will be diminished, its priorities will be unbalanced, and ultimately its flavor as the salt of the earth will be lost.

My desire is to see God's church functioning as He has ordained, with strength and purity in the midst of a weak and wicked society. My strong conviction is that when the church submits to God's pattern for leadership, we will begin to experience His blessing beyond anything we could ever ask or think.

Appendix 2

Answering the Key Questions About Deacons[*]

The title *deacon* seems to have as many different connotations as there are churches to bestow it. In some churches the deacons are the official board, the legally recognized managing body. Other churches appoint as deacons almost everyone who is a regular attender. Still other churches bestow the title as a badge of honor, like "reverend," but for laymen. The ministry of a deacon is so different from church to church that when a person says he is a deacon, you usually have to ask several questions to find out what, if anything, he actually does.

Scripture itself is vague about the specifics of what deacons are to do. We read a lot about what qualifies a man to be a deacon but little about how deacons are to minister in the local church. That fact in itself teaches us much about God's view of church leadership: the issue is character, not specific action.

Unfortunately, that point is often overlooked in debates about church government. My conviction is that when a church becomes as concerned about maintaining high standards of purity and integrity in leadership as it is about upholding a specific form of government, it will begin to fall more in line with Scripture in every other area as well.

* Unless otherwise noted, all Scripture references in this appendix are from the *New American Standard Bible*.

How Is the Word *Deacon* Used in the New Testament?

The New Testament text uses three primary words to refer to deacons: *diakonos,* which means "servant"; *diakonia,* which means "service"; and *diakoneō,* which means "to serve." The original use of this group of words seems to have been specific, meaning the service of waiting on tables or serving people food. But it broadened beyond that and came to mean any kind of service.

It is important to understand at the outset that in a biblical context, the group of Greek words from which we get the word *deacon* have meanings no more specific than the meanings of their English equivalents. In biblical usage, *diakonia* suggests all kinds of service, just as the English word *service* does. We might use the word *serve* to describe anything from the start of a volley in a tennis match to a convicted criminal who "serves" a term in prison. We use it to describe a slave who serves his master or a king who serves his people.

The Greek words *diakonos, diakoneō,* and *diakonia* have just as wide a variety of meanings, but in general they refer to any service that supplies the need of another person. The words are used at least a hundred times in the New Testament, and they are usually translated with variants of the English words *serve* or *ministry.* In a few places in the King James Version they are translated differently—*diakonia* is "administration" in 1 Corinthians 12:5 and 2 Corinthians 9:12, and "relief" in Acts 11:29. But in those verses and in every usage of the words throughout the New Testament, the primary meaning has to do with service and ministry.

What Kind of Service Is Implied by the Greek Word for "Deacon"?

SERVING FOOD

The original and most limited meaning of the word *diakoneō* has to do with serving food. The account of the wedding at Cana is a good illustration of that: "His mother said to the servants *[diakonoi],* Whatever He says to you, do it. . . . And when the headwaiter tasted the water which had become wine, and did not know where it came from (but the servants *[diakonoi]* who had drawn the water knew), the headwaiter called the bridegroom" (John 2:5, 9). That is clearly a reference to people who actually served tables, which is the traditional and original meaning of the word *deacon.*

Luke 4:39 tells us that after Christ healed Peter's mother-in-law, she "immediately arose and began to wait on them." The verb form of *diakoneō* appears there. Peter's mother-in-law waited on both Christ and Peter, which probably means she served them a meal. Three other texts in the gospels where the word *deacon* refers to serving a meal are John 12:2, Luke 10:40, and Luke 17:8.

GENERAL SERVICE

On some occasions, *diakoneō* or one of the related words is used without specifying what kind of service is involved. In John 12:26 Christ says, "If anyone serves Me, let him follow Me; and where I am, there shall My servant also be; if any one serves Me, the Father will honor him." The meaning of the word there is general and could refer to a number of forms of service.

Biblically, the word *diakonos* is not limited to describing believers. Romans 13:3-4 says, "Do you want to have no fear of authority? Do what is good, and you will have praise from the same; for it is a minister of God to you for good. But if you do what is evil, be afraid; for it does not bear the sword for nothing; for it is a minister of God, an avenger who brings wrath upon the one who practices evil." Here *diakonos*, translated "minister," is used twice of a policeman or soldier who isn't necessarily a Christian.

A passage in which both the original and the general usage of the word appear is Luke 22:27, where Christ says, "Who is greater, the one who reclines at the table, or the one who serves? Is it not the one who reclines at the table? But I am among you as the one who serves." In that verse *diakoneō* is used twice. The first usage clearly refers to serving a meal. The second speaks of general service.

SPIRITUAL SERVICE

Looking more directly at the term, we find it used of the believer's role as a servant. In Romans 15:25 Paul writes, "I am going to Jerusalem serving the saints." He identified himself as a servant (*diakonos*). From Acts 20:19 we learn that he kept busy "serving [*diakoneō*] the Lord with all humility."

In 2 Corinthians 8:3-4 Paul says of the churches in Macedonia, "I testify that according to their ability, and beyond their ability they gave of their own accord, begging us with much entreaty for the favor of participation in the support [*diakonia*] of the saints." The ministry of providing resources for meeting basic physical needs is a form of spiritual service.

In this spiritual sense of *diakonos* and the related words, any act of obedience done by a Christian should qualify as service to Christ. In the way the words are often used in Acts and the epistles, a believer in any form of ministry could be called the servant, or deacon, of Christ.

First Corinthians 12:5 tells us that "there are varieties of ministries [*diakonia*], and the same Lord." All Christians are involved in some form of service. All who serve the Lord are deacons, or ministers, if not in an official sense, at least in the general sense of the word.

Other verses that use a form of the word *deacon* to speak of spiritual service are 2 Corinthians 4:1; 9:1 and Revelation 2:19. In those and all the verses that we have looked at so far, we have not yet found the word used in reference to the office of deacon in the church.

DOES THE NEW TESTAMENT SPEAK ABOUT THE OFFICE OF A DEACON?

Because of the variety of meanings attached to *diakonos* and the related words, with one or two possible exceptions it is difficult to pin down any clear reference in the New Testament to an office of deacon in the early ecclesiastical government. Most occurrences of *diakonos* and the related words use their general meanings and clearly have nothing to do with a church office. Other passages are more ambiguous, but usually the clearest, most natural interpretation calls for the general meanings, not a reference to a special title belonging to a select group in the church.

For example, some say that Romans 12 contains a reference to the office of deacon: "Since we have gifts that differ according to the grace given to us, let each exercise them accordingly . . . if service, in his serving" (vv. 6- 7). But is the gift of serving equivalent to the function or office of a deacon? There is nothing in the text to support that. The other gifts listed in Romans 12 do not involve offices. Also, offices are not necessarily related to gifts. A person who has the gift of teaching, for example, does not have to be a pastor-teacher to exercise his gift. The gifts are related to calling and assignment, not just offices.

In 1 Corinthians 16:15 Paul says, "You know the household of Stephanas, that they were the first fruits of Achaia, and that they have devoted themselves for ministry [*diakonia*] to the saints." Was Paul saying that the household of Stephanas was a family of officially titled deacons? There is no way to affirm that on the basis of the terms used or the context—in fact, the most natural interpretation is to take it the way it is translated.

Some suggest that Ephesians 4:12 talks about deacons in the church. Starting with verse 11 we read, "[The Lord] gave some as apostles, and some as prophets, and some as evangelists, and some as pastors and teachers, for the equipping of the saints for the work of service, to the building up of the body of Christ." The "work of service" (*diakonia*) is not the work of the deacons, but rather the work of all saints in being servers. Paul was talking about Christians in general being equipped for spiritual service, not about the office of a deacon.

Is Anyone Specified
As a Deacon in the New Testament?

PAUL PROBABLY WASN'T

Some believe that Paul was a deacon. They point to Acts 20:24, where Paul says, "I do not consider my life of any account as dear to myself, in order that I may finish my course, and the ministry [*diakonia*] which I received from the Lord Jesus, to testify solemnly of the gospel of the grace of God." But Paul was saying that he had a special ministry given to him by Christ; he was not calling himself a deacon or minister in any official sense. In Romans 11:13 he writes, "I speak to you Gentiles, inasmuch as I am the apostle of the Gentiles, I magnify mine office [*diakonia*]" (KJV). *The New American Standard* uses the word *ministry* in that verse instead of "office." The use of "office" in the King James Version was arbitrary; it seems unlikely that Paul was using the word in reference to an official position. His office was that of apostle, which he called "my ministry" or "my service."

In 1 Timothy 1:12 Paul writes, "I thank Christ Jesus our Lord, who has strengthened me, because He considered me faithful, putting me into service." That translation is accurate; Paul is not saying that he was put into the office of a deacon. Other passages that talk about Paul as a minister or servant are 1 Corinthians 3:5; 2 Corinthians 3:6 and 6:4; and Ephesians 3:7. In each of those instances, there is no evidence to indicate that Paul was assigned the office of deacon. He was calling himself a servant of God in a general sense.

Paul was an apostle—he spends much of 2 Corinthians 10-12 emphasizing that point. The apostle's office was the highest of all in the early church, superseding that of the elder and deacon. In an official capacity Paul would never have claimed to be a deacon; he was an apostle.

TYCHICUS PROBABLY WASN'T

Paul said to the Ephesians, "[So] that you also may know about my circumstances, how I am doing, Tychicus, the beloved brother and faithful minister [*diakonos*] in the Lord, will make everything known to you" (Eph. 6:21). It could be that Paul was calling Tychicus a faithful deacon. But Paul also used *diakonos* in Ephesians 3:7 and *diakonia* in Ephesians 4:12 as references to general service, and there is no reason to assume he meant differently here.

EPAPHRAS PROBABLY WASN'T

In Colossians 1:7 Paul calls Epaphras "our beloved fellow bond-servant, who is a faithful servant [*diakonos*] of Christ on our behalf." In verses 23 and 25 he writes, "Continue in the faith firmly established and steadfast, and not moved away from the hope of the gospel that you have heard, which was proclaimed in all creation under heaven, and of which I, Paul, was made a minister [*diakonos*]. . . . Of this church I was made a minister according to the stewardship from God bestowed on me for your benefit." Paul used *diakonos* to describe both himself and Epaphras. Since we feel certain that the apostle Paul was not calling himself a deacon, it seems highly unlikely that he was referring to Epaphras as one. Principles of interpretation suggest that a word finds its meaning within the context of a book, and in the context of Colossians there is no indication that *diakonos* refers to the office of deacon.

THOSE MENTIONED IN PHILIPPIANS 1:1 PROBABLY WEREN'T

Another place that the word *deacon* appears is Philippians 1:1. The letter to the Philippians begins, "Paul and Timothy, bond servants of Christ Jesus, to all the saints in Christ Jesus who are in Philippi, including the overseers and deacons."

Up to now we have not seen the Greek word *diakonos* translated as "deacons." Why did the Bible translators suddenly introduce the word *deacon* here in an official sense when in virtually every other usage the word is translated "minister" or "servant"? Granted, the word here could refer to officers in the church, but the context does not seem to warrant such an interpretation.

The word in this verse translated "overseers" (*episkopos*) is not the word normally used to identify elders (*presbuteros*). The most natural interpretation of this verse is that Paul was addressing his letter to the whole church. He seems to be saying, "I write to the whole church, including the leadership and those who follow or serve." To say that Philippians 1:1 refers to the office of deacon might be correct, but it is an arbitrary choice. There is not enough evidence to be dogmatic about what Paul is saying.

We have already seen many uses of the Greek words *diakonos*, *diakoneō*, and *diakonia*, but none with a clear reference to a specific church office.

Doesn't Acts 6 Talk About Deacons?

Many view Acts 6 as the initiation of the deacon's office. Verses 1-2 say that "while the disciples were increasing in number, a complaint arose on the part of the Hellenistic Jews against the native Hebrews, because their widows were being overlooked in the daily serving of food. And the twelve summoned the congregation of the disciples and said, 'It is not desirable for us to neglect the word of God in order to serve tables.'" When food was being given out to care for the widows, the Hellenistic widows were not getting their fair share. Apparently the native Jews were concentrating on the needs of their own people.

It is important to realize the extent of the problem facing the church in trying to provide food for everyone. The church could well have exceeded twenty thousand people at that time. There was no way the twelve apostles would have the time to carry food all over town to meet the needs of hundreds of widows. Not only did food need to be distributed, but also people were needed to administer the whole distribution process. That included collecting and safeguarding the necessary finances, purchasing the food, and dispensing it fairly.

The apostles recognized the scope of the problem yet realized that they needed to solve it without sacrificing their own valuable time and priorities. They said to the congregation, "It is not desirable for us to neglect the word of God in order to serve tables" (v. 2).

The apostles' advice to the congregation is found in verse 3: "Select from among you, brethren, seven men of good reputation, full of the Spirit and of wisdom, whom we may put in charge of this task." It was important to select men who had a reputation for honesty because they were going to be entrusted with money. They did not have the checks or accounting procedures we have today. The men also had to be "full of the Spirit and of wisdom." It is difficult to work out an equitable system of distribution to people who have varying needs. They would have to determine whether someone's need was legitimate.

Seven men were to be chosen so that the apostles could be free to do what God had called them to do. In Acts 6:4 the apostles say, "We will devote ourselves to prayer, and to the ministry of the word." Verses 5-6 tell us that their "statement found approval with the whole congregation; and they chose Stephen, a man full of faith and of the Holy Spirit, and Philip, Prochorus, Nicanor, Timon, Parmenas, and Nicolas, a proselyte from Antioch. And these they brought before the apostles; and after praying, they laid their hands on them."

Were the seven men listed in Acts 6:5 fulfilling the office of deacon? The traditional interpretation of Acts 6 is that those men were the first deacons. Notice that verses 1-2 say, "[The Hellenistic] widows were being overlooked in the daily serving [*diakoneō*] of food. . . . It is not desirable for us to neglect the word of God in order to serve [*diakonia*] tables." Some say that the use of those words implies that these men were chosen to fill the office of deacon.

Another argument for viewing these men as deacons is that early church history confirms that in the postapostolic period deacons were assigned charge of administrative affairs—including the distribution of goods to the poor. In addition, the postapostolic church in Rome limited the number of deacons to seven for many years. They seem to have taken that number from the seven chosen in Acts 6.

Still, there are a number of reasons for rejecting the notion that these seven men were chosen to fill the office of deacon. The use of *diakonia* and *diakoneō* is inconclusive because *diakonia* is used in Acts 6:4 in reference to the work of the apostles themselves. So there is no reason to conclude that the office of a deacon is meant in verse 5. The New Testament never refers to the men listed in Acts 6:5 as deacons. Only two of the men are mentioned elsewhere in Scripture (Stephen and Philip), but they are nowhere called deacons.

Keep in mind that Acts was written in the earliest years of the church. We have already seen that none of the epistles written to specific churches recognized the office of deacon, except the possible indication in Philippians. There is no strong evidence in those epistles to claim that the office of deacon was instituted in Acts 6. Elders are mentioned later in the book of Acts and in several of the epistles to the churches, but not deacons. If Acts 6 is indeed the institution of the deacon's office, it seems strange that deacons are never referred to again in Acts.

Notice the word "task" in Acts 6:3. That suggests the seven men were called to help take care of a one-time crisis, not necessarily installed into a permanent office. Ongoing ministries seem to have been distinct from the immediate task. None of the seven is ever mentioned again in association with any food distribution ministry.

Note that all seven who were chosen had Greek names. If those men were being appointed to the Jerusalem church for an ongoing ministry, it would seem strange that only Greeks would be chosen. A permanent order of deacons in Jerusalem would not likely be made up of Greeks. On the other hand, it seems reasonable to conclude that seven Greeks would be chosen to take care of a short-term ministry to the Hellenistic widows who had been neglected. Those men knew the situation and their people.

It is best to see the events described in Acts 6 as an effort by the Jerusalem church to take care of a temporary crisis, and the calling of the seven men as a temporary ministry.

IF THE MEN IN ACTS 6:5 WEREN'T DEACONS, WHAT WERE THEY?

If the deaconate had been maintained as an official function, we would expect it to be mentioned in Acts 11. There was a famine in Judea six or seven years after the events of Acts 6. The church at Antioch, responding to the needs of the Jerusalem believers, sent relief food to help them: "In the proportion that any of the disciples had means, each of them determined to send a contribution for the relief of the brethren living in Judea. And this they did, sending it in charge of Barnabas and Saul to the elders" (Acts 11:29-30).

The comparison of Acts 6:1-6 and 11:29-30 suggests that the ongoing ministry of distributing goods in the Jerusalem church was entrusted to elders, not deacons. If there had been an officially constituted deaconate in Acts 6 with a continuing responsibility to distribute goods to the needy, the church at Antioch would have sent their contribution to that group.

Now let's look at the men selected in Acts 6. Verse 8 says that Stephen, "full of grace and power, was performing great wonders and signs among the people." His function was not typical of the office of deacon, as indicated later in 1 Timothy 3. He was articulate in the Word and almost apostolic in his gifts. He performed great wonders and signs.

In Acts 21:8 we read about Philip, who is described as an evangelist. Since Acts 7 shows Stephen preaching and Acts 8 shows Philip evangelizing, it appears that the seven men in Acts 6:5 were closer to being elders in function than they were to being deacons. The seven men had administrative responsibilities, they had oversight of a very broad task, some articulated the Word of God, and some evangelized the lost. They were full of the Spirit, faith, and wisdom, and some even performed signs and wonders (cf. Acts 6:8; 8:6-7).

It is noteworthy that only seven men were selected. How could seven men possibly meet the broad need that the Jerusalem church was faced with? It would take more than seven people to do the job of distribution alone! It is more likely that the seven were a group· of highly qualified spiritual leaders, teachers, and honorable men chosen to administrate the situation. By doing what they did, they freed the apostles to devote themselves to the priorities of prayer and the ministry of the Word.

Although we cannot say definitively that Acts 6 talks about the church offices of elder or deacon, we can clearly see there is a need for two areas of ministry: one is teaching and praying (v. 4), which involves spiritual care alone; the other is administration and oversight of needs (v. 1-3), which involves both spiritual and physical care.

The seven men in Acts 6:5 did more than just hand people food. We know that Stephen and Philip were dynamic preachers. Some might assume that the other men listed in Acts 6:5 were not. But immediately after the men were chosen, the church "brought [them] before the apostles; and after praying, they laid their hands on them. And the word of God kept on spreading; and the number of the disciples continued to increase greatly" (Acts 6:6-7). That indicates the seven were a part of the early church's growth. It also suggests that they were more like elders in function than deacons.

Nothing indicates that the seven continued to serve in their original capacity. Stephen was killed shortly thereafter, and Philip went to Samaria. The persecution of Christians in Jerusalem that soon began may have scattered the whole group. As was noted, by the time of Acts 11:29-30 there is no mention of the group. Rather we read of a group of elders. If any of the original seven did remain, they would probably have been elders or secondary apostles of the churches— not deacons.

IS THERE ANY SCRIPTURE PASSAGE THAT REFERS TO DEACONS IN THE OFFICIAL SENSE?

Having explored several general or questionable passages in reference to the office of deacon, it is necessary to turn to the one passage in the New Testament that can definitely be said to refer to that office: 1 Timothy 3. Verse 8 says, "Deacons likewise must be men of dignity, not double-tongued, or addicted to much wine or fond of sordid gain." An interpretive key to that verse is "likewise." It refers to verse 1, in which we find the statement, "If any man aspires to the office of overseer." That indicates deacons occupy a recognized office just as elders do.

So in the church there is to be a plurality of godly men—elders —who oversee the Lord's work in the church. They are assisted in their work by deacons. The basic offices of a church do not need to be more sophisticated than that.

By the A.D. 60s, when this epistle was probably written, the church had developed to the point where the spiritual qualifications for church leaders were specific, yet the instructions for organization were still quite limited. That is by divine design. There is great flexibility in individual church organization because God knew that situations and needs would differ over time and in different cultures. The biblical emphasis is not on the organization but on the leaders' purity and spiritual depth.

What Qualifies a Man to Be a Deacon?

The qualifications for deacons can be divided into two categories: personal character and spiritual character.

PERSONAL CHARACTER

Paul listed four personal qualifications. First, deacons must be men of dignity (1 Tim. 3:8). That means they must be worthy of respect and serious minded, not treating serious things lightly. The Greek word for "dignity" is *semnos,* which means "venerable, honorable, reputable, grave, serious, and stately." The same Greek word appears in Titus 2:2, which says that older men "are to be temperate, *dignified,* sensible, sound in faith, in love, in perseverance" (emphasis added).

First Timothy 3:8 also says a deacon must not be double-tongued or one who says one thing to one person and something else to another—a malicious gossip. He is always consistent and righteous in what he says. Next, deacons are not addicted to much wine. Rather they are noted for their clear thinking and self-control. Finally, Paul said that deacons should not be fond of gain. That would be important because deacons are sometimes responsible for handling funds. Therefore their goals in life must not be monetary. First Timothy 6:9 says that a pervasive desire for financial gain corrupts a man.

SPIRITUAL CHARACTER

Paul also listed four spiritual qualifications. First, a deacon must hold "to the mystery of the faith with a clear conscience" (1 Tim. 3:9). In other words, he must have convictions based on the knowledge of true biblical doctrine. His clear conscience implies that he lives out his convictions. He must hold to the faith and apply the truth in his life.

A second spiritual qualification for deacons is given in verse 10: "Let these also first be tested; then let them serve as deacons if they are beyond reproach." Before a man is officially appointed as a deacon, he must have proved himself faithful in serving the Lord. If he has proved himself to be beyond reproach, then let him serve.

Third, a deacon must be morally pure in every way, just as an elder. Literally verse 10 says, "Let them serve as deacons if they are in the process of being irreproachable." Those who are not above reproach are disqualified from serving as deacons. Verse 12, which says, "Let deacons be husbands of only one wife," also implies that deacons are to be morally pure. But that does not necessarily mean a deacon is to be someone who has never been divorced, although that would be a disqualification if his sin contributed to the divorce or if the circumstances of the divorce bring reproach on him. The main point is that a deacon must be totally consecrated and devoted to his wife. The Greek text actually reads, "Let deacons be one-woman men." Having one wife does not necessarily reflect one's character, but being single-mindedly devoted to one's wife does.

The fourth characteristic of a deacon's spiritual life is that he leads his family well. Deacons are to be "good managers of their children and their own households" (v. 12). A deacon must demonstrate management ability. The proving ground for leadership is how a man manages his children and household.

Although specific personal and spiritual qualifications must be met by those in the offices of elder and deacon, that does not mean the standard is lower for anyone else in the congregation. Everyone should seek to be in the role of a deacon—whether he is a recognized, office-holding deacon or simply a servant to the Body. The qualifications specified in 1 Timothy 3 should be a goal and a guideline for every believer.

WHAT DOES THE BIBLE SAY ABOUT DEACONESSES?

First Timothy 3:11 begins, "Women must likewise be dignified." Again, "likewise" relates back to an office of the church. Contrary to the King James Version's translation of that verse, we know Paul was not talking about the wives of deacons because he used no pronoun to refer to them. He didn't say *their* wives, or *their* women. Since there are no comments about the wives of elders, why would there be any comments about the wives of deacons?

In Romans 16:1 we read, "I commend to you our sister Phoebe, who is a servant [*diakonos*] of the church which is at Cenchrea." Phoebe was recognized by the church for her service. It is possible that she served in an official capacity as a deaconess at the church in Cenchrea.

The Greek word for "women" in 1 Timothy 3:11 is *gunaikas*. Apparently Paul used that term to be specific since there is no feminine form of *diakonos*. The same form of the word *diakonos* is both masculine and feminine; it would have been unclear for Paul to use just the term *diakonos* if he wanted to refer to women servers. He had to identify them as women.

We see, then, three distinct church offices described in 1 Timothy 3—elders, deacons, and deaconesses. This is what Paul had to say about deaconesses: they must be "dignified, not malicious gossips, but temperate, faithful in all things" (v. 11).

What Is the Difference Between Elders and Deacons?

It is essential to recognize that deacons are equally qualified with elders in terms of character and spiritual life. The one difference between their qualifications is that the elder must be able to teach, but the deacon doesn't have to be. In churches today, some who are called elders are really closer to being deacons and vice versa. They both should be proved servants of Christ who have the capability to manage their households and lead the members of their congregation. Elders should be given the primary responsibility of teaching the Word, and that can be accomplished as deacons share the work of the ministry with them.

Deacons are to administrate, shepherd, and care for the flock. Although their primary function is not teaching, they are no less spiritually qualified, honored, or respected than elders. They free up those who are more skilled in teaching to pray and study the Word.

In a special sense, the deacon's task sums up the essence of spiritual greatness. Our Lord said, "Whoever wishes to become great among you shall be your servant, and whoever wishes to be first among you shall be your slave; just as the Son of Man did not come to be served, but to serve" (Matt. 20:26-28).

The Lord Jesus Himself, then, is the model for those who would step into the deacon's role. It is a role of service, sacrifice, and commitment to others' needs. The reward of the deacon's office is not the temporal glory that comes from human adulation but the eternal blessing that comes from living a life of spiritual service to the glory of God.

Appendix 3

Qualifications for Spiritual Leadership*

The character and effectiveness of any church is directly related to the quality of its leadership. That's why the Bible stresses the importance of qualified church leadership and delineates specific standards for evaluating those who would serve in that sacred position. Failure to adhere to those standards has caused many of the problems that churches throughout the world currently face.

It is significant that in his description of the qualifications for elders, Paul focused on their character rather than their function. A man is qualified because of what he is, not because of what he does. If he sins and thereby soils his character, he is subject to discipline in front of the entire congregation (1 Tim. 5:20). The church must carefully guard that sacred office.

The spiritual qualifications for leadership are nonnegotiable. I am convinced they are part of what determines whether a man is indeed called by God to the ministry. Bible schools and seminaries can help equip a man for ministry, church boards and pulpit committees can extend opportunities for him to serve, but only God can call a man and make him fit for the ministry. The call to the ministry is not a matter of analyzing one's talents and then selecting the best career option. It's a Spirit-generated compulsion to be a man of God and

* From tapes GC 54-18–54-24.

serve Him in the church. Those whom God calls will meet the qualifications.

Why are the standards so high? Because whatever the leaders are, the people become. As Hosea said, "Like people, like priest" (4:9). Jesus said, "Everyone, after he has been fully trained, will be like his teacher" (Luke 6:40; NASB). Biblical history demonstrates that people will seldom rise above the spiritual level of their leadership.

First Timothy 3 carefully outlines the spiritual qualifications for men in leadership. Paul is speaking specifically of elders' qualifications in the verses we will examine (vv. 1-7), but note that the only significant difference between an elder's qualifications and those of a deacon is that an elder must be skilled as a teacher (cf. vv. 1-7 and 8-13).

Paul begins by asserting that the man who desires the office desires a good work (v. 1). But no one should ever be placed into church leadership based on desire alone. It is the responsibility of the church to affirm a man's qualifications for ministry by measuring him against God's standard for leadership as delineated in verses 2-7.

"Blameless"—
He Is a Man of Unquestionable Character

Paul began, "A bishop [or elder] . . . must be blameless" (v. 2). The Greek word translated "must" emphasizes an absolute necessity: blamelessness is mandatory for overseers. It is a fundamental, universal requirement. In fact, the other qualifications listed by Paul in verses 2-7 define and illustrate what he meant by "blameless."

The Greek text indicates this is referring to a present state of blamelessness. It doesn't refer to sins that the man committed before he matured as a Christian—unless such sins remain as a blight on his life. (No one is blameless in that sense.) The idea is that he has sustained a reputation for blamelessness.

"Blameless" (v. 2) means "not able to be held." A blameless man cannot be taken hold of as if he were a criminal in need of detention for his actions. There's nothing to accuse him of. He is irreproachable.

A church leader's life must not be marred by sin—be it an attitude, habit, or incident. That's not to say he must be perfect, but there must not be any obvious defect in his character. He must be a model of godliness so he can legitimately call his congregation to follow his example (Phil. 3:17). The people need to be confident that he won't lead them into sin.

Spiritual leaders must be blameless because they set the example for the congregation to follow. That is a high standard, but it isn't a double standard. Since you are responsible to follow the example of your godly leaders (Heb. 13:7, 17), God requires blamelessness of you as well. The difference is that certain sins can disqualify church leaders for life, whereas that's not necessarily true for less prominent roles in the church. Nevertheless, God requires blamelessness of all believers (cf. Eph. 1:4; 5:27; Phil. 1:10; 2:15; Col. 1:22; 2 Pet. 3:14; Jude 24).

A church leader becomes disqualified when there's a blight on his life that communicates to others that one can live in sin and still be a spiritual leader. There are always malicious people looking for ways to discredit the reputation of Christ and His church. A sinful leader plays right into their hands, giving them an unparalleled opportunity to justify their lack of belief.

It's not coincidental that many pastors fall into sin and disqualify themselves from ministry. Satan works hard to undermine the integrity of spiritual leaders because in so doing he destroys their ministries and brings reproach upon Christ. Therefore spiritual leaders must guard their thoughts and actions carefully, and congregations must pray earnestly for the strength of their leadership.

I believe the devil attacks spiritual leaders with more severe temptations than most Christians will ever experience. It stands to reason that those who lead the forces of truth and light against the kingdom of darkness will experience the strongest opposition from the enemy.

An unholy pastor is like a stained glass window: a religious symbol that keeps the light out. That's why the initial qualification for spiritual leadership is blamelessness. Puritan Richard Baxter wrote,

> Take heed to yourselves, lest you live in those sins which you preach against in others, and lest you be guilty of that which daily you condemn. Will you make it your work to magnify God, and when you have done, dishonor Him as much as others? Will you proclaim Christ's governing power, and yet condemn it, and rebel yourselves? Will you preach His laws, and willfully break them?
>
> If sin be evil, why do you live in it? If it be not, why do you dissuade men from it? If it be dangerous, how dare you venture on it? If it be not, why do you tell men so? If God's threatenings be true, why do you not fear them? If they be false, why do you needlessly trouble men with them, and put them into such frights without a cause?
>
> Do you "know the judgment of God, that they who commit such things are worthy of death"; and yet will you do them? "Thou that teachest another, teachest thou not thyself? Thou that sayest a man should not commit adultery," or be drunk, or covetous, art

thou such thyself? "Thou that makest thy boast of the law; through breaking the law dishonorest thou God?" What! Shall the same tongue speak evil that speakest against evil? Shall those lips censure, and slander, and backbite your neighbour, that cry down these and the like things in others?

Take heed to yourselves, lest you cry down sin, and yet do not overcome it; lest, while you seek to bring it down in others, you bow to it, and become its slave yourselves: "For of whom a man is overcome, the same he is brought into bondage." "To whom ye yield yourselves servants to obey, his servants ye are whom you obey, whether of sin unto death, or of obedience unto righteousness." O brethren! it is easier to chide at sin, than to overcome it. (*The Reformed Pastor* [Carlisle, Pa.: Banner of Truth, 1956], pp. 67-68)

Baxter also wrote,

When your minds are in a holy heavenly frame, your people are likely to partake of the fruits of it. Your prayers and praises, and doctrine will be sweet and heavenly to them. They will likely feel when you have been much with God: that which is most on your hearts, is like to be most in their ears. . . .

When I let my heart grow cold, my preaching is cold; and when it is confused, my preaching is confused; and so I can oft observe also in the best of my hearers, that when I have grown cold in preaching, they have grown cold too; and the next prayers which I have heard from them have been too like my preaching. . . .

O brethren, watch therefore over your own hearts: keep out lusts and passions, and worldly inclinations: keep up the life of faith, and love, and zeal: be much at home, and be much with God. . . . Take heed to yourselves, lest your example contradict your doctrine . . . lest you unsay with your lives what you say with your tongues; and be the greatest hinderers of the success of your own labours. . . . One proud, surly, lordly word, one needless contention, one covetous action may cut the throat of many a sermon and blast the fruit of all that you have been doing. (Pp. 61-63)

How does a spiritual leader protect himself from the onslaughts of Satan? The answer is threefold: Scripture, prayer, and fellowship. David said, "Thy word have I hidden in mine heart, that I might not sin against thee" (Ps. 119:11). Being continuously exposed to the living Word guards us from sin and makes us pure (cf. John 15:3). Tragically, many spiritual leaders allow themselves to be drawn away from God's Word. Perhaps the nature of their ministry doesn't require them to be studying the Word each day, so their lives aren't regularly exposed to its convicting truth. Or perhaps they have grown complacent in their commitment to the Word. If so, they have neglected the strength that comes as God's Spirit ministers through His Word and have created a serious weakness in their spiritual armor.

Prayer acknowledges our dependency on God for spiritual strength and victory. It is an admission that we need help. Fellowship is just as important. In my spiritual battles I draw great strength and encouragement from those around me who are engaged in the same struggles.

By saying overseers must be blameless, the apostle Paul was not saying a man must be perfect, or everyone would be disqualified. Clearly, however, he meant that there must be no blight of any kind of sin that taints a man's reputation or puts his character in question. As he delineates the other qualifications for overseers, he simply expands on the particulars of what it means to be blameless.

"THE HUSBAND OF ONE WIFE"— HE IS SEXUALLY PURE

"The husband of one wife" is not the best rendering according to my studies of the Greek text. I believe the words translated "wife" (*gunaikos*) and "husband" (*anēr*) are better translated "woman" and "man." The Greek construction places emphasis on the word *one*, thereby communicating the idea of a one-woman man.

It is appropriate that sexual fidelity is first on Paul's list of moral qualifications because that seems to be the area that most often disqualifies a man from ministry. It is therefore a matter of grave concern.

There have been many proposed interpretations of this qualification. The view that an elder can't have more than one wife at a time has been the traditional understanding of the English phrase "the husband of one wife," but the religious and cultural climate of Paul's day make it unlikely that he was referring to polygamy. Neither the Jews nor the Romans tended to engage in that practice.

Some people say that "the husband of one wife" means a man can't be an elder if he has remarried for any reason. But Paul couldn't have been referring to remarriage because he made clear that God permits remarriage after the death of one's spouse (1 Tim. 5:9-15; Rom. 7:2-3; 1 Cor. 7:39).

Others say that Paul was prohibiting divorced men from serving as elders. But if Paul were referring to divorce, he could have clarified the issue by saying, "An elder must be a man who has never been divorced." But even that statement would pose problems because the Bible teaches that remarriage after a divorce is within God's will under two circumstances.

First, divorce is justified when one partner commits continuous sexual sin. Jesus said to the religious leaders, "It hath been said [by your rabbinical tradition], Whosoever shall [divorce] his wife, let him give her a writing of divorcement" (Matt. 5:31). Many Jewish men were divorcing their wives for insignificant reasons, and the only requirement was to complete the necessary paperwork.

But Jesus said, "Whoever shall [divorce] his wife, except for the cause of fornication, causeth her to commit adultery [when she remarries]; and whosoever shall marry her that is divorced committeth adultery" (Matt. 5:32). That implies fornication is legitimate grounds for divorce.

I believe that the "fornication" mentioned in that context refers to extreme situations of unrelenting and unrepentant sexual sin. God graciously permits the innocent party to be free from bondage to such an evil partner. With that comes the freedom to remarry a believer.

Under Old Testament law, if a marriage partner committed adultery, he or she could be stoned to death. That would release the other partner from that marriage and free him or her to remarry. Although God no longer demands the death of an unfaithful spouse, the sin of adultery is no less serious. Should God's grace in sparing the life of the adulterer penalize the innocent party by demanding lifelong singleness? I don't think so. The grace that spares the adulterer's life also frees the innocent party to remarry.

Second, divorce is justified when an unbelieving partner leaves. In 1 Corinthians 7:15 Paul says, "If the unbelieving depart, let him depart. A brother or a sister is not under bondage in such cases; but God hath called us to peace." If an unbelieving partner wants out of the marriage, the believer is free to let him or her go. God doesn't require you to live in a state of war with such a partner.

Some people say 1 Timothy 3:2 prohibits single men from serving as elders. But that position is refuted by the fact that Paul, who was an elder (1 Tim. 4:14; 2 Tim. 1:6), was himself single (1 Cor. 7:7-9).

The phrase "one-woman man" doesn't refer to marital status at all. Paul is giving moral qualifications for spiritual leadership, not outlining what an elder's social status or external condition is to be. "One-woman man" speaks of the man's character, the state of his heart. If he is married, he is to be devoted solely to his wife. Whether or not he is married, he is not to be a ladies' man.

Unfortunately, it is possible to be married to one woman yet not be a one-woman man. Jesus said, "Whosoever looketh on a woman to lust after her hath committed adultery with her already in his heart" (Matt. 5:28). First Timothy 3:2 is saying that a married—or unmarried—man who lusts after many women is unfit for ministry. An elder must love, desire, and think only of the wife that God has given him.

Sexual purity is a major issue in the ministry. That's why Paul placed it at the top of his list.

"TEMPERATE"—
HE IS NOT GIVEN TO EXCESS

The Greek word translated "temperate" *(nēphalios)* means without wine or not mixed with wine. It speaks of sobriety—the opposite of intoxication. Wine was a common drink in biblical times. Because Palestine was so hot and dry, it was often necessary to consume a large volume of wine to replenish body fluids lost in the heat. To help avoid drunkenness, wine was normally mixed with large amounts of water. Even so, the lack of refrigeration and the fermentative properties of wine made intoxication a problem.

Even though wine could cheer a person's heart (Judg. 9:13) and was beneficial for medicinal purposes such as stomach ailments (1 Tim. 5:23) and relieving pain for those near death (Prov. 31:6), its abuse was common. That's why Proverbs 20:1 says, "Wine is a mocker, strong drink is raging, and whosoever is deceived thereby is not wise."

Proverbs 23:29-35 says, "Who hath woe? Who hath sorrow? Who hath contentions? Who hath babbling? Who hath wounds without cause? Who hath redness of eyes? They that tarry long at the wine; they that go to seek mixed wine Look not thou upon the wine when it is red, when it giveth its color in the cup, when it moveth itself aright. At the last it biteth like a serpent, and it stingeth like an adder. Thine eyes shall behold strange things, and thine heart shall utter perverse things. Yea, thou shalt be as he that lieth down in the midst of the sea, or as he that lieth upon the top of a mast. They have stricken me, shalt thou say, and I was not sick; they have beaten me, and I felt it not. When shall I awake? I will seek it yet again."

Genesis 9 records an example of the mocking effect of wine. Noah planted a vineyard, made wine, and became drunk. While he was drunk "he was uncovered within his tent" (v. 21). The Hebrew text implies some kind of sexual evil. Ham, one of his sons, saw him in that state and mocked him. His two other sons entered the tent backward to cover him up because they were ashamed of his sinfulness.

Because of their position, example, and influence, certain Jewish leaders abstained from wine. Priests could not enter God's house while under its influence (Lev. 10:9). Kings were also advised not to consume wine because it might hinder their judgment (Prov. 31:4-5).

The Nazirite vow, the highest vow of spiritual commitment in the Old Testament, forbade its participants from drinking wine (Num. 6:3). In the same way, spiritual leaders today must avoid intoxication so they may exercise responsible judgment and set an example of Spirit-controlled behavior.

It's likely that Paul's usage of *nēphalios* went beyond the literal sense of avoiding intoxication to the figurative sense of being alert and watchful. An elder must deny any excess in life that diminishes clear thinking and sound judgment.

Commentator William Hendriksen said, "Such a person lives deeply. His pleasures are not primarily those of the senses, like the pleasures of a drunkard for instance, but those of the soul. He is filled with spiritual and moral earnestness. He is not given to excess (in the use of wine, etc.), but is moderate, well-balanced, calm, careful, steady, and sane. This pertains to his physical, moral, and mental tastes and habits" *(Exposition of the Pastoral Epistles* [Grand Rapids: Baker, 1981], p. 122).

Drinking is only one area in which excess can occur. Overeating has been called the preacher's sin, and often that's a just criticism. But spiritual leaders are to be moderate and balanced in every area of life.

"SOBER-MINDED"—
HE IS SELF-DISCIPLINED

The Greek word translated "sober-minded" *(sōphrōn)* speaks of discipline or self-control. It's the result of being temperate (v. 2). The temperate man avoids excess so that he can see things clearly, and that clarity of thought leads to an orderly, disciplined life. He knows how to order his priorities.

Sōphrōn indicates a person who is serious about spiritual things. Such a man doesn't have the reputation of a clown. That doesn't mean he avoids humor—any good leader is able to use and enjoy humor. But he is to have an appreciation for what really matters in life.

Some young men have a frivolous mentality, but the longer they serve Christ and observe life, the more they see things through God's perspective. As time passes, their frivolity is tempered by their increased understanding of man's lostness and the inevitability of hell. That's part of being a sober-minded person.

I received a letter from a lady who thanked me because our radio program helped her break a ten-year addiction to soap operas. She has learned to study and meditate on God's Word rather than pursuing her five-hour-a-day viewing habit. She expressed her praise to God for His grace in her life. I rejoice with her because she is learning to set her mind on what is worthy of thought.

Paul said, "Whatever things are true, whatever things are honest, whatever things are just, whatever things are pure, whatever things are lovely, whatever things are of good report; if there be any virtue, and if there be any praise, think on these things" (Phil. 4:8). That's the focus of an ordered and well-disciplined mind.

"Good Behavior"— He Is Well-Organized

The Greek word translated "good behavior" is *kosmios*. It comes from the root word *kosmos*, which in its general sense refers to the interplay between human, divine, and satanic values. A man of "good behavior" approaches all the aspects of his life in a systematic, orderly manner.

This kind of person diligently fulfills his many duties and responsibilities. His disciplined mind produces disciplined actions— "good behavior."

The opposite of *kosmios* is chaos. Elders must not have a chaotic lifestyle. That's because their work involves administration, oversight, scheduling, and establishing priorities.

The ministry is no place for a man whose life is a continual confusion of unaccomplished plans and unorganized activities. Over the years I have seen many men who had difficulty ministering effectively because they couldn't get their lives into meaningful order. They couldn't concentrate on a task or systematically set and accomplish goals. Such disorder is a disqualification.

"Given to Hospitality"— He Is Hospitable

The Greek word translated "given to hospitality" is composed of the words *xenos* ("stranger") and *phileō* ("to love" or "show affection"). It means to love strangers.

Quite often I hear it said that So-and-so has the gift of hospitality because she is a great cook or because she likes to have friends over for a visit. As gracious and important as those virtues are, they are not examples of biblical hospitality.

Biblical hospitality is showing kindness to strangers, not friends. In Luke 14:12-14 Jesus says, "When you give a luncheon or a dinner, do not invite your friends or your brothers or your relatives or rich neighbors, lest they also invite you in return, and repayment come to you. But when you give a reception, invite the poor, the crippled, the lame, the blind, and you will be blessed, since they do not have the means to repay you; for you will be repaid at the resurrection of the righteous" (NASB).

I realize that showing love toward strangers requires vulnerability and can even be dangerous because some may take advantage of your kindness. Whereas God doesn't ask us to discard wisdom and discernment as we deal with strangers (cf. Matt. 10:16), He does require us to love them by being hospitable (Rom. 12:13; Heb. 13:2; 1 Pet. 4:9).

When I consider my responsibility to love strangers, I am reminded that God received into His family we who were "aliens from the commonwealth of Israel, and strangers from the covenants of promise, having no hope, and without God in the world" (Eph. 2:12). Since those of us who are Gentiles have been welcomed by God, how can we fail to welcome strangers into our homes? After all, everything we have belongs to God. We are simply His stewards.

"Apt to Teach"—
He Is Skilled in Teaching

The Greek word translated "apt to teach" (*didaktikon*) is used only two times in the New Testament (here and in 2 Tim. 2:24). It means "skilled in teaching." It's the only qualification listed here that relates to the function of an elder and sets the elder apart from the deacon.

Paul repeatedly reminded Timothy of the priority of teaching (1 Tim. 5:17; 2 Tim. 2:2, 15). Elders must be skilled in teaching. They must have the ability to communicate God's Word and the integrity to make their teaching believable.

The most powerful impetus to effective teaching is credibility. A skilled teacher will practice what he preaches. If you teach one thing and live another, you are contradicting and undermining your teaching.

Paul said to Timothy, "Let no man despise thy youth, but be thou an example [to] the believers" (1 Tim. 4:12). He wanted Timothy to be a model others could follow—a prototype of his own teaching. Paul went on to list the areas of life in which Timothy should be an example: "in word [what you say], in conduct [what you do], in love [what you feel], in spirit [what you think], in faith [what you believe], in purity [what motivates you]" (v. 12). That's exemplary behavior in every dimension of life and is the first and foremost factor in skilled teaching.

In 1 Corinthians 11:1 Paul says, "Be ye followers of me, even as I also am of Christ." You are not a skilled teacher unless you can call on people to follow your example.

The Holy Spirit gives the gift of teaching to those called to teach the church (Rom. 12:7; 1 Cor. 12:28; Eph. 4:11). It is not a natural ability but a Spirit-given endowment that enables one to teach the Word of God effectively.

First Timothy 4:6 describes a good minister as being "nourished up in the words of faith and of good doctrine." Even though Timothy was that kind of minister, Paul encouraged him to guard carefully the sound doctrine he had been taught. In 1 Timothy 6:20 Paul says, "O Timothy, keep that which is committed to thy trust." In 2 Timothy 1:13-14 he says, "Retain the standard of sound words which you have heard from me. . . . Guard, through the Holy Spirit . . . the treasure which has been entrusted to you."

Generally speaking, the more doctrinal knowledge a teacher has the more skilled his teaching will be. That doesn't mean a new Christian can't be a skilled teacher, but he will have to work hard to make up for his lack of knowledge.

A teacher's attitude is as important as what he knows. If you teach God's truth with arrogance, you will undermine what you say. That's why humility is essential to skilled teaching. Paul said, "The servant of the Lord must not strive, but be gentle unto all men, apt to teach, patient, in meekness instructing those that oppose him" (2 Tim. 2:24-25).

"Not Given to Wine"—
He Is Not a Drinker

The Greek word translated "given to wine" *(paroinos)* means "one who drinks." It doesn't refer to a drunkard—that's an obvious disqualification. The issue here is the man's reputation: Is he known as a drinker?

We saw that the Greek word translated "temperate" (v. 3) refers in its literal sense to one who is not intoxicated. *Paroinos,* on the other hand, refers to one's associations. Such a person doesn't frequent bars, taverns, and inns. He is not at home in the noisy scenes associated with drinking. His lifestyle is not that of a drinker.

"Not Violent"—
He Is Not a Fighter

You can't be an elder if you settle disputes with your fists or in other violent ways. The Greek word translated "violent" *(plēktēs)* means "a giver of blows" or "a striker." An elder isn't quick-tempered and doesn't resort to unnecessary physical violence. That qualification is closely related to "not given to wine" because such violence is usually connected with people who drink excessively.

A spiritual leader must be able to handle things with a cool mind and a gentle spirit. Paul said, "The servant of the Lord must not strive" (2 Tim. 2:24).

"PATIENT"—
HE EASILY PARDONS HUMAN FAILURE

We skipped "not greedy of filthy lucre," which appears in the King James Version but not in the better Greek manuscripts. That qualification is identical in meaning to "not covetous" (v. 3), which we will soon cover.

The Greek word translated "patient" *(epieikēs)* means "to be considerate, genial, forbearing, gracious, or gentle." Aristotle said it speaks of a person who easily pardons human failure (cited by William Barclay, *The Letter to Timothy, Titus and Philemon* [Philadelphia: Westminster, 1975), p. 83). It's also used in 2 Timothy 2:24: "The servant of the Lord must not strive, but be gentle unto all men, apt to teach, patient."

In a practical sense, patience is the ability to remember good and forget evil. You don't keep a record of wrongs people have committed against you (cf. 1 Cor. 13:5). That's an important virtue for a spiritual leader. I know people who have left the ministry because they couldn't get over someone's criticizing or upsetting them. They carry a list of grievances that eventually robs them of the joy of serving others.

Discipline yourself not to talk or even think about wrongs done against you because it serves no productive purpose. It simply rehearses the hurts and clouds your mind with anger.

"NOT A BRAWLER"—
HE IS NOT QUARRELSOME

The Greek word translated "not a brawler" *(amachos)* is similar in meaning to *mē plēktēs* ("not violent," v. 3). The difference is that the latter refers to not being physically violent, whereas the former refers to not being quarrelsome.

When you have a plurality of church leaders attempting to make decisions, you can't get very far if any of them are quarrelsome. That's why Paul said, "The servant of the Lord must not strive, but be gentle unto all men . . . patient" (2 Tim. 2:24). He must be a peace-maker.

"NOT COVETOUS"—
HE IS FREE FROM THE LOVE OF MONEY

The Greek word translated "not covetous" (*aphilarguros*) is a negation of the Greek words for "love" and "silver." It speaks of someone who doesn't love money.

Love of money can corrupt a man's ministry because it tempts him to view people as a means by which he can get more money. Paul said, "Godliness with contentment is great gain; for we brought nothing into this world, and it is certain we can carry nothing out. And having food and raiment let us be therewith content. But they that will be rich fall into temptation and a snare, and into many foolish and hurtful lusts, which drown men in destruction and perdition. For the love of money is the root of all evil, which, while some coveted after, they have erred from the faith, and pierced themselves through with many sorrows" (1 Tim. 6:6-10).

How do we keep from loving money? Here's a simple principle I've used. Don't place a price on your ministry. Sometimes people ask me how much I charge to teach or preach. I don't charge anything. If I'm paid, that's fine; if not, that's fine too. I leave that up to the Lord and those I minister to. I'll accept whatever He supplies, but I don't want my ministry to be influenced, distorted, or corrupted in any way by financial expectations.

If someone gives you a financial gift you didn't seek, you can accept it from the Lord and be thankful for it. But if you pursue money, you'll never know whether it comes from Him or from your own efforts. That robs you of the joy of recognizing God's provision for your needs.

"ONE THAT RULETH WELL"—
HE MAINTAINS A GODLY FAMILY

First Timothy 3:4-5 says that an overseer must be "one that ruleth well his own house, having his children in subjection with all gravity. (For if a man know not how to rule his own house, how shall he take care of the church of God?)." An elder's home life is an essential consideration. Before he can lead in the church he must demonstrate his spiritual leadership within the context of his family.

The Greek word translated "ruleth" means "to preside, having authority over, stand before, or manage." He is the manager of his home. That affirms the consistent biblical teaching on male headship in the home. Obviously there are shared responsibilities between husband and wife and many tasks that the wife manages within the home, but the husband must be the leader.

The same Greek word is used in 1 Timothy 5:17: "Let the elders that rule well be counted worthy of double honor." An elder's ability to rule the church is affirmed in his home. Therefore he must be a strong spiritual leader in the home before he is qualified to lead in the church.

He must rule his home "well." There are many men who rule their home, but they don't rule very well—they don't get the desired results.

By implication a man's home includes his resources. A man may love the Lord and be spiritually and morally qualified to be an elder. He may even be skilled in teaching and have a believing wife and children who follow his leadership in the home, but let's say he has mismanaged his funds and is in bankruptcy. Somehow he can't seem to pull his finances into proper order. Since in the area of finances he doesn't rule his household well, he is disqualified from spiritual leadership. Stewardship of possessions is a critical test of a man's leadership. His home is a proving ground where his administrative capabilities can be clearly demonstrated.

The Greek word translated "subjection" is a military term that speaks of lining up in rank under those in authority. His children are to be lined up under his authority: respectful, controlled, and disciplined. That qualification applies only if a man has children. He's not disqualified if he doesn't have children. But if God has given him children, they must be under control and respectful to their parents.

Titus 1:5-6 says an elder must have "children who believe, not accused of dissipation or rebellion" (NASB). The Greek word translated "believe" (*pistos*) refers in that context to believing the gospel. An elder's children must believe the message he's preaching and teaching. If they are unbelievers, they rob his ministry of credibility.

The Greek word translated "gravity" refers to dignity and respect. It blends the concept of dignity, courtesy, humility, and competence. It's been described as stateliness or refinement. His children bring honor to their parents.

It is possible that a man who is otherwise qualified for spiritual leadership could be disqualified on the family level. Perhaps his personal life is right before the Lord but he became a Christian after his wife or children had already established sinful patterns of behavior, so his family is in chaos. In that case he is not qualified to lead in the church.

He may have children who are not favored with the sovereign electing grace of Christ. In that case he does not qualify to be an elder, but God has other plans for him. He is in no way relegated to an inferior ministry. Church leadership is of high priority, but every ministry is important (1 Cor. 12:12-25). He needs faithfully to pursue the ministry opportunities God brings his way and not feel that his task is in any sense inferior to another's.

In the Old Testament there were certain physical disqualifications for a priest. Leviticus 21:16-20 says, "The Lord spoke to Moses, saying, 'Speak to Aaron, saying, "No man of your offspring throughout their generations who has a defect shall approach to offer the bread of his God. For no one who has a defect shall approach: a blind man, or a lame man, or he who has a disfigured face, or any deformed limb, or a man who has a broken foot or broken hand, or a hunchback or a dwarf, or one who has a defect in his eye or eczema or scabs or crushed testicles"'" (NASB).

Anyone with a physical deformity could not perform priestly duties. That wasn't a commentary on the character or spiritual life of a deformed man, but simply a matter of God's selecting a certain kind of man to serve as priest. He wanted unblemished men as models of spiritual service. It's the same with church leadership. God wants elders to have an unblemished and exemplary home life.

It is essential that a father exercise enough authority to make it advisable for his children to obey him. Where there's disobedience, there must be immediate and negative consequences. Because of the Fall, all human beings start out spiritually depraved. The only way you can train a depraved person to do what is right is to associate pain with disobedience (Prov. 13:24).

A father must also have enough wisdom to make it natural and reasonable for his children to obey him. Invariably a child will question authority: "Why can't I do that?" or, "Why should I do this?" Whether you like it or not, as long as you are raising your children you are their local neighborhood philosopher and theologian. That requires your being reasonable in what you expect of them.

In addition, a father must have enough love to make it easy for his children to obey him. Your children ought to long to obey you because they would never want to do anything that would hinder their relationship with you.

I believe there's no better place to see a man's commitment to meeting the needs of others than in his own home. Does he care about his family? Is he committed to each member? Does he work hard to meet their needs? If he doesn't, how could he ever care for the church?

"NOT A NOVICE"—
HE IS A MATURE CHRISTIAN

First Timothy 3:6 says an elder must not be "a novice, lest being lifted up with pride he fall into the condemnation of the devil." Although Paul didn't specifically mention humility in this passage, it is the obvious point of contrast in his caution against spiritual pride.

The Greek word translated "novice" (*neophutos*) means "newly planted." The idea is that an elder should not be a new convert or newly baptized. This is the only use of *neophutos* in the New Testament. It is used in its literal sense outside the New Testament to speak of planting trees in the ground (Fritz Rienecker and Cleon Rogers, *Linguistic Key to the Greek New Testament* [Grand Rapids: Zondervan, 1982], p. 623).

The opposite of a new believer is a mature Christian. An elder must be mature in the faith. Of course maturity is relative, so the standard of maturity will vary from congregation to congregation. The point is that an elder must be more spiritually mature than the people he leads.

The Greek word translated "lifted up" (*tuphoō*) means "to wrap in smoke" or "puff up." In its figurative sense it speaks of being clouded with pride. We don't want new Christians to get puffed up with a false sense of spirituality. We don't want their thinking to become clouded with prideful thoughts.

The issue in restricting a new convert from spiritual leadership is not his ability to teach—he may be a fine Bible teacher. It's not that he isn't a good leader—he may have strong leadership characteristics. It's not that he has inadequate knowledge of God's Word—he may be a diligent Bible student. But if you elevate him to spiritual leadership alongside mature godly men, he's going to have a battle with pride.

He may fulfill the qualifications of 1 Timothy 3:2-5 by having a blameless life and a marvelous family. But if he's a relatively new Christian, the tendency will be for him to feel proud about being elevated to the level of leadership occupied by older, more mature men who have been in the church for many years.

Grace Community Church has existed for more than thirty years and has taught God's Word throughout that time. Consequently we have many third, fourth, fifth, and sixth generation Christians in our congregation. Our elders are mature men who have spent many years preparing for leadership and know and teach the Word in great depth.

On the other hand, suppose you are a missionary who has led people to Christ in a primitive part of the world, established a church, ministered there for six months, and then have to return home. Before leaving you would have to select someone to be its pastor. That person would be a new Christian, but you'd look for someone who is mature in comparison to the rest of the congregation. It might take that same man ten years to become an elder at Grace Community Church, but he's rightfully pastoring a church because of the relative nature of what spiritual maturity means in any given congregation.

We have young seminary graduates ministering here who are not elders because the church's perception of elder leadership is so high. Many of those men are excellent teachers and are qualified in their moral character and family life, but to place them in that level of leadership so soon in their ministry would tempt them to be prideful.

Many of our young men have left our church to pastor other churches without ever having been an elder at Grace Church. But they were seen by those churches as men of spiritual maturity who could lead and teach them in God's Word.

You might expect Paul to say that prideful leaders will become ineffective or fall into sin, but instead he says they will fall into the "condemnation of the devil." That's a serious situation.

What is the condemnation of the devil? Some people think that means a prideful leader will be condemned by the devil, but Scripture never portrays the devil as a judge who condemns people. Since Scripture presents God as Judge, it's best to understand the condemnation of the devil as a reference to the judgment God pronounced on the devil. A prideful leader will incur that same type of condemnation. That conclusion is supported by the context, which deals with the issue of pride, and Scripture teaches that God opposes a proud man (James 4:6).

The condemnation of the devil was a demotion from high position on account of pride. God will do the same to any man whose thinking is clouded with pride and whose perception of his own spirituality is distorted because of a premature rise to spiritual leadership.

Lucifer's sin was pride, for which God cast him out of heaven. We see his prideful character on display in Isaiah 14:12-14: "How art thou fallen from heaven, O Lucifer, son of the morning! How art thou cut down to the ground, who didst weaken the nations! For thou hast said in thine heart, I will ascend into heaven, I will exalt my throne above the stars of God; I will sit also upon the mount of the congregation, in the sides of the north, I will ascend above the heights of the clouds, I will be like the Most High."

He wanted to usurp God's authority. Five times he said, "I will," but God said in effect, "No, you won't": "Yet thou shalt be brought down to sheol, to the sides of the pit. They that see thee shall narrowly look upon thee, and consider thee, saying, Is this the man who made the earth to tremble?" (vv. 15-16).

Satan was humiliated rather than exalted. To avoid exposing a man to that kind of humiliation, we must avoid placing him into spiritual leadership too quickly. It's not that a leader who becomes prideful will lose his salvation, for that is impossible, but he will lose his esteemed position.

"A GOOD REPORT OF THEM WHO ARE OUTSIDE"— HE IS WELL-RESPECTED BY NON-CHRISTIANS

The Greek word translated "good" (*kalōs*) embraces the ideas of internal and external goodness. An elder must have a good internal character and a good external reputation or testimony.

The Greek word translated "report" (*martureō*) is the word from which we get *martyr,* but its basic meaning is "a certifying testimony." An elder's character must be certified by the testimony of other people.

"Outside" has reference to those who are not in the church. An elder must have a reputation for integrity, love, kindness, generosity, and goodness among those in the community who know him. That doesn't mean people will agree with his theology. In fact, there might even be some antagonism toward his Christian convictions, but he is seen as a man of character. That's an important qualification because an elder can't have a godly influence on his community if it has no respect for him. That would bring reproach on Christ.

The Greek word translated "reproach" means disgrace. It is sad to consider how many men have disgraced the Lord and His church because of their sins. That's why an elder must be blameless in his reputation.

Incidentally, that qualification isn't limited to sins committed as an elder. It also includes any sins in the past that have given him a bad reputation. A man's ongoing reputation in the community must be considered before he is placed into spiritual leadership.

The importance of a good reputation in the community is illustrated throughout the New Testament. Romans 2:24 says of Israel, "The name of God is blasphemed among the Gentiles through you." Israel's sin brought reproach upon God, and it's no different for the church.

I'm constantly aware that many people know who I am and what I do. Consequently, I must carefully guard my testimony in the community. For example, I was in a store recently with my family, and we were discussing the purchase of a few furniture items. The salesman waited patiently as everyone contributed their comments and opinions about the various options available. When we had reached a consensus I told the salesman we were ready. He smiled and said to me,

"I know who you are." I immediately thought, *Oh no, what impression have we left on him?* He then said, "I appreciate your ministry very much." I was relieved that our somewhat lengthy family discussion had not hindered our testimony.

Every Christian has to deal with some level of visibility, and people need to see a blameless life. They may not agree with your beliefs, but they must see your godly character.

Paul wanted the Philippians to be "blameless and harmless, children of God, without rebuke, in the midst of a crooked and perverse nation . . . [shining] as lights in the world, holding forth the word of life" (2:15). The quality of their lives would bear witness to the reality of their God. That's a high calling and a sacred responsibility. In Colossians 4:5-6 Paul says, "Walk in wisdom toward them that are outside [unbelievers]. . . . Let your speech be always with grace, seasoned with salt, that ye may know how ye ought to answer every man." A good reputation includes wise words as well as godly deeds.

Elders need a good reputation with those outside the church so they don't fall into "the snare of the devil." Satan tries to entrap spiritual leaders so that he might destroy their credibility and integrity. He's like a roaring lion seeking to devour (1 Pet. 5:8), and spiritual leaders are a primary target.

Like all Christians, elders have areas of weakness and vulnerability, and they will sometimes fall into one of Satan's traps. Only a perfect man doesn't stumble (James 3:2). Elders must be particularly discerning and cautious to avoid the snares of the enemy. Then they can be effective in leading others away from his traps.

The Ephesian church needed to examine its leaders, and we do as well. The future of the church depends on the quality of today's leaders. God is building men to lead His flock. As a church we must identify them, place them into leadership, pray for them, and follow their example. In so doing we will bring glory to God.

Appendix 4

Elements of Church Discipline*

While trying to discover how to motivate people to be holy, I learned that you can't just preach holiness and then be indifferent to how the people respond. Matthew 18, Acts 5, 1 Corinthians 5, and 2 Thessalonians 3 make clear that the church is to enforce a biblical standard of holiness.

Sin has to be dealt with. It isn't enough to make announcements or post rules. Proverbs 3:11-12 says, "My son, despise not the chastening of the Lord, neither be weary of his correction; for whom the Lord loveth he correcteth, even as a father the son in whom he delighteth." As a father must discipline and correct his children, so the Lord must discipline His children.

People have often asked me, "Why is the church in America, even the evangelical church, so unholy?" The issue isn't necessarily that we have preached the wrong message but that we have neglected its implementation in the lives of the people. We have said in effect, "As long as the sermon is right doctrinally, we really don't care what you do." But you can't raise children in permissiveness that punishes only by reasoning with them.

In Matthew 18 our Lord explains to His disciples how to respond when a fellow believer sins against them. The principles He set forth are applicable as we seek to implement discipline in the church.

*From tapes GC 2330-2332.

These are guidelines for dealing with sin as it affects believers. The primary application of Matthew 18 addresses the personal offense of an individual believer's sin against his brother, giving the offended brother instructions on how to respond. Our Lord clearly teaches here that ultimately the entire assembly of believers has a responsibility to follow through in seeking restoration of a sinning member. My conviction is that the principles He sets forth here are applicable in every situation where sin affects the Body of Christ.

THE PLACE OF DISCIPLINE

Twice in verse 17 Jesus mentions "the church" (Gk., *ekklēsia,* "the called-out ones" or "the assembly"). Used in a nontechnical sense in Matthew, *ekklēsia* does not specifically refer to the church born at Pentecost, but it certainly anticipates the New Testament church that comes about by the baptism of the Spirit of God in Acts 2. Its immediate application was to the assembly of the disciples who were gathered in the house at Capernaum, but it gives a principle that goes beyond that small assembly and embraces the whole church.

Jesus wanted His disciples to know that discipline is to take place in the assembly of God's redeemed people. There is no exterior court of higher authority for the issue of discipline. We don't need to establish a national church court. If we were to establish some bishop, cardinal, synod, or any group of people unrelated to the local assembly of believers to carry out discipline, we would have created a court beyond that which the Word of Christ and the teachings of His apostles allow. Because Jesus refers to the church in general terms, a hierarchical structure of ecclesiastical rulers who sit as judges is not in view.

That principle is illustrated in 1 Corinthians 6, where Paul indicts the Corinthians for suing each other: "Dare any of you, having a matter against another, go to law before the unjust, and not before the saints?" (v. 1). In other words, "What are you doing taking your grievances and problems before the courts of unregenerate men and not before fellow believers?" Paul didn't mention a court appointed by the saints because the context of the Christian fellowship and family is the highest court there is. He proved that by saying, "Do ye not know that the saints shall judge the world? . . . Know ye not that we shall judge angels? How much more things that pertain to this life?" (vv. 2-3). The church is ultimately the highest court.

Therefore all church discipline is to occur within the community of believing people. It can be large like ours, or it can be very small. It might be on a mission field with three or four missionaries who don't yet have a church established. It may be in your Bible study or your fellowship group, because those are units of God's redeemed people. We're not interested in forming an inquisition committee because each local assembly is responsible for the purity of the individual members.

THE PURPOSE OF DISCIPLINE

"If he shall hear thee, thou hast gained thy brother" (v. 15). The purpose of discipline is restoration—restoring a sinning believer to holiness. God has always been concerned with restoration, as the following verses show.

> *Proverbs 11:30*—"He that winneth souls is wise."
> *Galatians 6:1*—"Brethren, if a man be overtaken in a fault [Gk., *paraptōma*, "a fall into sin"], ye who are spiritual restore such an one."
> *James 5:19-20*—"Brethren, if any of you do err from the truth, and one convert [restore] him, let him know that he who converteth the sinner from the error of his way shall save a soul from death."

The goal of church discipline is not to throw people out, embarrass them, be self-righteous, play God, or exercise authority and power in some unbiblical manner. The purpose of discipline is to bring people back into a pure relationship within the assembly.

Notice the word "gained" in verse 15. The Greek term spoke of accumulating wealth in the sense of monetary commodities. That pictures the sinning brother as a lost valuable treasure. That is, in fact, the heart of God: each soul is a treasure to Him. The church needs to have that same sense of concern. We can't allow one to just float away as we say, "Well, I don't know where that person is, but I really can't get involved." We must work to restore a sinning brother or sister because that soul is of value to God and to us.

Galatians 6:1, which says, "Ye who are spiritual restore [Gk., *katartizō*] such an one," conveys the idea of repairing something to bring it back to its original condition. The Greek word is used in reference to mending fractured bones, putting dislocated bones in place, and mending fishing nets. We are in the business of recovery. Why has the church strayed from such a noble venture?

PRIVACY

Some people feel that a disciplining church runs around checking on everyone's sin. I've had people ask me, "What do you have, the Grace CIA or Secret Service spying on everyone?" But that isn't the idea. We merely have a tremendous hunger to fulfill God's desire for His church to be holy, and we put a very high value on the worth of a soul that belongs to God. We refuse not to show the proper concern. We're not content with letting someone drift away.

PERMISSIVENESS

Some say, "Well, So-and-so went astray, but I'm not going to say anything because who am I? He chose his way. I'm not going to run his life."

PRIDE

Others secretly relish the fall of others because it makes them feel spiritually superior. But that is really a sickness called pride. If you can smugly remain indifferent to your brother's sin, thinking that you're better than he is, you are far afield from the heart of the Shepherd. In fact, you are guilty of sinning as much as your brother.

PERSECUTION

I was touched by what one Christian said of his own experience: "I've often thought that if I ever fall into a sin, I will pray that I don't fall into the hands of those censorious, critical, self-righteous judges in the church. I'd rather fall into the hands of the barkeepers, street walkers, or dope peddlers because the church people would tear me apart with their long, wagging, gossipy tongues, cutting me to shreds." I'm sure there are a lot of people who have had that experience.

Instead of making excuses about why we don't carry out our responsibility to discipline, we need to be obedient, having the heart of the Shepherd, who attempts to bring the lost sheep back into the fold.

THE PERSON OF DISCIPLINE

"If thy brother shall trespass against thee, go and tell him his fault between thee and him alone; if he shall hear thee, thou hast gained thy brother" (v. 15). Who is the star of verse 15? You, not some discipline committee. Discipline is not just for church officials; it's for everyone, including those who lead in the church. In fact, Galatians 6:1 tells us exactly who should do it: "Brethren, if a man be overtaken in a fault, ye who are spiritual restore such an one." Those who are walking in the Spirit, who are obeying the Word, and who are in the fellowship should restore the fallen brother. How should it be done? "In the spirit of meekness, considering thyself, lest thou also be tempted."

The purity of the church is every Christian's concern. We all need to humbly and lovingly confront that which makes it impure when we become aware of it. Don't just say, "Well, we're praying for So-and-so that he'll see the light." That may not be enough. You've got the light—take it and shine it in his eyes!

THE PROVOCATION OF DISCIPLINE

Just cause for discipline occurs "if thy brother shall trespass [Gk., *hamartanō*, "to sin"] against thee" (v. 15). That is the basic New Testament word for sin. What sins need to be corrected? All of them. That's why the text is general. Any sin is the antithesis of the utter holiness of God and puts a stain on the fellowship. The discipline process is to go into action whenever any member of a Christian fellowship violates God's Word.

Note that the sin is "against thee." There are two ways a fellow believer's sin can affect you:

DIRECTLY

If someone punched you in the nose because he was angry with you or stole from you, deceived you, lied to you, abused you, slandered you, or committed a crime of immorality against you, those would be sins directly against you. Matthew 18 instructs that if a Christian directly sins against you, you need to point out that what he has done is sin and encourage him to confess and repent of it. Such a gracious response would shock a person waiting for your retaliation because the human tendency is to hold a grudge against someone who directly sins against us.

How many Christians can you think of whom you've got a grudge against and with whom you refuse to speak? If you can think of some, note that Ephesians 4:32 says we should be "kind one to another, tenderhearted, forgiving one another, even as God, for Christ's sake, hath forgiven [us]." Who are we to hold a grudge when God has forgiven us so much?

INDIRECTLY

Not all sins against us are direct. Any sin that brings reproach on the assembly of God's people stains us all. When our brothers and sisters sin, they are in danger of being lost to our fellowship—a loss that affects us all. Furthermore when any believer lives a disobedient life, he brings reproach on Christ. Because we are Christ's representatives and bear His reproach, any sin is indirectly against us.

If you restrict discipline to direct sin against members of the church, then Christians could sin against people who aren't a part of the assembly and no one would confront them. It must be understood that any sin—whether direct or indirect—is a sin that stains the fellowship. As the apostle Paul says in Galatians 5:9, "A little leaven leaveneth the whole lump" (cf. 1 Cor. 5:6). Therefore if you know about sin in a fellow believer's life, you need to go to that brother or sister and lovingly confront him or her.

THE PROCESS OF DISCIPLINE

Four steps are clearly delineated in this passage:

STEP ONE—TELL HIM HIS SIN ALONE

"Go and tell him his fault between thee and him alone" (v. 15). In the present imperative, the first verb implies that you should go and pursue the brother without being distracted. The second verb, in the aorist imperative, conveys the idea of being convincing in getting the point across. From the Greek verb *elengchō*, it means "to expose to the light." Don't just say, "Hey, I haven't seen you at church, and I was just wondering—are you drifting around?" Confront the person, exposing the sin so that he is aware of it and understands that there is no escaping it. Take the time and effort needed to delicately handle this difficult task.

Discipline is difficult with people you know well because when you start talking about their sin, they may have something to say to you as well. It's also difficult with people you don't know well because you're apt to say, "Who am I to do that?" Consequently we tend to be intimidated by the people we know and indifferent toward the people we don't know. But it's a responsibility Jesus has given us.

Galatians 6:1 helps us to see the attitude we should have in confronting a sinning believer: "Brethren, if a man be overtaken in a fault, ye who are spiritual restore such an one in the spirit of meekness, considering thyself, lest thou also be tempted." In other words, you should go in humility, realizing that it could have been you who was tempted. Verse 2 says, "Bear ye one another's burdens, and so fulfill the law of Christ." And what is the law of Christ? It's the royal law (James 2:8), the law of liberty (James 1:25)—the law of love (John 15:12). So you go with a love that wants to help him carry the burden, and you go in meekness. You don't go in a pontificating, pious, and self-righteous manner to make yourself look good and him look bad. You go in loving, humble concern to restore him.

Also notice that you should go alone so that there are just the two of you. The first confrontation is to be "between thee and him alone." Instead our tendency is to say, "Did you hear about So-and-so? It's so sad, but we're praying for brother So-and-so." And the word starts spreading around. But this text tells us that if we know about a sin, we are to go alone to the one who has committed it. It doesn't need to get beyond that.

If you confront the person in love and humility without saying anything to anyone else and that person repents, you will have a bond of intimacy that nothing will be able to break. God doesn't say, "Shout it from the housetops." He says, "Just go by yourself, and let it be between the two of you." Verse 15 says, "If he shall hear thee, thou hast gained thy brother." That is what you are seeking to accomplish.

Is there any illustration in the New Testament of that kind of discipline? Note Galatians 2:11. After Peter had sinned in cutting himself off from the assembly of God's people to identify with some legalizers, Paul confronted him: "When Peter was come to Antioch, I withstood him to the face, because he was to be blamed." Did Peter respond? Yes, he did, because later he wrote in 2 Peter 3:15, "Even as our beloved brother Paul . . . " Evidently one reason for the bond between them was that Paul cared enough to be willing to confront Peter with his sin. Often after you confront a person on a one-to-one basis, your hearts will be knit together.

STEP TWO—TAKE SOME WITNESSES

"But if he will not hear thee, then take with thee one or two more, that in the mouth of two or three witnesses every word may be established" (v. 16). God had established that law in Deuteronomy 19:15 to prevent the passing on of slanderous information that was unconfirmed. Therefore in the second step of discipline, you must take one or two more believers with you.

Now that begins to put the pressure on. You take a couple of people with the same objective of gaining back your brother. As you pursue the individual, your objective is to show him his sin so that he truly understands it and so that there might be genuine confession, repentance, and restoration.

Verse 16 says that "in the mouth of two or three witnesses, every word may be established." These are not one or two people who saw the sin or originally knew about it. Rather they are witnesses of the confrontation who can come back and confirm what was said. Their presence is as much a protection for the one being approached as it is for the one approaching. After all, a biased person could erroneously say, "Well, I tried to confront him, but he's impenitent." It would be presumptuous to think that one person could make that ultimate determination, especially if he had been sinned against. The witnesses need to confirm whether there is a heart of repentance or one of indifference or rejection. Such a report provides the basis for further action because the situation has been verified beyond the report of one individual.

God wants two or three witnesses to confirm either the person's repentance or impenitence. Before discipline takes place, He wants to be sure that our analysis of a person's attitudes and actions are accurate. He doesn't want wrong reports given about His people. He doesn't want it to be said that they are not repenting when they are, or vice versa.

Hopefully the person confronted will respond to this second step. Second Corinthians 13:1-2 gives us an example of this step. Paul said, "This is the third time I am coming to you. In the mouth of two or three witnesses shall every word be established. I told you before, and tell you beforehand, as if I were present, the second time; and being absent now I write to them who heretofore have sinned, and to all others, that, if I come again, I will not spare." He was saying, "I talked to you about your sin and then confirmed it with witnesses. And if I come and you still have not repented, I won't spare the discipline."

After taking the witnesses to confirm the story, what happens if the one who has been confronted still refuses to repent?

STEP THREE—TELL THE CHURCH

"If he shall neglect to hear them, tell it unto the church" (v. 17). We are to tell the whole assembly when a sinning believer fails to respond to the confrontation of the witnesses. In our church that may or may not involve a public proclamation. Sometimes the leaders disseminate word through the fellowship or study groups in which the person is known. Other times it may be announced at a Communion service.

What is the purpose of discipline? Restoration. So tell the church to try to win him back. An individual went—no response. Two or three went—no response. Now we'll all pursue this person's restoration.

Remember that discipline isn't the task of one person. The apostle John said, "I wrote unto the church, but Diotrephes, who loveth to have the preeminence among them, receiveth us not. Wherefore, if I come, I will remember his deeds which he doeth, prating against us with malicious words; and not content with that, neither doth he himself receive the brethren, and forbiddeth them that would, and casteth them out of the church" (3 John 9-10).

Here was a self-appointed guy throwing people out of the church. But it is not one man's task to decide that. If we ever have to put a person out of the church, it is only because he refuses to repent after one person has gone to him, followed by two or three, who are in turn followed by other believers in the assembly. No single person is calling all the shots; many people are out there trying to restore the brother. And if he still does not respond, then the motion goes into effect to put him out.

In 2 Corinthians 2:5-8 Paul says, "If any has caused sorrow [to the assembly because of sin], he has caused sorrow not to me, but in some degree—in order not to say too much—to all of you. Sufficient for such a one is this punishment which was inflicted by the majority, so that on the contrary you should rather forgive and comfort him, lest somehow such a one be overwhelmed by excessive sorrows. Wherefore I urge you to reaffirm your love for him" (NASB). Here's a case where the whole church knew of a man's sinfulness. Apparently he responded with repentance. So Paul in essence said, "Now that he has responded, don't hold him at arm's length and browbeat him. Rather embrace him and forgive him in love."

How long should the church keep encouraging someone to repent? Perhaps until you think he's getting harder and harder and absolutely refuses to stop sinning. The Spirit of God has to give you subjective wisdom. I think it's usually a shorter time than we think because God wants a response.

STEP FOUR—TREAT HIM AS AN OUTSIDER

"But if he neglect to hear the church, let him be unto thee as an heathen man and a tax collector" (v. 17). In the parlance of the time of Christ, "heathen" referred to those who weren't Jewish, and a "tax collector" was a Jewish person who had sold himself to the Roman government to exact taxes from his own people.

Jesus' use of those terms doesn't mean that we should treat these people badly. The gospels show us clearly that He loved heathens and tax collectors. It simply means that when a professing brother (or sister) refuses to repent, we are to treat him as if he were outside our fellowship. We are not to let him associate and participate in the blessings and the benefits of the Christian assembly.

1 Corinthians 5—In the Corinthian church there was an unrepentant man who was having an incestuous relationship with his father's wife. Paul said, "He that hath done this deed might be taken away from among you. . . . [I have decided] in the name of our Lord

Jesus Christ, when ye are gathered together, and my spirit, with the power of our Lord Jesus Christ, to deliver such an one unto Satan for the destruction of the flesh, that the spirit may be saved in the day of the Lord Jesus" (vv. 2, 4-5). Professing Christians who refuse to repent need to be put out of the church and turned over to the Satan-controlled worldly system so that their fleshly desire to sin may be destroyed. They may have to go down to the very depths of sin before they repent. But it is something that must be done because, as verses 6 and 7 say, "Know ye not that a little leaven leaveneth the whole lump? Purge out, therefore, the old leaven, that ye may be a new lump." The unrepentant believer must be put out of the assembly to protect it.

Paul further said, "I wrote unto you in an epistle not to company with fornicators; yet not altogether with the fornicators of this world, or with the covetous, or extortioners, or with idolaters, for then must ye needs go out of the world. But now I have written unto you not to keep company, if any man that is called a brother be a fornicator, or covetous, or an idolater, or a railer, or a drunkard, or an extortioner; with such an one, no, not to eat" (vv. 9-11). Because sharing a meal with a person is symbolic of a hospitable and cordial fellowship, it is not to be allowed under the circumstances. When you put a person out of the church, you don't have him over for a meal. You don't treat him like a brother. You treat him like an outcast.

1 Timothy 1—"Hymenaeus and Alexander . . . I have delivered unto Satan, that they may learn not to blaspheme" (v. 20). That's remedial training. They needed to learn by experiencing the consequence of their sin. When you put someone out, the sanctifying graces of God's assembly are no longer there. Then they may begin to think about how much the fellowship of believers really meant to them. But if a person is accepted by the people of God along with his sin, he can unintentionally be encouraged to continue in his sin. Such people must be told that they have a choice: it's either the devil and the world or God and His people, but not both.

2 Thessalonians 3—"We command you, brethren, in the name of our Lord Jesus Christ, that ye withdraw yourselves from every brother that walketh disorderly and not after the tradition which he received of us" (v. 6). The word translated "withdraw" means "to flinch" or "avoid."

Now we're not talking about people who don't know the Lord. We want those people to be exposed to the church. We're talking about sinning members of the church family. Verse 14 reinforces that principle: "If any man obey not our word by this epistle, note that man, and have no company with him, that he may be ashamed."

Leave him to his shame and sin because if he truly belongs to God, He won't let him go, though He may have to drag him very low.

Romans 16—"I beseech you, brethren, mark them who cause divisions and offenses contrary to the doctrine which ye have learned; and avoid them. For they that are such serve not our Lord Jesus Christ but their own body, and by good words and fair speeches deceive the hearts of the innocent" (vv. 17-18).

Second Thessalonians 3:15 says, "Yet count him not as an enemy, but admonish him as a brother." There is a sense in which you never really let him go: though you are to put him outside of the sphere of fellowship, you keep calling him back. People say things such as, "My brother is a Christian, but he divorced his wife and has been living in adultery. Is it OK if I see him?" I reply, "It's fine for you to see him as long as you make sure you admonish him, encouraging him to get his life right by confessing and repenting of his sin." You put such a person out for the purity of the church, but you keep calling him back as well.

THE POWER OF DISCIPLINE

Jesus said, "Verily [truly], I say unto you, Whatsoever ye shall bind on earth shall be bound in heaven; and whatsoever ye shall loose on earth shall be loosed in heaven" (v. 18). It is inconceivable to me that I could be acting in concert with the infinite, holy God in terms of binding and loosening! Those are rabbinical terms undoubtedly familiar to our Lord's Jewish audience. They simply refer to the rabbi's telling a person whether he was still under the bondage of sin or freed from it.

If you are a sinning person in a church and somebody comes to you and you don't repent, and two or three come to you and you don't repent, and the whole church is pursuing you and you don't repent, we can say that your sins are bound on you. That is what the Father has already determined in heaven. On the other hand, if you are in sin and we come to you and you eventually repent with a broken heart, we can say that your sins are loosed, and thereupon we welcome you into the fullness of the fellowship. We are merely doing on earth what has already been done in heaven.

"Thy will be done in earth, as it is in heaven" says the Disciples' Prayer (Matt. 6:10). Do you want to do God's will on earth as it is in heaven? Then you must carry out the process of discipline, and heaven will have already done what you do down here.

It's comforting to know that heaven supports us in the process of discipline, because people often think that if you try to confront sin and call it what it is, you are being unloving. But what you're really doing is fighting God's battle and lining up with heaven.

In verse 19 Jesus says, "Again I say unto you that if two of you shall agree on earth as touching anything that they shall ask, it shall be done for them by My Father, who is in heaven." The Greek word for "agree" (*sumphoneō*, from which *symphony* is derived) literally means "to produce a sound together." Hence, when all of you are in harmony with regard to the person you are confronting, the Father also will be in agreement with you. I don't think that verse is talking about a blank check for prayer, although it has been taken out of its context and misapplied in that way. It certainly isn't saying that if you can get any two people to agree, God has to give you what you're agreeing for. The "two" here means two witnesses in a case of church discipline regarding a sinning person, and they really want God's will to be done. After having followed the biblical pattern, they can be confident that God's will indeed will be done.

Verse 20 says, "Where two or three are gathered together in my name, there am I in the midst of them." You've probably heard that verse applied to prayer meetings, but that is another misinterpretation. Remember the context: the "two or three" are the witnesses in a discipline situation. These common misinterpretations illustrate why it's so important to teach the context of Scripture.

We have the confidence that not only is the Father acting in heaven with us (v. 19), but the Son is here on earth with us as well (v. 20). Never are you more actively fulfilling the will of God and the work of the Son than when you are acting in the purging and the purifying of the church. We all have to be a part of that process as ministers of holiness.

In closing, remember that the goal of church discipline is to restore the sinning brother or sister. Dietrich Bonhoeffer, a German theologian who lived through some of the terrors of Nazi Germany, wrote a little book called *Life Together* that contains some penetrating thoughts. Although we would disagree with much of what Bonhoeffer taught, these profound words ring with insight:

> Sin demands to have a man by himself. It withdraws him from the community. The more isolated a person is, the more destructive will be the power of sin over him, and the more deeply he becomes involved in it, the more disastrous his isolation. Sin wants to remain unknown. It shuns the light. In the darkness of the unexpressed it poisons the whole being of a person. This can happen even in the midst of a pious community. In confession the light of the gospel breaks into the darkness and seclusion of the heart. The sin must be brought into the light. The unexpressed must be openly

spoken and acknowledged. All that is secret and hidden is made manifest. It is a hard struggle until the sin is openly admitted, but God breaks gates of brass and bars of iron (Ps. 107:16).

Since the confession of sin is made in the presence of a Christian brother, the last stronghold of self-justification is abandoned. The sinner surrenders; he gives up all his evil. He gives his heart to God, and he finds the forgiveness of all his sin in the fellowship of Jesus Christ and his brother. The expressed, acknowledged sin has lost all its power. It has been revealed and judged as sin. It can no longer tear the fellowship asunder. Now the fellowship bears the sin of the brother. He is no longer alone with his evil for he has cast off his sin in confession and handed it over to God. It has been taken away from him. Now he stands in the fellowship of sinners who live by the grace of God and the cross of Jesus Christ. . . . The sin concealed separated him from the fellowship, made all his apparent fellowship a sham; the sin confessed has helped him define true fellowship with the brethren in Jesus Christ." ([New York: Harper & Row, 1954], pp. 112-13)

Church discipline is the key to the purity of the church, which in turn will enable us to reach the world.

Appendix 5

Restoring a Sinning Brother*

We have seen in Matthew 18 how the Lord instructs His disciples in regard to disciplining and forgiving those who sin, having discussed the whole matter of reproving and rebuking sin (appendix 4). What do you do when a person repents and turn from sin? You forgive that brother or sister in the fullest sense. Then what do you do after the person is forgiven? You restore him.

In Galatians 6 Paul gives three important guidelines for this ministry of restoration:

Pick Him Up

Verse 1 says, "Brethren, if a man be overtaken in a fault, ye who are spiritual restore such an one in the spirit of meekness, considering thyself, lest thou also be tempted." The term "brethren" indicates that Paul's words are applicable to the church family when a Christian is "overtaken in a fault."

The word translated "fault" (Gk., *paraptōma*, "a stumbling," "blunder," or "fall") is taken by some to refer to something less than a sin. I believe it actually refers to a sin. In context, Paul had been talking about walking in the Spirit (5:16, 25). The idea of falling is not so

---

*From tape GC 1291.

much a theological definition of sin as it is consistent with his metaphor of the spiritual walk.

Notice the word "overtaken." I don't think that's referring to someone walking along who gets overtaken by a sin. Rather I think it is a believer who overtakes someone who has fallen into a sin. The Greek term for "overtaken" *(prolambanō)* means "to catch off guard." Sin doesn't take us unaware because, if we're walking in the Spirit, we have the faculty to discern its presence. Consequently, there is no such thing as unwilling sin.

The fact that you come across someone in sin is not implying, however, that you go through life looking for sin. The verse is merely saying that as you walk in the Spirit, you may come across someone in sin who needs your help.

Paul explicitly calls for restoration to be handled by "ye who are spiritual." What does it mean to be spiritual? We find this brief definition in 1 Corinthians 2:15-16: "He that is spiritual judgeth [discerns] all things, yet he himself is judged of no man. For who hath known the mind of the Lord, that he may instruct him? But we have the mind of Christ." To be spiritual is to have the mind of Christ.

To look at it another way, Ephesians 5:18 says, "Be filled with the Spirit." Colossians 3:16 says, "Let the word of Christ dwell in you richly." Notice that the same results come from following both commands. Therefore we conclude that being filled with the Spirit is the same as letting the Word of Christ dwell in you richly. The spiritual person is the one walking in obedience to God's will as revealed to him through the Word of God and energized by the Spirit of God.

The word translated "restore" (Gk., *katartizō*) in Galatians 6:1 speaks of repairing something in the sense of bringing it back to its former condition. It is used of reconciling two arguing factions, of setting bones that are broken, of putting a dislocated limb back into its proper place, and of mending broken nets.

"In the spirit of meekness" means the person who picks up a weaker brother ought to do so with an attitude of humility. Note the next phrase: "considering thyself, lest thou also be tempted." When we restore another person, we should do so understanding that we could be in the same position. There's no place for spiritual pride and vainglory among Christians who think that they are better than others. We must be meek enough to realize that we ourselves could also fall.

In 1 Corinthians 10 we see that those who have been mightily blessed by God can still sin. Israel had been taken out of Egypt "under the cloud, and all passed through the sea" (v. 1). Wandering in the wilderness, they were guided by the Shekinah of God, finally entering the Promised Land. But in spite of all the blessing and provision of God, twenty-three thousand of them committed fornication and fell in judgment. This nation with such great privilege still committed sin. Paul then applied the principle to Christians: "Now all these things happened unto them for examples, and they are written for our admonition, upon whom the ends of the ages are come. Wherefore, let him that thinketh he standeth take heed lest he fall. There hath no temptation taken you but such as is common to man" (vv. 11-13). You never want to get to the point where you think you are invincible.

You need to be willing to stoop to pick someone up, knowing that you could just as well be the one who needed picking up. Sooner or later there will be sin in your life from which you will need restoration.

Hold Him Up

Galatians 6:2 continues: "Bear ye one another's burdens, and so fulfill the law of Christ." Paul, maintaining the metaphor of walking, says that when you are going along the road and see someone who has fallen under a crushing burden too heavy for him, you should get under the load and help him carry it.

A burden is a spiritual weakness that threatens to induce a person to fall into sin—whatever chink Satan can find in a weakness of personality or character. A person might sin and repent many times and then be forgiven and brought back into the fellowship. But if no one bothers to get under the load, the person continues carrying the same load of temptation under the same difficult circumstances and is apt to fall again.

A distraught and tearful young man came to see me and said, "I've given my life to Christ, having been a homosexual before I was saved, but I still have terrible problems. I keep stumbling back into wrong relationships even though I repent and turn from them, asking God to forgive me." In attempting to help him, I said, "Every time you have a homosexual relationship over the next two weeks or cultivate ungodly thinking in that regard, I want you to write it out in a full paragraph and explain it to me. Then, in two weeks when we meet again, you can go through the list with me." Though he was stunned at what I said, two weeks later he came back with a smile on his face. He reported, "I didn't have anything to write because I didn't do anything—and that's the first time in two weeks." "What was the difference?" I asked. He said, "I didn't want to have to tell you about it." One way to carry a brother's load is to keep him accountable.

There are many other ways to carry someone's load. I can't tell you how many people I've said this to: "If you feel you are about to give in to temptation, I suggest that you pick up the telephone and get someone to carry the load with you." Restoration is more than just saying, "Be ye warmed and filled" (James 2:16). Nor should we merely quote Psalm 55:22, which says, "Cast thy burden upon the Lord, and he shall sustain thee" (cf. 1 Pet. 5:7). The Lord wants to sustain others through you and me. We have to be mutual burden bearers.

You will notice at the end of Galatians 6:2 that bearing others' burdens fulfills "the law of Christ." In John 13:34 Jesus says, "A new commandment I give unto you, that ye love one another." The law of Christ is the law of love. James calls it "the royal law" (2:8), "the perfect law of liberty" (1:25).

Who are you currently helping to carry the burden of temptation and weakness? Anyone? It's easy to be uninvolved, saying to ourselves, *I don't like to deal with other people's sin because I might get affected by it and taint my spirituality.*

If that's your perspective, read on: "If a man think himself to be something, when he is nothing, he deceiveth himself" (Gal. 6:3). Whenever I think I'm better than someone else, it's because I am comparing myself to the wrong standard. I can always find people worse than me. But Paul said, "We dare not make ourselves of the number, or compare ourselves with some that commend themselves; but they, measuring themselves by themselves, and comparing themselves among themselves, are not wise" (2 Cor. 10:12). That's because Christ—not someone of our choosing—is the standard. First John 2:6 says, "He that saith he abideth in him ought himself also so to walk, even as he walked." Because Christ is the standard, we are to compare ourselves to Him. But guess where we come out? On the low end.

Galatians 6:4 says, "Let every man prove his own work, and then shall he have rejoicing in himself alone, and not in another." You can claim you are working for the Lord and that you are spiritual, but you're going to have to prove it. Someday you are going to have to stand before Christ all by yourself with verification of your claim to spirituality. The *bema* judgment, which the following verses refer to, is the time when believers are going to be rewarded.

> *Revelation 22:12*—Jesus said, "Behold, I come quickly, and my reward is with me, to give every man according as his work shall be."
>
> *2 Corinthians 5:10*—"We must all appear before the judgment seat of Christ, that everyone may receive the things done in his body, according to that he hath done, whether it be good or bad."

1 Corinthians 3:12—Paul identified our works as "gold, silver, precious stones, wood, hay, stubble." The insignificant and worthless works—represented by the wood, hay, and stubble—are going to be burned up (v. 13).

Galatians 6:5 says, "Every man shall bear his own burden ["load"; NASB]." That is a different kind of burden from the one mentioned in verse 2. Even the Greek terms are different. *Baros* in verse 2 is a strong word, which means "a heavy weight"; whereas *phortion* in verse 5 refers to anything that is easily carried. It was often used of the general obligations of life that a person is responsible to bear on his own. One of those obligations is to help others with their crushing burdens, a kindness that will reap eternal rewards.

BUILD HIM UP

In verse 6 we read, "Let him that is taught in the word share with him that teacheth in all good things." Picture yourself as the teacher and the person you are restoring as the student. Though some people say this verse means that he who preaches or teaches should be paid, understanding the term "good things" (Gk., *agathos*) to refer to money, I would prefer to go to 1 Corinthians 9 to support that responsibility. I don't think this verse is talking money. *Agathos* as used in the New Testament is a general term referring to spiritual excellence. For example, Romans 10:15 talks about the proclamation of "good things," using the same term found in Galatians 6:6, Hebrews 9:11, and 10:1. It refers to the good things of God's kingdom.

In the restoration process, both the one who teaches and the one being restored are to share in the spiritual blessings resulting from that relationship. It is an ongoing, reciprocating edification process. Both share in all the spiritual benefits of growing strong in Christ.

We are to pick up weaker brothers who have fallen, hold them up, and then build them up. As Matthew 18 tells us, the process begins with confronting them with their sin. That can be discouraging because sometimes those you confront don't respond.

Second, we are to be forgiving. That also can be painful because the person you forgive may still not respond.

The third step is the ministry of restoration, where we bring the person back to a place of spiritual stability. This can be painful as well because it involves carrying a heavy burden. But don't let those realities prevent you from carrying out that vital ministry to which the Lord has called you. There is no greater joy than obeying Him, and He will be by your side every step of the way as He uses you to help purify His church (Matt. 18:19-20).

Appendix 6

Should Fallen Leaders Be Restored?

I have watched with alarm the latest trend in the church. I am shocked at how frequently we are seeing Christian leaders sin grossly, then step back into leadership almost as soon as the publicity dies away. Sadly, Christians don't expect much of their leaders anymore. We are in the midst of a disaster that is certain to have far-reaching consequences.

I recently received a cassette tape that disturbed me greatly. It was a recording of the recommissioning service of a pastor who had made national news by confessing to an adulterous affair. After little more than a year of "counseling and rehabilitation," this man was returning to public ministry with his church's blessing.

It is happening everywhere. I have received inquiries from other churches wondering if we have written guidelines or a workbook to help in restoring fallen pastors to leadership. Many no doubt expect that a church the size of ours would have a systematic rehabilitation program for sinning leaders.

Gross sin among Christian leaders is epidemic. That is a symptom that something is seriously wrong with the church. But an even greater problem is the lowering of standards to accommodate our leaders' sin. That the church is so eager to bring these men back into leadership indicates a rottenness to the core.

We must recognize that leadership in the church cannot be entered into lightly. The foremost requirement of a leader is that he be above reproach (1 Tim. 3:2, 10; Titus 1:7). That is a difficult prerequisite, and not everyone can meet it.

Some kinds of sin irreparably shatter a man's reputation and disqualify him from a ministry of leadership forever because he can no longer be above reproach. Even Paul, man of God that he was, said he feared such a possibility. In 1 Corinthians 9:27 he says, "I buffet my body and make it my slave, lest possibly, after I have preached to others, I myself should be disqualified" (NASB).

In referring to the body, Paul obviously had sexual immorality in view. In 1 Corinthians 6:18 he describes it as a sin against one's own body. It was almost as if he put sexual sin in its own category. Certainly it disqualifies a man from church leadership. First Timothy 3:1 demands that elders be one-woman men.

Where did we get the idea that a year's leave of absence can restore integrity to someone who has squandered his reputation and destroyed people's trust? Certainly not from the Bible. Trust forfeited is not so easily regained. Once purity is sacrificed, the ability to lead by example is lost forever. As my friend Chuck Swindoll has commented in referring to this issue, it takes only one pin to burst a balloon.

What about forgiveness? Shouldn't we be eager to restore our fallen brethren? To fellowship, yes. But not to leadership. It is not an act of love to return a disqualified man to public ministry; it is an act of disobedience.

By all means we should be forgiving. But we cannot erase the consequences of sin. I am not advocating that we "shoot our own wounded." I'm simply saying that we shouldn't rush them back to the front lines. Certainly the church should do everything possible to minister to those who have sinned and repented. But that does not include restoring the mantle of leadership to a man who has disqualified himself and forfeited the right to lead. Doing so is unbiblical and lowers the standard God has set.

Why is the contemporary church so eager to be tolerant? I'm certain a major reason is the sin and unbelief that pervade the church. If casual Christians can lower the level of leadership, they will be much more comfortable with their own sin. The man-centered focus of modern religion has spawned the erroneous notion that committing the worst kinds of sin makes a person more effective in ministering to sinners. The implications of such a philosophy are frightening. Our pattern for ministry is the sinless Son of God. The church is to be like Him and her leaders our models of Christlikeness.

Conservative Christians have for most of this century focused on the battle for doctrinal purity. And that is good. But we are losing the battle for moral purity. Some of the worst defeats have occurred among our most visible leaders. The church cannot lower the standard to accommodate them. We should hold it higher so that purity can be regained. If we lose here, we have utterly failed, no matter how orthodox our confession of faith. We can't win if we compromise the biblical standard.

Pray for your church's leaders. Keep them accountable. Encourage them. Follow their godly example. Understand that they are not perfect. But continue to call them to the highest level of godliness and purity. The church must have leaders who are genuinely above reproach. Anything less is an abomination.

Appendix 7

The Danger of False Teaching*

Scripture clearly affirms that God is truth and cannot lie. It also affirms that Satan is a liar and the father of lies. That dichotomy pervades every area of the universe. There is conflict between the holy angels and unholy demons. There is conflict on earth between the truth of God and the lies of Satan.

The people of God have always been plagued with false doctrine. They have endured the invasion of false prophets and teachers throughout the ages. Satan attempts to confuse the world by drowning it in a sea of deceit. It was Satan's misrepresentation of the truth to Eve that plunged the human race into sin (Gen. 3:1-6). The steady stream of false teaching has been so cumulative that it is wider and deeper now than it has ever been before. False teaching about God, Christ, the Bible, and spiritual reality is pandemic. The father of lies works overtime to destroy the saving, sanctifying truth God has given to us in His Word. The effects of false teaching have been devastating and damning. That's why the Bible calls them destructive heresies (2 Pet. 2:1). As we get closer to the return of Christ, these deceptions, lies, and misrepresentations will increase.

---

* From tape GC 55-9. Unless otherwise noted, all Scripture references in this appendix are from the *New American Standard Bible*.

Any servant of the Lord must be aware of false teachers and warn others about their lies. That is why the apostle Paul warned the believers and leaders in Ephesus (Acts 20:29-30).

Second Timothy 2:14-19 specifically tells us why we should avoid false teaching. Paul had called Timothy to be a faithful servant of the Lord. He asked him to rise above the influence of ungodliness, evil teaching, and evil people and to set the church right. To do so he had to keep his mind on the truth of God and be sure that he and his people avoided the impact of false teaching:

> Remind them of these things, and solemnly charge them in the presence of God not to wrangle about words, which is useless, and leads to the ruin of the hearers. Be diligent to present yourself approved to God as a workman who does not need to be ashamed, handling accurately the word of truth. But avoid worldly and empty chatter, for it will lead to further ungodliness, and their talk will spread like gangrene. Among them are Hymenaeus and Philetus, men who have gone astray from the truth saying that the resurrection has already taken place, and thus they upset the faith of some. Nevertheless, the firm foundation of God stands, having this seal, "The Lord knows those who are His," and, "Let everyone who names the name of the Lord abstain from wickedness."

REMINDING TRUE TEACHERS

The literal translation of verse 14 would read, "Remind of these things." The word "them" was added because it identifies who is being reminded—the faithful men of verse 2. What things were they to be reminded of? What Paul said in verses 1-13. He wanted Timothy to remind the church leaders and teachers of their responsibility to pass on the truth to others. They needed to be reminded of the noble cause they served and the loftiness of the gospel ministry.

AVOIDING FALSE TEACHING

A transition takes place from Paul's positive reminder to his negative command. In verse 14 he says, "Solemnly charge [Gk., *diamarturomai*, a legal term] them in the presence of God not to wrangle about words." *Diamarturomai* speaks of a continual reminder and a constant command. Timothy was constantly to remind the leaders of their positive duty and constantly to warn them to avoid false teaching. The warning is earnest, made even more serious by the next phrase: "Solemnly charge them *in the presence of God*" (emphasis added). The leaders were to do their duty out of a healthy fear of God. Paul had given such charges before:

1 Timothy 5:21—"I solemnly charge you in the presence of God and of Christ Jesus and of His chosen angels, to maintain these principles without bias."

1 Timothy 6:13-14—"I charge you in the presence of God, who gives life to all things, and of Christ Jesus, who testified the good confession before Pontius Pilate, that you keep the commandment without stain or reproach."

2 Timothy 4:1—"I solemnly charge you in the presence of God and of Christ Jesus, who is to judge the living and the dead, and by His appearing and His kingdom: preach the Word."

Those are all serious directives. They are not just words of advice but solemn commands—solemn commands in the presence of God. The intention is to put fear in the hearts of God's people by reminding them that they are directly accountable to God. Although there are times when the presence of the Lord is meant to comfort us, it is more often meant to increase our sense of accountability. We are always in the presence of God, and His presence acts as a controlling factor on how we live. He monitors each of our lives. A solemn charge in the presence of God makes its recipients accountable before the Holy One, the righteous judge.

Given the gravity of the command, you would expect Paul to name some heinous evil that Timothy was to command people to withdraw from. But he is warning them about engaging in word battles.

The Greek word translated "wrangle about words" (v. 14) speaks of waging a war of words. Paul called for the leadership to avoid futile debates because they would end up being sidetracked. Evidently the errorists in Ephesus tended to focus on worthless chatter based on speculation, not on the Word of God (1 Tim. 1:3-4; cf. 6:3-10).

The Screwtape Letters, by C. S. Lewis, tell of an older demon, Screwtape, writing to a younger demon, Wormwood, about how to be effective in dealing with people. In his first letter Screwtape said, "Your man has been accustomed, ever since he was a boy, to have a dozen incompatible philosophies dancing about together inside his head. He doesn't think of doctrines as primarily 'true' or 'false,' but as 'academic,' or 'practical.' Jargon, not argument, is your best ally in keeping him from the Church" ([N.Y.: Macmillan, 1961], p. 8). Demons know that true science and reason will not contribute to their cause—deception. Speculations, not facts, must fill men's minds. All "good" demons use that strategy because it obscures biblical truth by focusing on temporal concerns.

Such jargon has infiltrated many of today's colleges and seminaries. Many television evangelists and preachers barrage the church with jargon about their false religious systems, and the church has listened. How else can you explain why some churches have begun to advocate abortion, women preachers, homosexuality, and divorce for any reason? Why has the church allowed unholy leaders to remain in leadership? How it is that so many husbands no longer lead their homes and wives have no commitment to the lives of their children? How could the church ever buy into the self-esteem movement at the expense of humility and service to others? Jargon has invaded the church. That's because the church is willing to listen to the world. It is willing to put the Bible alongside the reason of man. In 2 Timothy 2:14 Paul calls the world's jargon useless. Worse than that, it's demonic. First Timothy 4:1-2 speaks of doctrines spawned by demons spoken through hypocritical liars.

Paul said word battles lead "to the ruin of the hearers." The Greek word translated "ruin" (*katastrophē*) means "to overturn," "subvert," "upset," or "overthrow." False teaching doesn't edify; it tears down. It doesn't strengthen; it weakens.

Katastrophē is used only one other time in the New Testament, in 2 Peter 2:6, which gives us insight into the kind of ruin Paul was referring to. Peter said God "condemned the cities of Sodom and Gomorrah to destruction [*katastrophē*] by reducing them to ashes." There *katastrophē* means "total devastation." Paul used it in the same sense in 2 Timothy 2:14—word battles totally destroy the hearers. They lead to the damnation of eternal souls. That's why 2 Peter 2:1 calls them destructive heresies that bring about swift destruction. Second Peter 3:16 says, "The untaught and unstable distort [Paul's teaching], as they do also the rest of the Scriptures, to their own destruction." We are called to stay away from false teaching because it has the potential to damn the eternal souls of those under its influence.

It also shames the teachers: "Be diligent to present yourself approved to God as a workman who does not need to be ashamed, handling accurately the word of truth" (v. 15). The key word is "ashamed." Anyone who teaches anything other than what accurately reflects the word of truth ought to be ashamed. Shame is the painful feeling that arises from an awareness of having done something dishonorable. Anyone who propagates false teaching has reason to be ashamed when he faces God. False teaching is worthy of condemnation by God. It doesn't matter to God how many degrees a minister has or how erudite he is; if he has mishandled God's precious Word, he has every reason to be ashamed.

If you're a teacher, how do you avoid being ashamed before the Lord? Second Timothy 2:15 says to "be diligent" (Gk., *spoudazō*, "to give diligence," "to give maximum effort," or "to do your best"). Teaching God's Word requires maximum effort. That's why 1 Timothy 5:17 says, "Let the elders who rule well be considered worthy of double honor, especially those who work hard at preaching and teaching." It is hard work.

In 2 Timothy 2:15 Paul says to "handle accurately the word of truth." The literal meaning of the Greek word translated "handling accurately" *(orthotomeō)* is cutting a straight line. It was used, for example, of cutting a straight line with a saw, making a straight path through the woods, or cutting a straight line on cloth or leather.

Paul was a leather worker. We often say he was a tentmaker, but a better translation of the Greek word is leather worker. He used animal hides, skins, and perhaps woven hair to make things, possibly tents. You can imagine that anyone making a tent would have to piece together a lot of hides. He would have cut each one just right so he could fit them together. It would be similar to dressmaking. If you don't cut the pieces right from the pattern, the dress won't look or fit right.

If you don't know how to cut the pieces, you can't make the whole product fit. The same is true in the spiritual realm—biblical theology and exegesis are interdependent. Every teacher must be committed to handling accurately (cutting straight) the Word of truth.

"Word of truth" (2 Tim. 2:15) is used other times in Scripture:

> *Ephesians 1:13*—"After listening to the message of truth, the gospel of your salvation." The message, or word, of truth refers to the gospel.
> *James 1:18*—"He [God] brought us forth by the word of truth."
> *John 17:17*—Jesus said, "Thy word is truth." Here the word of truth refers to all of God's revelation.

When you realize the importance of handling the gospel correctly, you've got to acknowledge that there is a lot of preaching today that doesn't. We have to handle the Word accurately so we don't misrepresent the gospel. We have to represent all of the Word of God, not in a flippant, offhanded way but properly. That requires diligence and a desire to be approved by God, not men. It demands that you be a workman.

First Timothy 2:16 says to "avoid worldly and empty chatter, for it will lead to further ungodliness." Such chatter is the common, profane, unholy talk of men. It is also "empty," which means it has no benefit—it yields no return. Empty words soon become evil words because their emptiness is a vacuum that sin rushes in to fill. Useless talk on useless matters becomes wicked talk. Words that are not of God soon become unholy words.

False teachers claim to be advancing our thinking, expanding our minds, and leading us to new truth. But what they're saying actually "will lead to further ungodliness" (v. 16). False teachers are ungodly, and they pull down the people who hear them. Peter said "many will follow their sensuality" (2 Pet. 2:2). Ungodly conduct is always the fruit of ungodly doctrine.

"Their talk will spread like gangrene" (2 Tim. 2:17). Gangrene is dead flesh. The bacterial kind spreads very quickly. The Greek word translated "gangrene" (*gangraina*) can refer to a spreading, consuming disease. To cure gangrene, the patient is sometimes placed in a hyperbaric chamber to expose the affected tissues to oxygen at high pressure, thereby killing the bacteria, which need an oxygen-free environment. The patient is then treated with antibiotics. Gangrene is like a prairie fire. Jude 23 tells us to "save others, snatching them out of the fire." False teaching is a malignancy—it eats up the surrounding tissue and spreads its corrupting doctrine to infect others.

Hymenaeus and Philetus (v. 17) were apostates, having erred from the truth like those referred to in Hebrews 6:4-6: "In the case of those who have once been enlightened and have tasted of the heavenly gift and have been made partakers of the Holy Spirit, and have tasted the good word of God and the powers of the age to come, and then have fallen away, it is impossible to renew them again to repentance." That's because they essentially "trampled under foot the Son of God, . . . regarded as unclean the blood of the covenant, [and] . . . insulted the Spirit of grace" (Heb. 10:29).

These apostates probably believed that the resurrection was nothing more than a mystical experience you had when you went from the unenlightened life to the enlightened life (cf. 2 Tim. 2:18). They probably were buying into a philosophical heresy that was prevalent at the time.

A denial of the resurrection is a major error. In 1 Corinthians 15:13-14 Paul says that if there were no resurrection of the dead, then Christ never rose. And if Christ never rose, neither will we. A doctrine that denies the resurrection cuts the heart out of the gospel. It's a denial of eternal life in a glorified body like Christ's, which is the essence of the Christian hope.

The error of Hymenaeus and Philetus "upset the faith of some" (2 Tim. 2:18). The Greek word translated "upset" literally means "to overturn." The people whose faith was overturned obviously had a nonsaving faith. That's because no one can overturn real faith (e.g., John 10:27-29; Rom. 8:30). Second Peter 2:18 says false teachers speak "out arrogant words of vanity [and] entice by fleshly desires, by sensuality, those who barely escape from the ones who live in error." Those who are overturned are looking for God, wanting to believe, and are beginning to open up to the gospel. But they encounter false teaching, and it destroys their weak, nonsaving faith. False religious systems prey on those who are looking for answers to the pains and pressures of life.

Verse 19 says, "Nevertheless, the firm foundation of God stands." The firm foundation of God is the church—the redeemed. We are the true people of God who form the solid, immovable foundation that false teachers can't uproot. False teachers will ruin some, shame some, lead some into ungodliness, corrupt some, and overturn the faith of some, but they won't affect the elect of God. We are a building not made with hands. We are the temple of the living God. We are the church Christ is building. The gates of hell will not prevail against us (Matt. 16:18). We are those who, having had a good work begun in us, will see it completed on the day of Jesus Christ (Phil. 1:6). We will never be separated from the love of God in Christ (Rom. 8:35). We are those of whom Jesus said, "All that the Father gives Me shall come to Me. . . . Of all that He has given Me I lose nothing, but raise it up on the last day" (John 6:37, 39). False teaching may devastate the souls of many people, and it may confuse believers from time to time, but the foundation of the church of God in Christ is firm. First John 2:14 says, "You are strong, and the word of God abides in you, and you have overcome the evil one." God called out a people for salvation and eternal glory before the world began.

The church can never be touched by false teachers because we are His: "The firm foundation of God stands, having this seal, 'The Lord knows those who are His'" (v. 19). He holds us in His sovereign powers. We are His for eternity. The first seal we have is that we are the elect. That seal is affixed to God's foundation. It guarantees permanence and makes dissolution impossible. In Matthew 7:22-23 the Lord says, "Many will say to Me on that day, 'Lord, Lord' . . . and then I will declare to them, 'I never knew you; depart from Me, you who practice lawlessness.'" They can't disturb the divine foundation. It will stand because we are the elect and the Lord knows who we are. Second Thessalonians 2:13 says, "God has chosen you from the beginning for salvation."

Notice the rest of 2 Timothy 2:19: "Let everyone who names the name of the Lord abstain from wickedness." To name the name of the Lord is to be identified with Him. If you belong to the Lord, abstain from wickedness. God's people are not only elect but also called to righteousness. God's election is an election to holiness. Our salvation is made up of God's predestining mercy and our inevitable duty. Paul said, "You have been bought with a price: therefore glorify God in your body" (1 Cor. 6:20). If we name the name of the Lord, we'll abstain from wickedness. It is both an exhortation and an affirmation. The one who names the name of the Lord does not apostatize but turns away from sin.

The two quotations in 2 Timothy 2:19 appear to be from Numbers 16. Korah rebelled against Moses and God, and many people joined him. But God judged them. In verse 5 Moses says, "The Lord will show who is His." That is almost the same wording as the first statement in 2 Timothy 2:19: "The Lord knows those who are His." When Korah and his friends gathered against Moses and the rest of the people, Moses affirmed that the Lord knew who belonged to Him. The second statement in 2 Timothy 2:19 parallels Moses' command to the people in Numbers 16:26: "Depart now from the tents of these wicked men, and touch nothing that belongs to them."

God will come in judgment, but He knows whom He will spare because they belong to Him. We'll know who they are because they will depart from the tents of wickedness. From the divine side, they're elect; on the human side, they're obedient. All the false teaching Satan wants to bring across our path will avail nothing because we stand firm on the foundation of God. Just as the rebellion under Korah ended in judgment, so will that of every false teacher.

INDEXES

Scripture Index

Topical Index

Accountability, 47-49
Amaziah, King, apostasy of, 139
Anatomy of a church. *See* Church
Apathy, 22-24
Apostasy
  character of, 142-43
  chronology of, 142
  definition of, 139-41
  predictability of, 141-42
  source of, 142-43
  teaching of. *See* False teaching
Armor of God. *See* Warfare, spiritual
Attendance. *See* Church
Authority, teaching with, 26-29, 58, 158-59

Balance. *See* Moderation

Barclay, William, on 1 Corinthians 15:58, 128-29
Baxter, Richard
  on blamelessness, 217-18
  on the work of the ministry, 158
Bestiality, 33
Blamelessness, 216-19
Bonhoeffer, Dietrich, on the danger of isolation, 246-47
Bowen, W.G., *Why the Shepherd*, 172-75

Calling
  of the church. *See* Church
  of the minister. *See* Ministry
Carey, William, vision of, 130
Change, willingness to. *See* Flexibility